Leadership for Pharmacists
Facilitating Change
in Pharmacy Practice

David A. Holdford, RPh, PhD

Notices

The author and the publisher have made every effort to ensure the accuracy and completeness of the information presented in this book. However, the author and the publisher cannot be held responsible for the continued currency of the information, any inadvertent errors or omissions, or the application of this information. Therefore, the author and the publisher shall have no liability to any person or entity with regard to claims, loss, or damage caused or alleged to be caused, directly or indirectly, by the use of information contained herein.

The inclusion in this book of any product in respect to which patent or trademark rights may exist shall not be deemed, and is not intended as, a grant of or authority to exercise any right or privilege protected by such patent or trademark. All such rights or trademarks are vested in the patent or trademark owner, and no other person may exercise the same without express permission, authority, or license secured from such patent or trademark owner.

Leadership for Pharmacists
Facilitating Change in Pharmacy Practice

David A. Holdford, RPh, PhD

Professor
Department of Pharmacotherapy and Outcomes Science
School of Pharmacy, Virginia Commonwealth University
Richmond, Virginia 23298

This book is dedicated with love to my brothers and sisters; Tom, Jeanne, Jack, and Ruth Ann.

They taught me empathy, communication, conflict management, advocacy, relationship management, fair play, and loyalty.

Contents

Preface

ORIGIN OF THIS TEXT

This introductory leadership textbook is the culmination of decades of observation, real-world application, teaching, and study of leadership and leaders in the pharmacy profession. The text provides didactic educational content to achieve core competencies for leadership established by the American Association of Colleges of Pharmacy, the American Council of Pharmaceutical Education, and other professional organizations. It provides a basic introduction into ideas and concepts that establish a foundation for application in experiential, cocurricular, and on-the-job training in leadership.

APPROACH AND ORGANIZATION

Leadership for Pharmacists: Facilitating Change in Pharmacy Practices summarizes and introduces readers to best practices in the leadership literature to meet the curriculum needs of schools and colleges of pharmacy. This text presents an overview of essential terms, concepts, and processes in leadership in a concise, practical, and understandable way. Content comes from published leadership and management literature and from class material developed over years of teaching. Emphasis is on explaining, developing comprehension, and encouraging application.

This book consists of 12 chapters divided into three sections. The first section, Introduction to Leadership and Management, consists of four chapters that provide an overview of leadership, management, and major concepts associated with the influencing of others. The second section, Foundations of Leadership, has five chapters that cover the important leadership topics of advocacy, management of yourself, decision-making, and motivation theories and strategies. The final section, Managing Relationships, contains three chapters that present ways to develop strong professional relationships and to negotiate conflicts productively and effectively.

This book is designed to provide pharmacy students, pharmacists, and others in the profession with a basic overview of leadership principles and best practices. The subtitle—*Facilitating Change in Pharmacy Practice*—foreshadows the primary purpose of the book—to help pharmacists lead change in pharmacy practice. This book is not a management book because it does not discuss management responsibilities, such as planning, finance, and inventory control. Instead, it emphasizes understanding human behavior and influencing change through people.

Leadership for Pharmacists: Facilitating Change in Pharmacy Practice is based on theories and research from the leadership, management, and business literature, but it is written in a way that is comprehensible and immediately applicable to the lives of pharmacists, pharmacy students, and others. Each chapter has learning objectives, key terms and concepts, discussion and review questions, and references, as well as case studies in boxes titled "Leadership in Action." Resources are also available for faculty in the form of PowerPoint slides; teaching tips; exercises for class and homework; additional resource material to supplement the book; links to podcasts, Web sites, and other online material; and access to self-assessment material.

INTENDED READERS

This book is written for any pharmacy student or pharmacist interested in influencing the practice of pharmacy. For students with limited work and career experience, the text provides a foundation in leadership and management that can be immediately applied to their personal and professional lives. For individuals with significant training and practice experience, the book presents a discussion about leadership best practices that will allow readers to place their experience into context. The book's content is universal to all practice settings, health care systems, and countries.

██ ██ EDUCATORS

This book can be used as the core text around which an elective or required course in leading change can be built. It can also serve as a text to integrate leadership training throughout didactic courses, experiential training, and cocurricular experiences in professional associations and student government. Educators can build learning experiences around individual book chapters and supplement the readings with presentations by practitioners, classroom exercises, and active learning projects.

SECTION I

INTRODUCTION TO LEADERSHIP AND MANAGEMENT

CHAPTER 1

Introduction to Leadership
How to Lead Change in Pharmacy

■■ OBJECTIVES

■ Explain why pharmacists need to learn about leadership.

■ Discuss the primary forms of power that individuals possess.

■ Define leadership, and contrast it with management.

■ Compare and contrast "push" and "pull" forms of influence.

Leadership [is] the art of getting someone else to do something that you want done because he wants to do it.

—Dwight D. Eisenhower

◼◼ INTRODUCTION

Leadership is an important and commonly discussed topic in the pharmacy profession today. Leadership is a desired outcome of pharmacy school education.[1-5] All student graduates are expected to understand and apply the basic concepts of leadership in pharmacy practice situations. Practicing pharmacists are expected to lead and participate in change in the profession.[6-9] Nevertheless, resistance is common from students and pharmacists regarding the need to learn about leadership and influencing change.

Resistance comes from multiple sources. One common lament is, "I went to pharmacy school to be a clinician, not a manager." Another is, "I am not very good in dealing with conflict. I would rather learn about serving patients and leave it at that." Others include, "Things are fine the way they are. Why change?" and "Things never change. Why try?" Several compelling reasons can be given in response to this resistance.

◼ Leading Change Is a Fundamental Responsibility of Being a Pharmacist

There is widespread agreement in the pharmacy profession that leading change is an essential responsibility of pharmacists.[2,5,10] Several reasons have been given in support of this assertion. One is that leading change is essential for meeting the promises made in the *Oath of a Pharmacist* (Box 1.1).

Pharmacy students and pharmacists take the oath voluntarily as a public statement of the roles and responsibilities of pharmacists. Because the fundamental responsibility of pharmacists is to influence appropriate medication use and desired health outcomes, the oath supports the importance of leadership development in pharmacists and students. It emphasizes the obligation of pharmacists to develop the capability to improve welfare and relieve suffering of patients. The ability to influence others is essential for pharmacists to be able to achieve these obligations.

◼ The Status Quo Is No Longer Acceptable in Pharmacy Practice

Leaders in the medical profession have made a persuasive case that the status quo in health care is unacceptable. The case for changing the status quo is substantiated throughout the health care literature, especially by a series of reports by the Institute of Medicine (IOM). The IOM, now the Health and Medicine Division of the National Academies of Sciences, Engineering, and Medicine, conducted extensive studies to guide and inform public health and health care

BOX 1.1 Oath of a Pharmacist[a]

The American Pharmacists Association has adopted the following Oath of a Pharmacist:

I promise to devote myself to a lifetime of service to others through the profession of pharmacy. In fulfilling this vow:

* I will consider the welfare of humanity and relief of suffering my primary concerns.
* I will apply my knowledge, experience, and skills to the best of my ability to assure optimal outcomes for my patients.
* I will respect and protect all personal and health information entrusted to me.
* I will accept the lifelong obligation to improve my professional knowledge and competence.
* I will hold myself and my colleagues to the highest principles of our profession's moral, ethical and legal conduct.
* I will embrace and advocate changes that improve patient care.
* I will utilize my knowledge, skills, experiences, and values to prepare the next generation of pharmacists.

I take these vows voluntarily with the full realization of the responsibility with which I am entrusted by the public.

a. See reference 11.

policy. Since 1999, the IOM made a case through the following reports that change is essential in health care:

* "To Err Is Human" establishes that economic and clinical consequences of medication error and misuse have cost the United States tens of thousands of preventable deaths and billions of dollars in waste.[12] It suggests that many of the errors in health care result from both poor applications of basic leadership functions, such as planning, and ineffective execution of planned actions.

* *Crossing the Quality Chasm: A New Health System for the 21st Century* calls for fundamental changes to improve the quality of health care.[13] In particular, the report emphasizes the need for training leaders and practitioners to change the way they currently work and innovate the delivery of health care. This approach requires individuals to take greater responsibility for managing themselves, their practice settings, the individuals with whom they work, and their patients.

* *Health Professions Education: A Bridge to Quality*, an IOM report, identifies gaps in health care education.[14] This report argues for better training in people skills, including teamwork, leadership, and communication.

To achieve the improvements recommended by IOM and other leaders in health care, pharmacists must know how to deal with people (patients, coworkers, other professionals), solve problems using a systems-based approach, communicate effectively, collaborate, manage themselves, and lead change in a manner that addresses the needs and preferences of patients. These are foundational ideas and concepts associated with leadership and the ability of pharmacy students and professionals to influence the future of pharmacy practice.

⬛ Change Is Happening

Students entering the pharmacy profession today face major transformations in health care, pharmacy practice, the world, and themselves. Technology is changing how pharmacists practice — patients are more demanding; payers expect more of health care providers; pharmacists demand greater influence in medication therapy; and other health care providers compete for roles within the evolving health care system.

Students and pharmacists have two primary paths for dealing with transformations in pharmacy practice. One strategy is to "go with the flow" and adapt to changes as they occur. This strategy may work if the transformations are positive for pharmacists and for the profession. In that case, they can ride that wave and reap the benefits. Indeed, until recently, a go-with-the-flow strategy has been ideal for many pharmacists who have benefited from a booming job market, steady work, and high salaries earned with relatively low levels of engagement in their jobs and the profession.

However, a go-with-the-flow path may not work well for pharmacists in the future. Currently, the job market for pharmacists is tightening, fueled in part by the increasing number of pharmacy graduates and improved efficiencies in the dispensing process. Pharmacists are now being asked to justify the value of the high salary being paid to them. Increasingly, they are being held accountable for achieving positive business results and positive patient health outcomes. They are competing with other health care professionals for a piece of the health care dollar and looking for new sources of revenue for nondispensing services. Pharmacists who choose to disengage, keep their heads down, and do what they are told will likely struggle with changes in the profession. They will either need to change or hope that they and their jobs will still be relevant until they retire.

A second, more hopeful path exists for students and pharmacists. This path consists of being a part of, even leading, change in pharmacy practice and the profession. Instead of complaining about the current situation, pharmacists can engage in changing circumstances for the better. This approach means taking ownership of the profession and one's practice and influencing its transformation. The remainder of this text is for students and pharmacists who choose the second path.

■ ■ WHAT IS LEADERSHIP?

Leadership has been defined by many people in numerous ways. This text uses the following concise and meaningful definition of leadership: "the process through which an individual attempts to intentionally influence another individual or group in order to accomplish a goal."[15] This definition highlights key characteristics of leaders.

Leadership has a purpose. Its purpose is to achieve specified and desired goals. Sometimes those goals are controversial or conflict with someone else's goals. The challenge to pharmacist leaders is to balance the needs and wants of various parties including patients, coworkers, employers, and oneself.

Leadership is a process. It is not an outcome or a formal title. One is a leader as long as one effectively influences others to accomplish goals. Individuals are not leaders, no matter their formal title, if they do not effectively influence others to achieve a purpose.

Leadership is intentional. It cannot happen by luck or error. Leadership is not something that happens by chance, although luck can play an important part of being a successful leader. True leadership is deliberate, and it requires leaders to accept responsibility and to be intentional in their actions and inactions.

Leadership is about people. Effective leaders build strong relationships with others to achieve ordinary and extraordinary things. Leaders achieve results through others, and effective leaders help others make a difference.

Finally, leadership is not about the leader. Good leaders realize that their goal is to serve others. Although leaders may personally benefit by leading others, the purpose of leadership is to benefit the people served by the leader.

■ *Leadership and Power*

Power is a fundamental aspect of leadership and management. *Power* is the ability to influence the behaviors of others. Leaders and managers use various sources of available power to influence change. Leaders typically have six sources of power available to them in differing amounts depending on the leader and individual circumstances (Table 1.1).

Pharmacists can lead by being both *willing* and *able* to exert their power to influence. Pharmacists have six forms of power available to them—a formal position, the capability to reward, the ability to punish, unique expertise, particular information, and the ability to inspire. Some pharmacists choose not to use their

TABLE 1.1 Sources of Power Available to Pharmacists

Power	Description
Legitimate	Sometimes called "formal" or "positional power," this power describes a person's authority originating from a formal title or position in an organization. Legitimate power is granted by organizations and institutions. Pharmacists are awarded legitimate power by state boards of pharmacy, their employers, and other institutions.
Reward	This power comes from one's ability to influence behavior in exchange for something desirable, such as money or public recognition. It is usually linked to legitimate power, although anyone can reward another person with respect, kind words, supportive behavior, openness, and fair treatment.
Punishment	This power, also called "coercive power," comes from one's ability to influence behavior in exchange for avoiding something undesirable, such as being fired, docked for pay, or reprimanded. Like reward power, it too is linked to legitimate power. Punishment can come from words (e.g., warnings) or overt actions (e.g., job termination).
Expert	This power is based on a person's knowledge, expertise, experience, and skills. Expertise is most influential when it is in short supply and can be wielded by anyone to influence decisions and ideas. Expertise is based on the perceptions of others, and it needs to be demonstrated, built, and earned over time.
Information	This power originates from the possession of information that is needed or desired. Like expertise, it is most influential when it is in short supply, and it too can be wielded by anyone to influence events. It occurs when one knows where to find information, how to access it, how it relates to things desired by others, and how to effectively use it to influence behaviors.
Charismatic	Also called "referent power," charismatic power describes one's ability to inspire devotion in others through force of character, attractiveness, or charm. It is associated with peoples' identification of and admiration for a leader. Charismatic leaders exert influence through a desire by followers to emulate or please them. Charismatic power is typically associated with inspirational leaders and transformational leaders.

power, "I don't see why I have to supervise my technicians." or "I can't inspire anyone!" Others wield their power ineffectively, "If I tell you to jump, your response should be 'How high?'" or "John can't be trusted. He never shares information with anyone." The positive aspect is that these deficiencies can be overcome when pharmacists learn how to effectively use their power.

⬛⬛ "BIG L" AND "LITTLE L" LEADERS

Pharmacists influence change by being "big L" and "little L" leaders.[16] *Big L leaders* are pharmacists with titles of authority who have the potential to influence others through their positions. Their formal positions tend to give them greater access to information, more contact with other influential people, and greater ability to reward and punish. Nevertheless, formal positions offer only an opportunity, not a guarantee, to lead.

Many new managers are surprised to learn of constraints placed on them by their positions. Managers may have authority to reward and to punish, but this power is often constrained by an organization's policies and culture. Their positions may provide greater access to information unavailable to those without titles (e.g., sensitive personnel histories), but new managers often find themselves cut off from some information power because of their ability to reward and punish, "Better to keep quiet than to risk taking a chance of something bad happening." Ultimately, the power of leaders is largely based on the perceptions of others, and these perceptions must be earned by carefully wielding the power available to big L leaders. As Maxwell[17] notes: "The only thing a title can buy is a little time—either to increase your level of influence with others or to erase it."

In reality, pharmacists can lead change without a title because everyone has the power to influence others. Pharmacists who influence without formal titles are called "little L" leaders by White.[16] *Little L leaders* influence patients, coworkers, other health care professionals, and management by using the various sources of power available to them. They accept responsibility for the outcomes of their patients and take charge of the success of their practice setting and what is going on around them. Increasingly, all front-line pharmacists are expected to be leaders in their everyday responsibilities. Box 1.2 illustrates how one does not need to have a formal leadership position to lead.

■ ● WHAT IS THE DIFFERENCE BETWEEN LEADERSHIP AND MANAGEMENT?

Leadership and management are two distinct but related activities. They are often confused because they have the same goal—to influence the behavior of individuals. Kotter[18] differentiates leaders and managers in the following way:

- Managers influence by providing order and consistency. Managers plan, budget, organize, hire staff, and control. They provide structure in day-to-day operations. Managers are most effective when conditions are calm and change is unnecessary. They are less effective in turbulent and changing circumstances because they tend to be more rigid and inflexible in behavioral expectations. In dynamic situations, adaptability is more important in responding to fluid circumstances.

- Leaders influence by inspiring people to work independently, without much direction, toward the mission of the organization. Leaders encourage adaptability, set direction, communicate a common vision, and inspire followers

BOX 1.2 Leadership in Action: Everyday Leadership

In 2001, an example of everyday leadership occurred at a small hospital in the southern United States. It did not make the news, but it was significant because it resulted from an act of bravery by someone who did not fall into the category of what people usually call a leader.

The pharmacy department personnel at this small hospital consisted primarily of technicians and pharmacists who were born and raised in the South. The pharmacy staff members got along fairly well, but there were some tensions between groups.

Pharmacists and technicians seemed to live in two different worlds. The majority of the department's pharmacists were well educated, financially secure, and Caucasian. Technicians were a mix of Caucasians and African Americans, but nearly all were less educated than the pharmacists and were living from paycheck to paycheck.

Joe Grubbs, MBA, PharmD, was the director of pharmacy at the hospital. He was 50 years old and a traditional southern white man. He took great pride in family, church, community, and southern traditions.

Joe truly cared about his staff members and consistently went out of his way to make their work life pleasant and productive. In fact, he was a really good director of pharmacy except for one aspect.

He was culturally insensitive in dealing with issues of workplace diversity. Some days, he would openly complain about working with women. He would say, "We need less estrogen in this department!" But his biggest cultural blind spot was a belief that there was nothing wrong with keeping a small Confederate flag on his work desk. Most of the employees, both African-American and Caucasian, found having a confederate flag in the workplace to be disrespectful and inappropriate. However, no one was willing to confront Joe about it. They would rather talk about him behind his back.

The situation changed one day. Michael Bates, a 25-year-old African-American pharmacy technician, quietly decided to act. Michael was always a soft-spoken, nonconfrontational individual whom no one really thought of as a leader. Always pleasant and easy-going, Michael had been working at the pharmacy since graduating from high school.

Like Joe, Michael also valued many southern traditions, but he and his family had suffered racial prejudice on many occasions.

In the afternoon of that day, Michael asked if he could talk to Joe privately in his office. Behind closed doors, Joe and Michael talked. No one knew what was said, but a few days later, someone noted that the Confederate flag was no longer on Joe's desk.

To this day, no one knows what went on in that meeting except the two participants. But everyone in the pharmacy department believes that Michael used his power to get Joe to do the right thing for the department.

Questions

1. Describe your impression of Joe Grubbs. Do you think he is a good and honorable man?

2. Do you think it was appropriate for Joe Grubbs to talk about people that way? Isn't he just "telling it like it is" or "being real"? What are the downsides of Joe's behavior?

3. What is your impression of Michael? Would you consider him brave? Do you think his action was difficult to do? Could you do it? Is Michael a leader?

to take responsibility. Leaders exert influence by relinquishing much of the structure and order of managerial tasks and instead encourage followers to take responsibility for their work and work settings.

In truth, the distinction may be irrelevant because organizations need individuals who are both good leaders *and* managers. Few people are pure managers or leaders—rather a blend of the two. In certain situations, they may provide order and consistency, whereas in other situations, they may inspire individuals to work independently, without much direction. Nevertheless, the distinction can highlight different strategies employed in influencing individuals.

The major distinction is that *leaders encourage commitment toward a common goal*, whereas *managers ask for compliant action toward that goal*. The choice between encouraging commitment or cultivating compliance is critical to this difference. Managers want people to do what they are told. They are less interested in the reasons for doing so. In contrast, leaders seek commitment over compliance. They believe that committed individuals will be more motivated and engaged in achieving common goals. Leaders believe that if they can capture the hearts of people, a greater commitment to goals and tasks will result.

Managers push individuals to complete tasks by providing an organized framework of rules and controls to guide them. Compliance to this normative framework is rewarded, and noncompliance is punished. A structured system of behavioral rules is essential for complex organizations like those seen in health care. Still, a rigid system based primarily on rewards and punishments will rarely encourage the high levels of commitment needed to rise to the challenge of extraordinary or changing conditions.[19]

Leaders pull individuals toward a shared vision (e.g., patient health) and leave the steps for achieving this vision to followers. Commitment inspired by leaders can help deal with difficult times like budget cuts and staff shortages. Committed individuals are less likely to quit or reduce effort when deteriorating working condition cause stress, uncertainty, anxiety, or conflict.

Pharmacists need to effectively employ both *push* (i.e., management) and *pull* (i.e., leadership) strategies depending on the circumstances. Even the most motivated followers need to be pushed sometimes. Both management and leadership are essential to the success of organizations, and the distinction between the two is often irrelevant in practice.

Daniel Goleman,[20] a leadership expert, argues for the need to seamlessly apply push and pull strategies depending on the situation. In his article, "Leadership that Gets Results," he ignores the leadership versus management dichotomy by

BOX 1.3 Leadership or Management? Does It Really Matter?

The difference between the two matters in that managerial practices are needed in some situations while leadership is required for other situations. Without knowing the difference, identifying the correct response to a situation can be difficult. Sometimes, managers are needed to provide order and structure. Other times, the commitment associated with leaders is required. Few individuals are pure managers or leaders. Instead, individuals have tendencies toward one or the other because of experience, habits, and personal preference.

At one time, separating management from leadership may have been useful, but in knowledge industries like pharmacy, they are often inseparable. A pharmacist may need to assign tasks but also give the tasks meaning by defining their purpose. The pharmacist might enforce rules and processes, but empower people to make choices. Pharmacists may help motivate with rewards and punishments, but still inspire coworkers to push their capabilities to serve patients' needs. With training and experience, people can develop both their leadership skills and their management skills, giving them the resilience to adapt to changing circumstances.

combining push and pull strategies into the concepts of leadership. Individuals who primarily influence by providing order and consistency simply employ different leadership styles than those who influence by communicating a common vision and inspiring. Leaders who cannot switch from one style to another style are less able to adapt to and succeed in dynamic situations.

Further, the acceptance of our leadership definition noted earlier in this chapter — "the process through which an individual attempts to intentionally influence another individual or group in order to accomplish a goal" — means that the outcome of management and leadership are the same. Any attempt to decouple them as an idea tends to cause more problems than it solves. The discussion in Box 1.3 makes a case for seeing leadership and management as inseparable. Therefore, the remainder of this chapter and book will view leadership and management as complementary and interrelated processes and will use the terms interchangeably.

◼️ ◼️ WHAT IT TAKES TO BE A LEADER

Many books and articles are dedicated to understanding and explaining leadership. A search of the Amazon online book site returns more than 100,000 titles under "leadership books." Many of the books are written as biographies or personal how-to summaries from leaders in business, politics, and other fields. Other books are scientific explorations of established and emerging theories in organizational behavior, psychology, and other social sciences. Despite the overwhelming number of ideas and explanations about leadership, this section describes the most widely recognized concepts reflecting what it takes to be a leader.

Leaders have identifiable traits that differentiate them from nonleaders. Traits are qualities that differentiate people, such as personality or physical characteristics. Many traits are inherited and cannot be changed (e.g., height, basic intelligence), leading to the belief that leaders are born, not made. Other traits are just tendencies to behave in a certain way and can be altered (e.g., confidence, decisiveness). Certain traits are associated with leaders and are key for leadership success (see Chapter 2 of this book). Individuals without these traits still have the capacity for leadership, and it may be possible through self-improvement to enhance certain traits to improve an individual's ability to lead.

Leaders have abilities and skills that distinguish their success as leaders. Leadership abilities and skills refer to one's capacity to lead, and these skills can be innate or developed through experience. For instance, some people have an innate or natural ability to communicate well verbally and in writing, but people can also learn to develop these abilities through practice. The ability and capacity to lead only refers to one's potential as a leader. Actual leadership occurs when an individual uses these abilities and skills to effect change.

Effective leaders behave differently. Leadership requires action that influences positive change. Behaviors differ from traits, abilities, and skills because they are observable and easier to evaluate objectively. Traits, abilities, and skills are only the foundations on which behaviors occur—leaders are most commonly held accountable for their words and actions. Leadership behaviors fall into two categories—tasks and processes. *Tasks* are work duties assigned to people. Task leadership behaviors, such as monitoring and giving feedback to team members, are those used to complete these assigned duties. *Processes* are a series of actions designed to achieve a goal. Leaders implement process behaviors to develop effective relationships within their team, such as giving public recognition for exceptional work or listening to a team member's concerns about conflict within the group. Task and process behaviors are both needed to achieve goals, although the relative balance can be difficult to determine. For example, incessantly driving team members to complete the job can damage professional relationships, which can in turn reduce the ability of the team to complete the job.

Leadership is about the relationships between people. In the past, the focus of leadership was on the leader; however, greater emphasis is now placed on the relationship between leaders and followers. Today, the process of leading is viewed as a collaboration between leaders and followers, where each party influences the other. Followers are encouraged to "lead up," to work with the people above them in the organization to meet the organization's goals. Good leaders are just as likely to lead up as they are to lead down. The traditional top-down leadership viewpoint is that the leader directs the followers and the followers do what is asked of them. Relational leaders accept that leadership is not a one-way, linear process, but rather more of an interactive, iterative progression between individuals. Although this type of leadership requires more of leaders, it can lead to a more adaptable, creative team.

Effective leaders adapt to changing situations. Changing situations require different approaches to leadership. The more dynamic the environment, the more important it is for leaders to identify the needs of the moment and to match the appropriate style of leadership to the problem at hand. A day that begins as routine may end in crisis mode. Effective leaders in changing situations need to be able to seamlessly switch from one leadership style to another as required. Applying the same leadership style to each event might generate significantly contrasting results. These concepts will be explored in more detail in the following chapters.

Some people are natural leaders—they have the capabilities and personality to lead others without any training or guidance. Humans have been leading change for centuries by relying completely on their own common sense and personal experience.

However, personal experience in leadership can be supplemented with knowledge about leadership theories and best practices. Evidence from the leadership literature can help pharmacists avoid making unnecessary mistakes based on incorrect assumptions about what works in leading others. Trial-and-error learning, although effective with the proper coaching and feedback, results in errors that can be avoided with a basic familiarity of the literature. In addition, a general understanding of leadership can provide a framework to test a pharmacist's personal experiences with what the literature suggests. This can result in deeper learning from experience and help pharmacists deal with difficulties that are not easily managed through common sense or intuition. This book makes the case that the application of evidence-based leadership will help pharmacists be more effective on the job and will help them avoid unnecessary problems when influencing individuals and groups.

⬤ ⬤ SUMMARY

This chapter provides an overview of current leadership theories and recommendations for pharmacists. It condenses extensive leadership literature into a relatively limited number of pages. As a result, some ideas are simplified for the reader and other ideas are omitted. For example, the chapter does not address emerging leadership theories such as servant leadership. Nevertheless, the chapter summarizes most of the key concepts pharmacists need to know about leading others.

Therefore, pharmacists must now begin their leadership journey. Every pharmacist in an organization can be a leader. Each of us has the ability to improve the quality of health care through leadership. Many problems faced by the profession could be improved if more pharmacists would exercise leadership at different levels of pharmacy organizations. And any leadership deficiencies can be overcome by developing leadership capabilities over time.

KEY TERMS AND CONCEPTS

- Oath of a pharmacist
- Institute of Medicine (IOM)
- "To Err is Human"
- *Crossing the Quality Chasm: A New Health System for the 21st Century*
- *Health Professions Education: A Bridge to Quality*
- Leadership
- Management
- Power
- Big L leaders
- Little L leaders
- Push strategies
- Pull strategies

DISCUSSION AND REVIEW QUESTIONS

1. Why would a pharmacist want to be a leader? Why not avoid conflict and leave change in the profession to other people?

2. What sources of power do pharmacy technicians have to influence change in their work settings? Do they have any power? If so, what types?

3. If you had to choose between working for a pure manager or a pure leader, which one would you select? What is missing in a work setting when people in formal positions of power are either a pure manager or pure a leader and not a blend of both?

4. Think of your best boss. Would you call that person a manager or a leader? Did your boss use primarily push or pull strategies to influence people?

5. What aspects of pharmacy practice do you think need changing? How can leadership help change these aspects?

▓▓ ● REFERENCES

1. Medina MS, Plaza CM, Stowe CD, et al. Center for the Advancement of Pharmacy Education 2013 educational outcomes. *Am J Pharm Educ*. 2013;77(8):162. doi:10.5688/ajpe778162.
2. Kerr RA, Beck DE, Doss J, et al. Building a sustainable system of leadership development for pharmacy: report of the 2008–09 Argus commission. *Am J Pharm Educ*. 2009;73(8). doi:10.5688/aj7308S05.
3. Bradley-Baker LR, Murphy NL. Leadership development of student pharmacists. *Am J Pharm Educ*. 2013;77(10). doi:10.5688/ajpe7710219.
4. Eriksen M. Authentic leadership. *J Manag Educ*. 2009;33(6):747–771. doi:10.1177/1052562909339307.
5. Janke KK, Traynor AP, Boyle CJ. Competencies for student leadership development in doctor of pharmacy curricula to assist curriculum committees and leadership instructors. *Am J Pharm Educ*. 2013;77(10):222. doi:10.5688/ajpe7710222.
6. Ivey MF, Farber MS. Pharmacy residency training and pharmacy leadership: an important relationship. *Am J Health Pharm*. 2011;68(1):73–76. doi:10.2146/ajhp100051.
7. American College of Clinical Pharmacy. A vision of pharmacy's future roles, responsibilities, and manpower needs in the United States. *Pharmacotherapy*. 2000;20(8): 991–1020. doi:10.1592/phco.20.11.991.35270.
8. Zilz DA, Woodward BW, Thielke TS, et al. Leadership skills for a high-performance pharmacy practice. *Am J Health Syst Pharm*. 2004;61(23):2562–2574.
9. Tsuyuki RT, Schindel TJ. Changing pharmacy practice: the leadership challenge. *Can Pharm J*. 2008;141(3):174–180. doi:10.3821/1913-701X(2008)141[174:CPPTL C]2.0.CO;2.
10. ASHP statement on leadership as a professional obligation. *Am J Health Syst Pharm*. 2011;68(23):2293–2295. http://www.ncbi.nlm.nih.gov/pubmed/22201191. Accessed May 15, 2018.
11. Oath of a Pharmacist. American Pharmacists Association. https://www.pharmacist.com/oath-pharmacist. Accessed May 15, 2018.
12. Kohn LT, Corrigan JM, Molla S. To err is human. *Medicine* (Baltimore). 1999; 126(November):312. doi:10.1017/S095026880100509X.
13. Institute of Medicine. *Crossing the Quality Chasm: A New Health System for the 21st Century*. Washington, DC: National Academies Press; 2001. doi:10.17226/10027.

14. Institute of Medicine. *Health Professions Education: A Bridge to Quality*. Greiner AC, Knebel E, eds. Washington, DC: National Academies Press; 2003.

15. Holdford DA. Leadership theories and their lessons for pharmacists. *Am J Health Syst Pharm*. 2003;60(17):1780–1786. http://www.ncbi.nlm.nih.gov/pubmed/14503115. Accessed January 9, 2016.

16. White SJ. Leadership: successful alchemy. *Am J Health Syst Pharm*. 2006;63(16): 1497–1503. doi:10.2146/ajhp060263.

17. Maxwell JC. *The 21 Indispensable Qualities of a Leader: Becoming the Person Others Will Want to Follow*. Nashville, TN: Thomas Nelson; 1999.

18. Kotter JP. What leaders really do. *Harv Bus Rev*. 1990;68(3):103–111. doi:10.1109 /EMR.2009.5235494.

19. Herzberg F. One more time: how do you motivate employees?. *Harv Bus Rev*. 2003;81(1):87–96. doi:10.1108/eb055227.

20. Goleman D. Leadership that gets results. *Harv Bus Rev*. 2000;78(2):78–90. doi:10.1147 /rd.433.0245.

CHAPTER 2

What Does It Take to Be a Leader?

Are Leaders Made or Born?

■■ OBJECTIVES

- Describe the leadership theories that focus on the individual natures of leaders and their effectiveness.

- Explain how leaders' expectations influence followers' behaviors.

- Discuss the differences between narcissistic leaders and servant leaders.

- Make a case for the effectiveness of task orientation or follower orientation as a general leadership behavior.

Some are born great, some achieve greatness, and some have greatness thrust upon them.

—William Shakespeare

◼ ◼ INTRODUCTION

Leadership theories can help explain and predict how leadership works by placing what is known about leading and managing people into coherent frameworks. Our understanding of leadership is built on tests of hypothesized relationships within these frameworks.

Leadership theories are more than just opinion. Opinions are viewpoints or judgments that may or may not be based on knowledge or fact.

Leadership theories have been tested; they represent our best understanding of the topic. In general, leadership theories can help answer the following questions:

1. What are the criteria for selecting effective leaders?

2. What characteristics and behaviors are associated with good leaders?

3. Under what conditions do different leadership behaviors work best?

4. How can pharmacists be more effective leaders?

No single theory provides *the answer* to any of these questions because people are complex and their behavior is often unpredictable. Leadership theories *can* provide possible solutions to problems within organizations.

Leadership deals with people engaged in difficult, messy, and often chaotic situations. People often respond in complex, inconsistent, and contradictory ways. Therefore, the science of leadership rarely offers the high level of validity seen in medicinal chemistry or pharmaceutical laboratories.

Instead, leadership theories provide basic "take-home" lessons regarding relationships, and the challenge is to determine how well a particular lesson applies to a given situation. For example, there is evidence that leaders are more likely to have certain traits, such as intelligence and personality, but there are limits to the reliability and usefulness of these traits in the identification and development of future leaders.

Pharmacists can learn a great deal from the accumulated wisdom of the leadership literature to help them lead others. Consequently, this chapter and the following chapter provide a brief review of leadership theories and what pharmacists can learn from them. Because the leadership literature is so extensive, these chapters can provide only a brief overview. Nevertheless, this information suggests nuanced approaches that pharmacists can use to develop effective solutions to problems.

FIGURE 2.1 Major Perspectives on Leadership

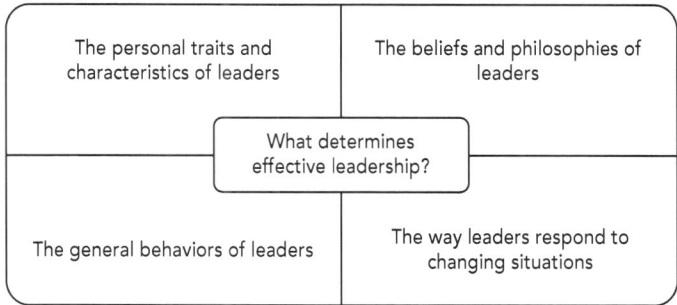

▨▨ MAJOR PERSPECTIVES ON LEADERSHIP

Leadership theories can be categorized as relating to one of four major perspectives (see Figure 2.1). The first perspective is the nature of leaders: their traits, skills, and abilities that give them the ability to lead. The second perspective deals with the general philosophies and attitudes that guide leaders' behaviors. The third perspective focuses on the behaviors associated with good leaders. The fourth and final perspective considers the situations faced by leaders and their responses to those situations.

The four perspectives overlap because the major variables—traits, philosophies, behaviors, and situation—are not independent of each other. The first three perspectives are discussed in this chapter, and the fourth, situational leadership, is discussed in Chapter 3 of this book.

▨▨ INDIVIDUAL NATURE OF A LEADER

▨ *Innate Traits or Abilities*

How can pharmacy organizations recognize good leaders? What makes some leaders effective and others not? What does it take to be a leader? Are leaders born or made? These are the questions that trait theories of leadership attempt to answer.

Trait perspectives of leadership are a group of theories founded on the idea that the greatest predictors of good leadership are the traits and dispositions with which people are endowed at birth or develop early in life.[1] The theories argue that the ability to lead is mostly fixed. By the time a person reaches a leadership position, these characteristics are difficult to obtain or to change. Therefore, proponents of these theories advocate that time is better spent on identifying and choosing individuals who have traits associated with effective leaders. Any leadership development should focus on providing these individuals with opportunities to develop their innate capabilities over time.

Trait theories are closely associated with the phrase "born leader," an individual who leads naturally and effectively. This phrase suggests that individuals have innate abilities or traits that make them effective in leading, and this suggestion forms the basis of theories focusing on traits and on skills.

One of the earliest trait theories was the *great man* (or person) theory, which argued that most of history can be explained by great people doing great things.[2] Greatness in people came from genetic blood lines of kings, queens, and highborn individuals. Although the great man theory has largely fallen out of favor in the scientific literature, the importance of leadership traits is still promoted in the popular literature in articles that discuss X traits of great leaders, Y essential qualities of a leader, and Z characteristics of remarkable leadership.

Numerous scientific studies have attempted to identify specific traits in people that might be predictive of leadership capability. These traits include physical characteristics (e.g., height, age, beauty), social traits (e.g., charm, tact, popularity), personality (e.g., Type A, extrovert, emotional stability), intelligence (e.g., IQ), and task-related traits (e.g., general motivation, energy level). Some traits are fixed because they are genetic; others are not fixed, and therefore can be learned. Reviews of the literature suggest the traits most consistently associated with leadership are as follows:[1,3]

- Determination

- Integrity

- Self-confidence

- Intelligence

- Social skills

The association between these traits and effective leaders makes sense on the face of it. However, the trait approach to leadership has been challenged because the relationship between traits and good leadership is relatively weak and not strongly predictive.

Lord et al.[4] observed that the relationship between traits and leadership capabilities is weak and inconsistent at best, making many traits poor predictors of good leaders. Intelligence, for instance, may be seen in many good leaders because leaders need a sharp mind to address the demands placed on them (e.g., complex problem solving, understanding of complex systems). However, many intelligent people are terrible leaders because they lack other characteristics, such as self-control or interpersonal skills, needed by effective leaders. Similarly, the positive trait of self-confidence may be associated with undesirable traits, such as self-deception or an unwillingness to listen to others.

In addition, traits and behaviors are different concepts. For instance, being intelligent does not mean that a leader will act intelligently. Likewise, a person with a reputation for integrity may not behave with integrity when faced with a difficult problem.

Nevertheless, traits are still widely used to identify and select leaders. A trait that has gained significant support in the recent literature, emotional intelligence, is closely associated with leadership capabilities.

⬤ Emotional Intelligence

Emotional intelligence (EI) describes a person's ability to perceive, monitor, and regulate one's emotions and to use that understanding to manage relationships with people.[5] EI deals with one's ability to integrate cognitive and emotional understanding to manage his or her life, and it can be learned and developed over time.

EI is a multidimensional construct. The number of dimensions vary depending on the researcher. Goleman identified five dimensions ("components") associated with leaders (Table 2.1).[5-7] These five components are necessary to identify and apply various leadership styles to different situations.

Leaders with greater EI are likely to be more effective and adaptable to challenges of leadership.[6] In contrast, leaders who are deficient in some dimensions of EI will be less adaptable. For example, an individual who lacks empathy may have difficulty using a supportive style of leadership, or a socially inept person may struggle with being inspirational.

As a trait, EI is important for pharmacists and pharmacy leadership. It has been promoted as important in leading,[8] in being a competent professional,[9] and in enjoying professional success.[10]

The premise of EI is that pharmacists who are more sensitive to their emotions and their effect on professional relationships will be more successful in managing them.

TABLE 2.1 Components and Competencies of Emotional Intelligence[a]

Component	Description	Competencies
Self-awareness	Recognizing and understanding one's emotions, drives, values, and goals, and their effect on others	Emotional awareness: Recognizing one's emotions and their effects Accurate self-assessment: Knowing one's strengths and weaknesses Self-confidence: Having a strong sense of one's self-worth and capacities
Self-regulation	Controlling or redirecting disruptive emotions and impulses; includes the ability to think before acting	Self-control: Keeping disruptive emotions and impulses in check Trustworthiness: Maintaining standards of honesty and integrity Conscientiousness: Taking responsibility for personal performance Adaptability: Flexibility with change Innovativeness: Being comfortable with novel ideas, approaches, and new information
Self-motivation	One's internal drive to achieve; requires understanding what one really wants	Drive: Striving to improve or meet a standard of excellence Organizational commitment: Aligning personal goals with the goals of the group or organization Initiative: Having a readiness to act Optimism: Persisting despite obstacles and setbacks
Empathy	Considering others' feelings, especially when making decisions	Understanding others: Sensing others' feelings and perspectives and taking an active interest in their concerns Developing others: Sensing others' development needs and encouraging their abilities Service orientation: Anticipating, recognizing, and meeting customers' needs Encouraging diversity: Cultivating diverse relationships Political awareness: Reading power relationships in groups
Social skills	Managing relationships with others to get things done	Communication: Listening and articulating views Conflict management: Resolving disagreements Leading change: Initiating or managing change Collaboration and cooperation: Working with others toward shared goals Team capabilities: Using groups to pursue collective goals Influence: Being persuasive

a. See reference 7.

◼ Skills of Leaders

Skills are another variable that describes the individual nature of leaders. Unlike traits, skills can be more easily learned; therefore, leaders can be developed through a *skills approach to leadership*. Research notes that some skills are natural depending on the person.[11] The skills approach seeks to build on individuals' baseline capabilities to maximize their leadership potential.

Anyone who directs and is responsible for the activities of others needs three basic skills—technical, human, and conceptual.[11] These three skills are interrelated and can be developed:

1. Technical skills require specialized knowledge and proficiency in an activity. For pharmacy managers, they might include personnel management or quality assurance.

2. Human skills refer to a person's ability to work well in groups and with individuals. People skills are primarily concerned with working with people (e.g., pharmacists, technicians), while technical skills primarily address working with "things," such as processes (e.g., medication selection) and physical objects (e.g., drugs).

3. Conceptual skills describe a person's ability to see the "big picture" within an organization (e.g., pharmacy chain) or system (e.g., U.S. health care). These skills are more abstract and deal with working with ideas and concepts, including the ability to understand relationships between individuals and groups and visualize ways to best influence these individuals and groups.

All three skills are important in management positions, but their relative importance in hierarchical organizations depends on one's level of responsibility. In a pharmacy organization, technical and human skills are more important for pharmacists, supervisors, and middle managers. This ideal is consistent with the Center for the Advancement of Pharmacy Education outcomes expected for all pharmacy graduates[12] that emphasize technical and human competencies in pharmaceutical sciences, pharmacy practice, and people skills.

Conceptual skills are more abstract and strategic in nature. Conceptual and human skills are more important for individuals at the top of hierarchical organizations, and these skills are central for developing an organization's vision and crafting strategies for success.

In leadership development, the three-skills framework indicates that pharmacists, supervisors, and middle managers benefit more from job-specific training in technical skills and human skills and that upper-level managers benefit more from conceptual skills and human skills training.

The skills approach presents a map for developing effective leadership in organizations, but it has two limitations. First, it deals primarily with hierarchies at a time when many organizations are decreasing their organizational levels. It is not clear whether the skills framework can be sustained in "flattened" organizations where lower-level workers are asked to take greater ownership for the organization's success. The second limitation is that the framework assumes that people start at the bottom of organizations and that they must master basic technical skills before they can move up and exercise conceptual skills.

But what happens to individuals who may be conceptually brilliant but technically inept? In these cases, the Peter Principle is likely to come into play.

The *Peter Principle* is a management concept stating that individuals advance within organizations because they are competent in current positions.[13] When they are promoted to a position where they are not competent, they no longer advance past their level of incompetence. That concept also means that individuals who may excel in higher-level positions may never reach those positions because they are stuck in current roles.[14]

The Peter Principle suggests that over time, every position in an organization will be occupied by someone who is incompetent to carry out the duties of the position. This mismatch in job capabilities has a significant effect on organizations.[15]

Realizing that incompetence in leaders may just be a mismatch of one's skills or training to a job is important. The solution is to recognize this mismatch and be willing to move individuals who are a poor match for a position.

▨ ● LEADERSHIP PHILOSOPHIES AND ATTITUDES

Certain leadership theories revolve around the general philosophies and attitudes of leaders and the way these philosophies and attitudes affect their relationships with followers. For instance, some leaders are laid-back while others are intense. Other leaders focus on helping themselves, and still other leaders emphasize service to others. How do these various philosophies affect leaders' behaviors and their relationships with team members?

Three major philosophies are discussed in this section—Theory X and Theory Y, narcissistic leaders, and servant leaders. These philosophies are based on leaders' general perceptions and focus. They are not a specific set of leadership tasks or methods; rather, these leadership philosophies are based on leaders' personal philosophies and belief systems.

● Theory X and Theory Y

Theory X and Theory Y is a theory dealing with a leader's attitudes and beliefs toward followers. Developed by MacGregor in the early 1960s, it divides leaders into two categories: Theory X leaders and Theory Y leaders.[16]

Theory X leaders believe that people are generally lazy, lack ambition, avoid responsibility, and seek security instead of challenge. Given freedom, they will slack off; provided with more time, they will waste it; and offered more responsibility, they will complain. According to this attitude, Theory X leaders believe that people cannot be trusted to behave ethically. Instead, they must be carefully watched and managed. Tight controls must be placed on them to keep them busy. They must be continually told what to do, rewarded when they do what they are told, and punished when they do not do as told. Common phrases associated with Theory X managers include, "I need eyes in the back of my head. If I don't constantly watch them, they will goof off!"; "They have no pride in their work and don't care about this place."; and "Do I have to do everything around here?" Given this attitude, Theory X leaders rely on coercive and controlling leadership methods to spur effort.

In contrast, *Theory Y leaders* have a more positive attitude toward people. They believe that people are generally ambitious and will achieve fantastic results when properly challenged. They believe that people are not lazy and that people enjoy mental and physical challenges. For such people, work can be as much fun as play. According to Theory Y leaders, people want to achieve mastery in their jobs and will seek out and accept responsibility that stretches their capabilities.

As a result of their beliefs and attitudes, Theory Y leaders treat followers differently than Theory X leaders treat followers. Theory Y leaders treat people with respect and ask as much from followers as they ask of themselves. They challenge followers to achieve and assume that followers will succeed. Phrases common to Theory Y leaders are, "When I give my employees the right conditions and tools to do a job, they always impress me." and "How do you think we should handle this problem? I value your judgment." With this attitude, Theory Y leaders use democratic, coaching, and supportive leadership techniques to engage workers.

Ultimately, the Theory X and Theory Y philosophy suggests that a leader's attitude toward followers can act as a self-fulfilling prophecy. Leaders who perceive followers to be lazy and inept will treat them that way. Followers who are treated as lazy and inept will respond in kind, or they will seek opportunities elsewhere. However, if leaders set high expectations for followers, support their work, and treat them as respected professionals, they will reward the leader's faith in them with exceptional effort and performance.

▉ Narcissistic Leadership

Narcissism is a mental state characterized by extreme self-absorption, an exaggerated sense of self-importance, and a need for attention and admiration

TABLE 2.2 Degrees of Narcissism in Leaders

Productive narcissism	Unproductive narcissism	Clinical narcissism
Healthy degree of self-interest and pride	Inability or unwillingness to control narcissistic behaviors	Narcissistic Personality Disorder Diagnosis
Ability to align self-interest with the organization's mission and control narcissistic behaviors when they get in the way of the mission	Excessive self-absorption, self-importance, and attention seeking that damages professional relationships and follower engagement	Inability to function in normal daily activities and roles

from others.[17] In the extreme, it is considered a psychiatric condition that is associated with a lack of both empathy and ability to appreciate the views of others (Table 2.2).

Similarly, *narcissistic leaders* are self-absorbed, self-important, and attention-seeking individuals who are in positions of responsibility over others. Narcissistic leadership is an approach that puts the leader's interests and desires above all else.[18] Although an uncomplimentary comment about a person, perhaps, it is a common characteristic of many leaders.[19] In fact, many of these narcissistic characteristics are unmistakable in well-known leaders. When asked to name a leader, most people will list individuals with larger-than-life, dominating personalities—two characteristics of narcissistic leaders. Many well-known leaders, such as Catherine the Great, Napoleon, Winston Churchill, Margaret Thatcher, Bill Gates, Steve Jobs, and Bill Clinton, fall into the narcissistic leader category. These and other narcissistic leaders are driven by their personal egos, rather than by an empathetic concern for those they lead. Indeed, they tend to take leadership positions to support their grandiose needs.

In extreme circumstances, narcissism in leaders can make the difference between success and failure because narcissistic leaders are more likely to take bold actions that more empathetic and considerate individuals might avoid. For instance, Steve Jobs is infamous for his intensity (and his mistreatment of his workers, according to some people), but he is highly respected for what he achieved at Apple. Many people credit his force of will and vision for making Apple one of the most successful companies in the world at the time of his death.

But narcissistic leaders have a dark side.[20,21] They pursue personal needs instead of the needs of the people they are meant to serve. They are self-promoters, and they often attain positions for which they are not qualified. Nevertheless, they are able to hide their lack of ability by being charismatic, confident, and bold. These leaders are more likely to damage the careers of the people they manage because they lack empathy for the concerns of subordinates, take unfair credit for the work of others, and blame anyone but themselves when things go wrong. Their tendency toward grandiose thoughts often leads to close-mindedness and distrust in anyone who does not agree with them. Therefore, they either surround themselves with sycophants or with people who will not challenge them.

Why are so many leaders in organizations narcissists? One reason is that they are perceived to be leader like. Their confidence and bold vision are traits that people expect in leaders. This expectation inspires people to choose narcissists for leadership positions. Once in a position, the narcissist's charisma and ability to cultivate a positive public image can hide potential flaws.

In addition, narcissistic leaders can succeed when matched with the correct followers and the right situation.[19] For example, narcissists can provide the bold vision and deeds needed by a leader in a crisis situation. Narcissists can also succeed when their personal agenda meets the needs of an organization. For example, professional athletes' extreme narcissism on the field is often glorified on television highlight films, which results in increased visibility for the athlete and the team and more people buying tickets to attend games.

Michael Maccoby argues that narcissistic leaders can be highly productive.[19] In today's chaotic world, he advocates that there is a need for leaders who ignore the concerns and thoughts of the crowd and put forth a grand, innovative vision. They are often unreasonable in their expectations—something necessary to achieve what others believe is impossible. These "productive narcissists," as Maccoby calls them, shape the future rather than try to understand it.[19] He includes Bill Gates, Steve Jobs, and Jack Welch among their number.

Still, narcissists can become tyrants in organizations when left unchecked.[21] Narcissistic leaders need to be able to restrain their worst behaviors and channel their efforts toward the good of the organization. With the proper oversight and mentoring from their bosses, narcissists can overcome their weaknesses and successfully lead change. Without restraints, however, narcissistic leaders can be a disaster for an organization (as illustrated in the in Box 2.1).

In summary, narcissistic leadership is common in business and government because narcissists can persuade people with their vision, confidence, boldness, and charisma. Narcissism is positively associated with attaining leadership positions, but it is not necessarily associated with performing well in them, especially over the long run.[18] In some cases, ego-driven narcissists can lead

---

BOX 2.1 Leadership in Action: The Narcissistic District Pharmacy Manager

Terri and Norm, senior managers in a pharmacy chain, are discussing their concerns about the new district manager.

Terri: "I'm really disappointed in our new district manager, Glen. He really seemed qualified on paper. His resume was as good as any I've seen in years, and he really impressed us in the job interviews."

Norm: "You know, I was completely surprised too. He hit the ground running when he started the job. Had a real vision for what he wanted to achieve, and his charm and energy were contagious—getting everyone to pitch in. Now, people want to strangle him."

Terri: "Me too! It started when I started receiving complaints about Glen being a jerk to the store pharmacists. Even Jennie complained, and she never says a bad thing about anyone. It seems that he has a hand-picked group of guys (no women), who he personally hired from other chains. He calls them his 'dream team' and in their eyes, he can do no wrong. When he makes it clear to them that he doesn't like someone, they make that person's life very difficult. Remember Jeanne? She got fed up and quit after 16 years in her job. I hated to see her go, and there is a rumor that she has hired a lawyer to look into a possible lawsuit."

Norm: "The thing that bothers me about Glen is that he pretends he cares about people, but he really doesn't. It's like there is some synapse associated with empathy missing in his brain. He thinks he is above our company's rules and doesn't listen to anyone else, even his dream team.

Terri: "It looks like things aren't going to work out with him. Now we are going to have to replace him. Probably his dream team, too."

Questions

1. Why might a narcissist like Glen be impressive in job interviews?
2. What narcissistic characteristics are being shown by Glen in this case?
3. What other options, besides firing Glen, do Terri and Norm have to deal with the problem?

---

bold innovation and social change. In many other cases, they leave damaged relationships and organizations in their wake.

◼ *Servant Leadership*

Servant leadership is a popular philosophy that is the opposite of narcissistic leadership. Servant leadership is an approach that puts others first.[22] Rather than accumulate power for personal ends and glory, servant leaders share and help others develop power to influence change. *Servant leaders* are coaches, teachers, and supporters who help develop the capacity of followers to make a difference. They help a group develop a collective vision of what it wants to achieve and use a variety of leadership styles to help the group get there.

Despite widespread enthusiasm for servant leadership, the exact behaviors associated with it are not very clear. However, the literature generally identifies the following dimensions of servant leadership:[23]

▪ Emotional healing: Showing sensitivity to others' personal concerns

▪ Creating value for the community: Possessing a conscious, genuine concern for helping the community

▪ Conceptual skills: Possessing knowledge of the organization and tasks at hand to be in a position to effectively support and assist others, especially immediate followers

▪ Empowering: Encouraging and facilitating the ability of others, especially immediate followers, to complete work tasks

▪ Helping subordinates grow and succeed: Demonstrating genuine concern for others' career growth and development by providing support and mentoring

▪ Putting subordinates first: Using actions and words to demonstrate to everyone that the work of subordinates is a priority

▪ Behaving ethically: Interacting openly, fairly, and honestly with others

▪ Relationships: Making a genuine effort to know, understand, and support others in the organization, with an emphasis on building long-term relationships with immediate followers

▪ Servanthood: Acting in a way to be marked by one's self-categorization and desire to be characterized by others as someone who serves others first, even when self-sacrifice is required

The servant leadership philosophy is linked to many leadership theories. It defines both traits (e.g., ethical) and behaviors (e.g., empowerment) associated with effective leaders. It also employs a situational approach by promoting an individualized manner in handling followers depending on the individual and organizational circumstances.

The servant leadership philosophy is intuitively appealing for several reasons. It can have a positive effect on an organization's culture and on the morale of individuals within an organization. There is a natural desire in individuals to strive for personal development and achievement of ideals and items of importance—both foundational concepts in servant leadership. Better professional relationships between individuals are also likely to result because behaviors associated with servant leadership will encourage commitment and trust,[22,24] as noted in the Oath of a Pharmacist:[25] "I promise to devote myself to a lifetime of service to others through the profession of pharmacy."

Despite the potential benefits of servant leadership, its dissemination in organizations may be limited.[24] The culture of some organizations in the United States is highly competitive, where getting ahead requires beating, not serving, others. In this environment, selflessness can be viewed as a sign of weakness and can be taken advantage of by opportunistic colleagues. In addition, servant leadership requires individuals to suppress their personal desires for those of the team. A pharmacist might ask why he or she might give up the freedom of a highly paid position to take on the greater responsibilities and the headaches of leading others. This leadership role requires a great deal of self-control, selflessness, lack of ego, and a vision for the greater good. Although many pharmacists have these characteristics, the path to leadership may not always be accessible to them. Individuals with a desire to serve may not have the chance to serve if they are not visible within an organization of self-promoters. In many cases, organizations reward those who put their needs above others.

⬤ ⬤ GENERAL BEHAVIORS OF LEADERS

Behavioral theories recognize that knowing the nature of leaders only provides a foundation for understanding leadership. The knowledge of the behaviors associated with good leaders is what can help in identifying and training them. *Behavioral theories* argue that the greatest predictors of leadership effectiveness are the behaviors that people learn and adopt over time.[26–28] Behavioral theories attempt to answer the question, "What leadership behaviors are most effective?" They are discussed in the popular literature in articles that discuss the X leadership behaviors that every business needs, the top Y most desired leadership behaviors, and the Z habits of successful leaders.

A variety of behavioral theories have been proposed.[26–28] However, they all revolve around two primary dimensions of behavioral orientation adopted by leaders—task orientation and follower orientation.

⬤ *Task-Oriented Leaders*

Task-oriented leaders have a greater concern for results than for people. They focus on accomplishing the assigned job, while the welfare of followers takes a back seat. Task-oriented leaders concentrate on providing the necessary structure (defined as setting goals, providing training, defining behavior expectations and limits, and establishing rules and procedures) that followers need to complete their work. A shortcoming of task-orientation leadership is that followers can feel disrespected and unsupported.

Some task orientation in leaders is essential because followers need some structure to complete most tasks. However, there is a point where structure is no longer useful and becomes restrictive, even irritating. For example, a pharmacist typically needs to provide technicians with general procedures and expected outcomes for tasks and to follow up to ensure tasks have been accomplished. However, if the pharmacist continually monitors a technician every few minutes and frequently interrupts the task with unsolicited advice or suggestions, the technician will probably find the guidance overbearing and unhelpful.

A high task orientation without empathy for followers is associated with an autocratic (also called authoritarian) leadership style. An autocratic leader tries to take control over all processes. Decisions are made without accepting input or suggestions. Little thought is given to the effect of these decisions on others. Task orientation is also seen in a command-and-control style of leadership, which demands the immediate compliance of followers, with no excuses.

▣ Follower-Oriented Leaders

Follower-oriented leaders are more concerned with people than with results. They concentrate less on the job at hand and focus more on the welfare of the follower. Such leaders actively support followers by treating them as human beings—not as cogs in a machine attempting to achieve some task. These leaders demonstrate supportive behavior by showing respect, gaining trust, demonstrating consideration, and being friendly and approachable.

A follower orientation is associated with affiliative styles of leadership. These leaders are more likely to accommodate the needs and concerns of followers. A follower-oriented leader promotes a pleasant work atmosphere and works to build strong professional relationships with team members. Typically, positive feedback is encouraged over negative feedback. A potential downside of this orientation is that poor performance can continue unchecked.

Both orientations are necessary in organizations, but either orientation can be problematic when taken to the extreme. Too much focus on the task may cause followers to chafe at the restrictions. Task orientation can lead to followers labeling the leader as a "micromanager" or a "slave driver" and feeling mistreated or exploited. In contrast, too much emphasis on the followers will result in failure to meet deadlines and goals.

Effective leaders are able to balance a task orientation with a follower orientation. They are able to demand high levels of performance while also treating their team members with respect and compassion. Box 2.2 describes the way

BOX 2.2 How to Provide Structure with Autonomy

Task-oriented leaders can offer structure that does not stifle independence and engagement.[a] Structure can facilitate teamwork, collaboration, communication, and positive relationships given the proper framework.

People need and want structure, but structure that is controlling and coercing can dampen commitment, innovation, and performance. Leaders who give people a clear sense of the organization's purpose, priorities, and principles provide structure that does not stifle or restrict people's ability to work independently in an organization's best interests.

A coherent "freedom within a framework" can boost performance, engagement, quality, creativity, and customer service.[b] There are three core elements of this framework:

* **A clearly articulated purpose.** This is a single shared goal that sums up the "why." Simon Sinek describes a golden circle when talking about the importance of why in accomplishing great things.[c] At the center of the circle is why. Why we do what we do? What is our purpose? Sinek says, "People don't buy what you do; they buy why you do it. And what you do simply proves what you believe." Theory X and Theory Y leaders have different opinions about the importance of "why?" Theory X leaders assume people do not care. Therefore, the why is irrelevant in managing people. Just focus on the "what" and the "how." Theory Y leaders assume that understanding the why is essential for taking ownership.
* **Priorities.** The why needs to be tethered to identified priorities—behavioral rules that reflect the organization's goals. Priorities clarify the choices that must be made to achieve the why. For example, should we focus on patient outcomes or the company's bottom line if a choice must be made?
* **Principles.** Principles are a simple set of behavioral guidelines growing out of the organization's purpose and priorities. For example, a company may state, "Rule number 1: The customer is always right. Rule number 2: Refer back to rule number 1." This suggests a different set of principles than a company that asserts, "Rule number 1: Use your best judgment. Rule number 2: There are no other rules."

If pharmacy schools offered "freedom within a framework" to student learning, they might suggest the following:

* **Purpose.** The purpose of the Doctor of Pharmacy education is to educate and train exceptional pharmacists and pharmacy leaders.
* **Priorities.** We place an emphasis on self-direction, mastery, collaboration, integrity, mutual respect, and making a difference.
* **Principles.** (1) Take responsibility for your own education. (2) Master the material—you will need it long after the test. (3) Our job is to help you do your job. Your job is to develop mastery. (4) Learning is better as a team sport. Be a good team member. (5) Give us reasons to brag about you to potential employers, alumni, and future students before and after graduation. (6) Prepare yourself for your life 5 to 10 years after graduation. (7) Have fun.

---

a. See reference 28.
b. See reference 28.
c. See reference 29.

to provide structure to a team while still offering the autonomy needed for independence and engagement.

In truth, task and follower orientations are compatible approaches in leading teams that share common goals. Working on important tasks with people who like and respect each other are elements of a highly performing organization.

■■ CONCLUSION

Individuals become effective leaders, in part, because of their individual natures, philosophies, attitudes, and behaviors. Changing a leader's individual nature is difficult, but a leader's philosophies, attitudes, and behaviors can be influenced through willpower, training, and experience. The ability to change and adapt to new challenges and situations is what makes one an exceptional leader. Exceptional leaders are able to adapt to circumstances, while so-so leaders can succeed only under specific, limited situations. A leader's ability to adapt will be discussed in Chapter 3 on situational leadership.

■■ KEY TERMS AND CONCEPTS

- Trait perspectives of leadership
- Emotional intelligence
- Skills approach to leadership
- Peter Principle
- Theory X leader
- Theory Y leader
- Narcissism
- Narcissistic leaders
- Servant leaders
- Behavioral theories of leadership
- Task-oriented leaders
- Follower-oriented leaders

◼◼ DISCUSSION AND REVIEW QUESTIONS

1. In your experience, what are the characteristics of effective leaders? Of these characteristics, which are genetic and which have been learned? Based on your experience, do you think leadership can be learned?

2. Can leaders with low levels of self-awareness be effective leaders? If leaders do not practice self-introspection, can they learn from their mistakes and successes? How can leaders with low self-awareness develop feedback strategies to improve their leadership capabilities?

3. Which skills are most important for a pharmacy technician: technical, human, or conceptual? What about for a pharmacist or a pharmacist manager? What about for a pharmacist district manager or a director of pharmacy? What about for a pharmacist chief executive officer or owner?

4. In your experience, which types of managers are more prevalent in pharmacy practice: Theory X or Theory Y managers? Why?

5. What are the upsides of narcissism in leaders? What are the downsides? At what point is narcissism a problem in leaders?

6. Can a narcissist ever be a servant leader? If so, how?

7. Describe situations in pharmacy practice that require high levels of structure and other situations that require high levels of support from managers. Compare the characteristics of individuals who require more structure with the characteristics of individuals who need less structure in completing tasks.

◼◼ REFERENCES

1. Kirkpatrick SA, Locke EA. Leadership: do traits matter? *Executive*. 1991;5(2): 48–60. doi:10.5465/AME.1991.4274679.

2. Bolden R, Gosling J, Marturano A, et al. *A Review of Leadership Theory and Competency Frameworks*. Exeter, United Kingdom: Centre for Leadership Studies, University of Exeter; 2003.

3. Zaccaro SJ. Trait-based perspectives of leadership. *Am Psychol*. 2007;62(1):6–16. doi:10.1037/0003-066X.62.1.6.

4. Lord RG, de Vader CL, Alliger GM. A meta-analysis of the relation between personality traits and leadership perceptions: an application of validity generalization procedures. *J Appl Psychol*. 1986;71(3):402–410. doi:10.1037/0021-9010.71.3.402.

5. Goleman D. What makes a leader? *Harv Bus Rev*. 1998;76(6):93–102. doi:10.4135 /9781446213704.

6. Goleman D. Leadership that gets results. *Harv Bus Rev.* 2000;78(2):78–90. doi:10.1147/rd.433.0245.

7. Goleman D. *Emotional Intelligence.* New York, NY: Bantam Books; 1995. doi:10.1016/j.paid.2003.12.003.

8. Haight RC, Kolar C, Nelson MH, et al. Assessing emotionally intelligent leadership in pharmacy students. *Am J Pharm Educ.* 2017;81(2). doi:10.5688/ajpe81229.

9. Vogt EM, Finley PR. Heart of pharmacy: a course exploring the psychosocial issues of patient care. *Am J Pharm Educ.* 2009;73(8):149. http://www.ncbi.nlm.nih.gov/pubmed/20221342. Accessed May 18, 2018.

10. Romanelli F, Cain J, Smith KM. Emotional intelligence as a predictor of academic and/or professional success. *Am J Pharm Educ.* 2006;70(3):69. http://www.ncbi.nlm.nih.gov/pubmed/17136189. Accessed May 18, 2018.

11. Mumford MD, Zaccaro SJ, Connelly MS, et al. Leadership skills: conclusions and future directions. *Leadersh Q.* 2000;11(1):155–170. doi:10.1016/S1048-9843(99)00047-8.

12. Medina MS, Plaza CM, Stowe CD, et al. Center for the Advancement of Pharmacy Education 2013 educational outcomes. *Am J Pharm Educ.* 2013;77(8):162. doi:10.5688/ajpe778162.

13. Romaine J. The Peter Principle resuscitated: are promotion systems useless? *Hum Resour Manag J.* 2014;24(4):410–423. doi:10.1111/1748-8583.12034.

14. Popper M, Gluskinos UM. Is there an inverse "Peter Principle"? *Manag Decis.* 1993;31(4):59. doi:10.1108/00251749310037558.

15. Benson A, Li D, Shue K. Promotions and the Peter Principle. NBER Working Paper 24343. National Bureau of Economic Research; 2018. doi:10.3386/w24343.

16. Sorensen P, Yaeger T. Theory X and Theory Y. *Hum Side Enterp.* 2015:358–374. doi:10.1093/OBO/9780199846740-0078.

17. Oxford English Dictionary Online. http://www.oed.com/.

18. Rosenthal SA, Pittinsky TL. Narcissistic leadership. *Leadersh Q.* 2006;17(6):617–633. doi:10.1016/j.leaqua.2006.10.005.

19. Maccoby M. Narcissistic leaders: the incredible pros, the inevitable cons. *Harv Bus Rev.* 2004;(January):92–101.

20. Nevicka B, Ten Velden FS, de Hoogh AHB, et al. Reality at odds with perceptions: narcissistic leaders and group performance. *Psychol Sci.* 2011;22(10):1259–1264. doi:10.1177/0956797611417259.

21. Doty J, Fenlason J. Narcissism and toxic leaders. *Mil Rev.* 2013;93(1):55–60. http://search.proquest.com/docview/1319774388?accountid=35812.

22. Greenleaf RK. *Servant Leadership: A Journey into the Nature of Legitimate Power and Greatness.* Spears LC, ed. Mahwah, NJ: Paulist Press; 1977. https://books.google.com/books?hl=en&lr=&id=AfjUgMJlDK4C&oi=fnd&pg=PT33&dq=greenleaf+servant+leadership+and+healthcare&ots=iBTHKTGeu6&sig=kwm381x o49RXJ6l1jSDl0An5wl0#v=onepage&q=greenleaf servant leadership and healthcare &f=false. Accessed May 5, 2018.

23. Liden RC, Wayne SJ, Zhao H, et al. Servant leadership: development of a multidimensional measure and multi-level assessment. *Leadersh Q.* 2008;19(2):161–177. doi:10.1016/j.leaqua.2008.01.006.

24. Heskett J. Why isn't "servant leadership" more prevalent? *Harv Bus Rev.* 2013;(May):1–2.

25. Oath of a Pharmacist. American Pharmacists Association. https://www.pharmacist .com/oath-pharmacist. Accessed May 15, 2018.

26. Schriesheim CA, Bird BJ. Contributions of the Ohio State Studies to the field of leadership. *J Manage*. 1979;5(2):135–145. doi:10.1177/014920637900500204.

27. Blake RR, Mouton JS, Bidwell AC. Managerial grid. *Adv Manag - Off Exec*. 1962;1(9):1–5.

28. Gulati R. Structure that's not stifling. *Harv Bus Rev*. 2018;96(3):69–79.

29. Sinek S. How great leaders inspire action. *TED*. 2010. https://www.ted.com/talks /simon_sinek_how_great_leaders_inspire_action/transcript?language=en.

CHAPTER 3

Situational Leadership
Adapting Leadership to the Circumstances

■ ■ OBJECTIVES

■ Explain the primary situational variables that influence which leadership styles to employ.

■ Define the basic leadership styles that are applied in situational leadership.

■ Compare and contrast the effectiveness of various leadership styles in different situations.

■ Describe the characteristics of adaptive leadership and tribal leadership.

■ Make a case for developing multiple leadership styles to lead change in pharmacy practice.

The ultimate measure of a man is not where he stands in moments of comfort and convenience, but where he stands at times of challenge and controversy.

—Martin Luther King Jr.

◼️ ◼️ INTRODUCTION

Chapter 2 of this book discusses leadership theories that emphasize the traits and skills of leaders, the philosophies that guide leaders' approach to leadership, and the behaviors leaders use to influence change. The theory of situational leadership highlights the role of context in effective leadership.

As the name implies, situational leadership depends on the circumstances faced by a leader. Situational theories are based on the common assumption that the greatest predictor of leadership effectiveness and success is the situation faced by leaders and the way leaders react to those situations.[1-3] The leadership traits, competencies, and behaviors that lead to success are specific to the circumstances. In one circumstance, certain traits and behaviors serve a leader well, while in another situation, they may be disastrous. For example, an egotistical and single-minded leader might be an ideal figure in a crisis but an utter failure in collaborative, creative conditions. Box 3.1 describes the frustration new pharmacists feel when facing leadership styles and work tasks that do not match their

BOX 3.1 Leadership in Action: The Frustration of New Pharmacists

Natalie Bishoff is frustrated at work. The district manager of the pharmacy chain where she works is ignoring her suggestions to improve the operations at her store and other pharmacies in the area. The 25-year-old newly graduated pharmacist from the University of Cincinnati accepted the job in the chain because she was promised an opportunity to make a difference in her job and to use her entrepreneurial skills to develop new clinical services. But the majority of her time is spent filling prescriptions and calling insurance companies. Natalie says, "If the company doesn't let me use my full abilities to make things better, why should I continue to work here?"

Ron Springs, the district manager, realizes that Natalie has skills but believes she is too impatient to carry out change. Ron noted, "In pharmacy school, Natalie was used to meeting short-term assignments over one-semester periods. Everything in pharmacy school is a sprint to the finish. She needs to gird herself for the marathon of a 40-year career in community practice. She needs to pay her dues before we start taking her seriously."

Natalie is wondering whether she made the right choice working for the chain. She is satisfied with the pay but really wants meaningful work. She is thinking about joining the Peace Corps or getting a law degree.

Questions

1. Summarize the problem between Natalie and Ron. Are either of them unreasonable in their viewpoints? What is the consequence to the pharmacy of not resolving this issue?

2. What leadership style do you think Ron should use with Natalie? Should he emphasize structure or support? Should he tell her to just accept the circumstances, or should he adopt a more empathetic, nurturing style? Which type of leadership approach do you think Ron is most likely to adopt given his comments about her?

perceived needs and expectations. A key to leadership success is the ability to recognize and understand the dynamics of a situation and adapt behaviors accordingly.

Although individual situational theories vary in content and emphasis,[3-6] they generally provide that the appropriate leadership style depends on the job, the followers, the relationship between the leader and the led, organizational constraints, and the leader's abilities:

- **The nature of the job.** Jobs can be classified as (1) routine and nonroutine or (2) structured and unstructured. Leading people in routine, structured tasks requires different strategies than in nonroutine, unstructured tasks. Simple tasks such as counting, lifting, and reading instructions require different oversight than more complex professional tasks like designing therapeutic plans or evaluating the source of a medication error.

- **Follower characteristics.** Some followers are highly motivated, energetic, willing to accept responsibility, and competent. These individuals may need little direction and structure in their jobs, while unmotivated and less capable people require close oversight and direction.

- **Relationship between leader and followers**. A strong relationship based on mutual trust and respect gives leaders the ability to collaborate and cooperate as a team with followers. A bad relationship leads to suspicion, second guessing of each other's motives, and adversarial interactions.

- **Organizational constraints.** Leaders are often constrained by organizational policies and procedures, corporate culture, and lack of time and resources. Thus, leaders are often hindered in their ability to communicate with, hire, fire, discipline, and reward staff members.

- **The leader's abilities**. Some leaders are more capable and experienced in dealing with leadership situations than others. A leader's ability to adapt to changing situations helps him or her adjust to different tasks, followers, and organizational constraints.

Leaders have little control over many factors influencing leadership situations. For the most part, leaders cannot substantially change the nature of the job, the characteristics of the followers, or the organizational constraints. Most pharmacy leaders "inherit" their workers and are given tasks that must be accomplished within the constraints of the organization. According to situational theory, leadership success depends more on the leader's ability to adapt to a situation than the ability to change it.

Leaders can act in different ways in circumstances varying along several dimensions. One dimension is the degree to which a leader will be directive or supportive to followers (see Table 3.1). *Directive leaders* decide what to do and instruct followers what to do. They establish deadlines and standards of performance, expecting them to be accomplished without much input from followers. In contrast, *supportive leaders* communicate more with followers, collaborate with them in decisions, and provide social and emotional support. As described in behavioral theories discussed in Chapter 2 of this book, supportive leaders emphasize the concerns of the followers, while directive leaders focus on the task at hand.

Another dimension of situational leadership is the degree to which leaders motivate by *pushing* (i.e., using rewards, punishments) or *pulling* (i.e., showing followers the way). Styles that emphasize a push strategy are transactional in nature where the leader says, "If you do this, I will do that." If a follower performs, a reward is given or a punishment is withheld, but if the follower does not perform, a punishment or no reward results. Styles using pull strategies are more persuasive and less transactional. They show the way by (1) establishing a vision of a desirable future, (2) including followers as active members of a team or movement, (3) setting a good example for followers, and (4) challenging them to achieve more than they thought was possible.

In most situations, pull strategies are better because they encourage intrinsically motivated behavior (i.e., motivated by the task and not the reward for the task) and reduce conflicts between leaders and followers. Nevertheless, pull strategies are less effective for some followers and situations, such as when an individual makes a conscious and determined decision not to perform as expected. Showing the way to individuals who refuse to look or follow is difficult.

A final dimension is the degree to which there is a mutual need or desire for a strong leader–follower relationship. Many tasks and jobs do not require close

TABLE 3.1 Directive and Supportive Behaviors in Leadership Styles[a]

Leadership style	Support and direction	Illustration
Delegating	Low support, low direction	"Here is the task. Let me know if you need any help or guidance."
Supporting	High support, low direction	"Here is the task. How are you feeling? Are you up for doing this? Is there anything I can do to help?"
Coaching	High support, high direction	"Here is the task. You can do this. It will help you develop your skills. I will be with you the entire way."
Directive	Low support, high direction	"Here is the task. Here is how to do it. Here is when I expect it to be completed."

a. See reference 1.

interaction between leaders and followers. Also, some individuals do not want to have close relationships with coworkers, bosses, and subordinates. However, modern work settings increasingly demand teamwork and commitment to the team and teammates as a means to achieve top performance.[7–9]

Because relationships are between two or more people, the level of mutual commitment between leaders and followers influences the needed leadership style. Leaders who wish to remain aloof or who lack social intelligence may have difficulty employing some leadership styles. Similarly, followers may not respond well to some relational leadership behaviors. In these cases, leaders need to employ the styles that work best for them and that will be accepted by team members.

STYLES OF LEADERSHIP

Leadership styles are patterns of behavior adopted by a leader to influence change. Styles differ by the way leaders direct (e.g., directive or supportive) and motivate (e.g., inspire, reward, set an example) people and by the types of relationships they have with team members (e.g., emotional bonds, distant and detached). Numerous leadership styles exist in the literature. Several are shown in Table 3.2.

Daniel Goleman identified six basic styles of leadership that address the fundamental influence patterns used by leaders. The six styles are likely to be familiar to anyone who has any work experience. They are coercive, transformational, affiliative, democratic, pacesetting, and coaching styles (Table 3.3).[10]

TABLE 3.2 Leadership Styles in Different Models

Style in a phrase	Goleman's styles[a]	Lewin's styles[b]	Blanchard's SLII[c]
"Do what I say. Now."	Coercive	Authoritarian	Directing
"Come with me."	Transformational[d]		
"People come first."	Affiliative		Supporting
"What do you think?"	Democratic	Participative	
"Follow me."	Pacesetting		
"Try this."	Coaching		Coaching
"You are on your own."		Delegative	Delegative

SLII, situational leadership II.
a. See reference 10.
b. See reference 11.
c. See reference 12.
d. Called "authoritative" by Goleman.

TABLE 3.3 Leadership Styles

Leadership style	Type of influence	Pros and cons
Coercive	Uses rewards and punishments to demand immediate compliance	Motivates quick action; damages relationships and only encourages compliance
Transformational	Mobilizes people toward a vision articulated by a leader	Is highly motivational; not all leaders are visionary
Affiliative	Revolves around meeting the emotional needs of followers	Focuses on people over the task; can neglect task
Democratic	Gives followers a say in decisions that affect their work lives	Solicits input from everyone; can be slow to reach consensus
Pacesetting	Sets extremely high performance standards for both followers and themselves	Works best with highly motivated and skilled teams; can overwhelm and offer confusing expectations
Coaching	Develops followers to work more independently and effectively	Works with motivated people who want to learn; requires time for coaching

Coercive Style

A coercive (or directive) leadership style uses rewards and punishments to influence behavior. This type of leader is very task oriented and controlling of others. Coercive leaders demand immediate compliance with their directions. They expect followers to do as told without question and bristle if they receive suggestions or are asked for feedback. Coercive leaders assume that rewards will be enough to motivate, but they are quick to punish too, if needed. The meme, "The beatings will continue until morale improves," is probably referring to coercive leaders who are not concerned with a team's morale or the overall climate of the organization.

The coercive leadership style is one of the most recognizable, being closely associated with authoritarian, command-and-control, and transactional leaders. It motivates through a simple reward–punishment feedback loop. If followers enact the leader's directions, something good or nothing bad will happen. It is the foundation of grading scales used in education and performance–reward systems in business.

Of all leadership styles, the coercive style appears to be the least effective when used as the primary form of leadership.[10] The coercive leader's emphasis on rewards and punishments often damages professional relationships by reducing human interactions into simple transactions of value. Instead of doing the job for intrinsically motivated reasons—such as the wish to be part of a team, a desire to do good work, or the drive to make a difference—followers work to get a reward or avoid a punishment. Instead of being engaged in their work, workers comply.

The transactional nature of coercive leadership tends to create an us-versus-them environment in which followers feel manipulated and disrespected. Any interaction between leader and follower is seen as a risky event for a gain or loss instead of contact between humans. Conversations devolve into negotiations of expectations instead of collaborations to achieve a goal. Followers avoid enthusiastic participation in new initiatives or programs because of a fear of making mistakes or a perception that their input is not appreciated. Instead, they wait for the leader to tell them what to do and are likely to say, "I just do what I'm told."

Furthermore, coercive leadership negatively affects an organization's culture by increasing competition for rewards and causing conflicts and decreased teamwork. Information is less likely to be shared if it gives an advantage over competitors for rewards. Pitching in to help coworkers is also unlikely if it reduces the chances for raises or bonuses. Focus moves from doing a good job to doing a good enough job to get a reward.

Although often ineffective when used as the primary leadership style, coercive leadership is essential as a supplement to other styles. Coercion is sometimes necessary to have individuals assume undesirable but necessary responsibilities. Some tasks are just not desirable, and coercive incentives (e.g., extra pay for working overtime) are needed sometimes. Coercion can also be indispensable for dealing with difficult coworkers who are apathetic, disruptive to team productivity, or noncompliant in completing their responsibilities. Occasionally, people need to be shocked into changing their behavior. Finally, coercion methods are critical in crises, such as when a business is failing and people resist initiatives that potentially can save the business. Fear through coercion may be the only way of getting people to change their entrenched behaviors.

Nevertheless, even under these conditions, coercive leadership should be used sparingly and for limited periods.[10] During crises, too much fear can cause people to give up hope or obsess over their personal concerns. Often, they need someone to attend to their emotional needs too. Similarly, people who have lost hope can regain it when leaders communicate a path for achieving success in the future.

● Transformational Style

The transformational style (labeled "authoritative" by Goleman) mobilizes people toward a vision articulated by a leader.[10] The transformational leader works with followers to identify the change needed, create a vision of the desired future, and facilitate their efforts toward the vision. This style is inclusive by developing a collective group identity and engaging the group in the change, "We see a future where pharmacists work in interprofessional teams to maximize patient health. Let's make it happen." Team members are challenged to take ownership of their work toward the vision.

Transformational leaders rely on charismatic power, not rewards and punishments, to influence others. They influence others because followers identify with them and their collective message. Martin Luther King Jr. is an example of a transformational leader. King shared a dream of what society could be like in America, "It is a dream deeply rooted in the American dream. I have a dream that one day this nation will rise up, live out the true meaning of its creed: 'We hold these truths to be self-evident, that all men are created equal.'" Through actions and words, he inspired millions to make that dream their own.

Of the six leadership styles, the transformational style is considered to have the most positive effect on the culture of organizations in the greatest number of situations.[10,13] Transformational leaders can inspire people by clearly defining how their work fits into a larger vision for the organization. This, in turn, maximizes the commitment of followers to the vision and energizes them to seek the best path for achieving it. Feedback from the leader focuses less on the process of achieving goals and more on the outcomes, encouraging individuals to innovate and take risks. The culture of the organization is energized toward achieving the vision.

The transformational style can fail when the leader is unable to articulate a clear vision. Not every leader can effectively communicate such a vision. Poor attempts at inspirational leadership may be seen as pompous or out of touch. Trust in the vision can also be broken when transformational leaders fail to model behaviors consistent with the vision or when they lose sight of their dream. Such a leader can have difficulty sustaining the inspiration of others.

■ Affiliative Style

The affiliative style of leadership revolves around meeting the emotional needs of followers. It is often associated with so-called maternal characteristics such as nurturing, benevolence, and caring.

The affiliative style focuses on people, whereas coercive leadership focuses on the task. Affiliative leaders seek happiness, harmony, and, ultimately, mutual loyalty between leaders and followers. They attempt to build trust by demonstrating respect to others and communicating openly. They offer positive feedback for good work to build confidence and self-esteem. When affiliative leaders are critical, the feedback is provided with the greatest care and concern for an individual's feelings. The goal is to increase productivity by enhancing communication, loyalty, trust, and innovation.

Affiliative leaders have a positive effect on the culture of an organization, particularly during times of stress or when the culture has been damaged by poor leadership in the past. Affiliative leaders make members of the team feel appreciated, welcome, and at ease.

Nevertheless, overreliance on the affiliative style can have negative effects. Just as coercive leadership can overemphasize the task to the detriment of people, the affiliative leader can stress the people over the job at hand. For instance, followers who hear only praise will not know when or how they need to improve their behavior. Poor performance can go uncorrected if followers feel that mediocrity is acceptable. Necessary conflicts that allow airing of differences may be papered over to avoid any stress. Too much nurturing may also lead to a sense of entitlement.[14,15]

Concerns have been voiced that recent generations of workers have received so much praise from their parents, teachers, and sports coaches that they expect kudos for just showing up.[14] There are worries that overnurturing has reduced the resilience of young people and caused an increase in emotional fragility to negative feedback.

Whether this is true or not, all workers — young and old — need structure to do their jobs well. Too much of one or the other can negatively influence the performance of pharmacy teams. Therefore, affiliative leaders need to supplement supportive behaviors with styles that offer more structure.

▆ Democratic Style

Leaders who practice the democratic style give followers a say in decisions that affect the followers' work lives. They solicit input from followers and attain the followers' buy-in for major decisions and initiatives. This approach generates a sense of ownership by the staff in an organization's goals, nurtures the generation of ideas by including more individuals in the process, and helps build mutual trust and respect.

The downside is that democracy can be frustratingly inefficient. It often leads people to debate trivial issues and haggle over decisions rather than take action. Another pitfall is that reaching consensus can lead to compromises that produce less-than-optimal results. This is a real problem when the pressure of deadlines looms or when individuals lack the qualifications to help with the decision. Democracy also fails when people are cynical and unwilling to participate in the democratic process. Finally, some leaders use the democratic style to avoid making difficult decisions (i.e., those that might have a negative effect on a leader's career). Instead, they attempt to shift responsibility—and potential blame—to followers.

The key is to choose those situations where democratic leadership works well and does not work well. The democratic style works optimally when the democratic process has sufficient time to unfold, the best course is uncertain, and followers are sufficiently competent to contribute. Everyone's understanding of and agreement to the process in which decisions will be made is also important. When these conditions are in place, the democratic leadership style can be very successful in developing a positive and collaborative culture in organizations and teams.

Pacesetting Style

Pacesetting leaders set extremely high performance standards for both followers and themselves.[10] Pacesetters lead by example—demonstrating effort and sacrifice and asking the same of others. If the pacesetter puts in long hours or gives up weekends for work-related projects, everyone else is expected to do the same. In essence, the pacesetter says, "Do as I do." Followers who cannot keep up with the leader are replaced by others who will.

Pacesetting leaders are often praised as admirable, and the pacesetting style is adopted by many pharmacy leaders. It is a common style adopted by people who have been in the military or who have participated in competitive athletics. When applied appropriately, a pacesetter's leadership style often builds credibility with followers by setting a good example.

The problem is that the pacesetting style can have an unintended negative effect on morale and performance.[10] A pacesetter's demands for total job commitment can seem unreasonable and overwhelming to many followers. Not everyone has the same dedication to the job as the pacesetter, especially if the leader has not inspired the followers toward a shared vision.

Another problem is that some pacesetters are not clear in the performance they expect of others. A pacesetter may believe that his or her actions are sending a clear message, but the meaning of actions can be ambiguous and misinterpreted. For instance, a leader may try to communicate through his or her actions the message, "If we all work as hard, we are going to be the best pharmacy in town." However, the follower may misinterpret the leader's message as, "If you do not work as hard as I do, you aren't good enough." When a pacesetting leader does not supplement actions with clear statements of expectations, followers are left to guess the leader's intentions. When they are not made explicit, perceived expectations of performance boil down to "be as good as me."

Nevertheless, the pacesetting style can be effective when done well. It is effective in leading self-motivated and highly competent people who need little direction to complete tasks, such as in professional sports and medical professions. It also works well when combined with other styles that supplement the pacesetter's actions with explicit written and spoken communication. Finally, it succeeds when pacesetters use the style humbly, in a way that does not appear arrogant or narcissistic.

Coaching Style

Coaching leaders strive to develop the abilities of their followers so the followers can work more independently and effectively toward organizational goals. They help followers set personal and professional goals and achieve them through career development, training, and skill development. Coaches work cooperatively with followers to improve productivity and performance, and they provide followers with the tools necessary to attain success. They challenge followers and delegate tasks to help followers develop skills.

Coaching can be a very effective leadership style, but it is often underused because managerial demands frequently do not permit leaders sufficient time for the slow and laborious work involved.[10] In many cases, leaders can do a task more easily themselves than teach others to do it. However, subordinates' learning a new skill can free leaders for other commitments. People who are taught to do a task can take over the responsibility for its completion. They may even do a better job than the coach. This style can positively affect an organization's culture by building highly productive teams that continually seek to be better.

Coaches do better with followers who are motivated to improve their performance and mature enough to accept feedback. Coaching also requires individuals who are willing to take responsibility for their personal development, instead of expecting it to be provided by the leader. Coaching does not work as well when followers resist change or new ideas. It can also be ineffective in a crisis, when quick actions are necessary. Coaching requires time and investment in developing people. Not all organizations are willing to invest the effort and money needed to benefit from the coaching style of leadership.

■ *Summary*

One can argue that Goleman's six leadership styles capture the major approaches to influencing others, although knowing other commonly discussed styles is useful. Box 3.2 describes additional leadership styles and the way they relate to Goleman's six styles.

■ ■ LEADERS NEED MANY STYLES

The more leadership styles a person masters, the better he or she can adapt to changing leadership situations. Leaders who have mastered four or more styles—especially the transformational, democratic, affiliative, and coaching styles—tend to establish and maintain the best working environment and show better business performance.[10] Equally important to mastery of leadership styles is the ability to switch among them as the situation demands (Figure 3.1).

Some leaders adapt to their leadership deficiencies by finding environments that match their styles and abilities. For example, a coercive leader might try to find a

---

BOX 3.2 Additional Leadership Styles

The following are additional leadership styles:

※ **Authoritarian.** An authoritarian leader is similar to the coercive leader in that he or she tells people what to do and how to do it and controls others without any meaningful input from them. Autocrats and dictators use this style.

※ **Bureaucratic.** This style relies on following policies and procedures and adhering to lines of authority. It is closest to the characteristics that people associate with managers: follow and enforce the rules, and discourage any imagination or creative solutions.

※ **Command and control.** This style is normally used to describe military leaders who blend a mix of authoritarianism and bureaucracy in leading soldiers to obey commands at any cost. In the modern military, this type of leadership style is becoming less prevalent.

※ **Laissez-faire.** Laissez-faire in French means "Let people do as they choose." Therefore, it describes a hands-off leadership style that gives the least possible guidance to followers. This style assumes that people excel when left on their own and is the opposite of the authoritarian style. It differs from the coaching style in which coaches delegate authority to followers to allow them a chance to learn and grow. Laissez-faire leaders cede authority to followers.

※ **Transactional.** This style views every interaction with team members as an exchange of value, " will do this for you if you do that for me." It can be seen as the same as coercive leadership because it is manipulative and motivates with rewards or punishments.

FIGURE 3.1 Matching Leadership Style to Situational Characteristics

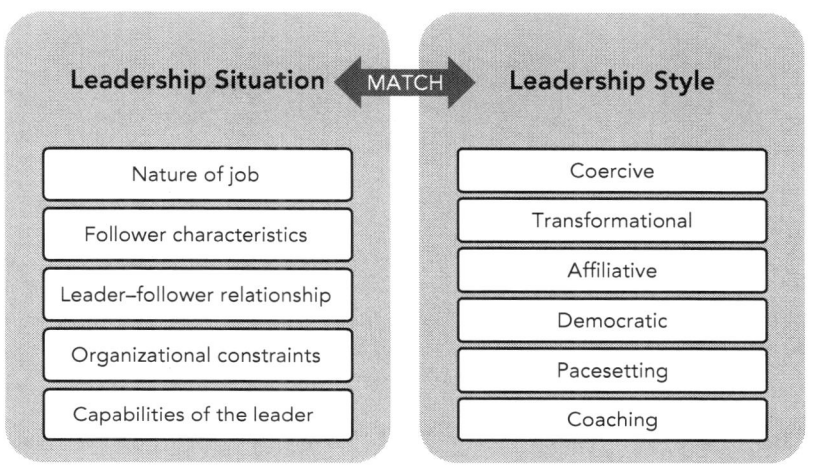

situation in which the staff prefers significant structure and the tasks are routine and standardized, or a democratic leader might seek followers who are participative and circumstances where democracy can thrive. The problem is that situations constantly change. Several famous wartime leaders, including Ulysses S. Grant, Winston Churchill, and George S. Patton, failed as peacetime leaders because they were unable to adapt their leadership to the new environment.

Other leaders adapt by working with individuals who are willing and able to cover up their leadership weaknesses. This adaptation requires leaders to understand their own weaknesses, identify individuals who have skills they lack, and be willing to delegate key responsibilities to those individuals with the requisite skills. For instance, a leader who lacks good interpersonal skills may try to delegate sensitive personnel issues to subordinates with such skills. The major problem with this solution is that the leader relies on others to do key aspects of his or her job. When key subordinates are not available or they leave for other jobs, the leader is left in a difficult position. The leader can also lose credibility with followers if too many responsibilities are delegated because the leader cannot or will not handle them.

Ultimately, leaders should develop the ability to apply multiple leadership styles to different situations. This approach requires the leader to expand his or her repertoire of leadership styles as much as possible. It also requires the leader to learn to identify effective styles for various leadership situations.

ADAPTIVE LEADERSHIP

A relatively new situational leadership framework has been proposed—adaptive leadership. *Adaptive leadership* is a framework that regards leadership as a process, not the application of styles.[16] The process consists of identifying and focusing on specific problems and adapting with new solutions. It is a framework designed primarily to adapt to extreme and continuous changes such as those currently occurring in health care. It is highly collaborative and consists of the following steps:[17]

1. Identify whether the problem is technical (common problems with relatively clear solutions) or adaptive (uncommon, challenging, or new situation without easy solutions).

2. Focus people's attention on the important aspects and away from distractions. Secure commitment from individuals to implement and support change.

3. Frame the issues to be considered. Ensure that there is a focus on the overall situation.

4. Secure ownership by stakeholders. Sustain conditions that make them take responsibility for offering solutions and solving problems.

5. Manage the conflict that inevitably occurs with change.

6. Create a safe haven where stakeholders maintain the change. Protect them from naysayers and doubters who may try to pressure them to revert to the status quo.

Adaptive leadership relies heavily on collaborative problem-solving processes and team behaviors. The argument for adaptive leadership is that chaotic conditions and crises are becoming the norm in life and work, and adaptive processes do not require the ability to predict the future, only to adapt to it.

CONCLUSION

Situational leadership considers the changing nature of leadership challenges and argues that leaders need to change as situations vary. Leaders can respond to challenges by assessing the circumstances and applying the appropriate leadership style. Sometimes, adjustments in style may be needed from one minute to the next.

Alternatively, leaders may choose adaptive processes to respond to leadership challenges. The best situational approach depends on the nature of the job, the individuals and their relationships, the organization in which the change is needed, and the capabilities of leaders.

██ ██ KEY TERMS AND CONCEPTS

- Situational leadership
- Directive leaders
- Supportive leaders
- Coercive leadership style
- Transformational leadership style
- Affiliative leadership style
- Democratic leadership style
- Pacesetting leadership style
- Coaching leadership style
- Authoritarian leadership style
- Bureaucratic leadership style
- Command-and-control leadership style
- Laissez-faire leadership style
- Transactional leadership style
- Adaptive leadership

██ ██ DISCUSSION AND REVIEW QUESTIONS

1. How do situational leaders identify the correct style to apply?

2. Why are pacesetting leaders so ineffective?

3. Which leadership style is most effective in developing other leaders?

4. Is laissez-faire leadership really leadership? Does a hands-off approach really influence change?

5. Why do transactional leaders have difficulty gaining anything more than compliance in followers? Why not commitment?

⬛⬤ REFERENCES

1. Blanchard KH, Zigarmi D, Nelson RB. Situational leadership after 25 years: a retrospective. *J Leadersh Organ Stud.* 1993;1(1):21–36.

2. Ayman R, Chemers MM, Fiedler F. The contingency model of leadership effectiveness: its levels of analysis. *Leadership Q.* 1995;6(2):147–167.

3. House RJ. Path-goal theory of leadership: lessons, legacy, and a reformulated theory. *Leadersh Q.* 1996;7(3):323–352.

4. Fiedler FE, Garcia JE. *New Approaches to Effective Leadership: Cognitive Resources and Organizational Performance.* New York, NY: John Wiley; 1987.

5. House RJ, Mitchell RR. Path-goal theory of leadership. *J Contemp Bus.* 1974; (Autumn):81–97.

6. Vroom V, Yetton P. *Leadership and Decision Making.* Pittsburgh, PA: University of Pittsburgh Press; 1973.

7. Hersey P, Blanchard KH. *Management of Organizational Behavior.* Englewood Cliffs, NJ: Prentice Hall; 1993.

8. Gabarro JJ, Kotter JP. Managing your boss: a compatible relationship with your superior is essential to being effective in your job. *Harv Bus Rev.* 1980;58(1): 92–100.

9. Erin W. Healthcare employee commitment rises among strong leaders. *Managed Healthc Exec.* 2004;14(6):44.

10. Goleman D. Leadership that gets results. *Harv Bus Rev.* 2000;(March–April):78–90.

11. Lewin K, Lippitt R, White RK. Patterns of aggressive behavior in experimentally created "social climates." *J Soc Psych.* 1939;10(2):269–308. doi:10.1080/00224545 .1939.9713366.

12. Blanchard KH, Hersey P. Great ideas revisited: revisiting the life-cycle theory of leadership. *Train Dev J.* 1996;(January):42–47.

13. Bass BM. From transactional to transformational leadership: learning to share the vision. *Organ Dyn.* 1990;18(3):19–31.

14. Zaslow J. Blame it on Mr. Rogers: why young adults feel so entitled. *Wall Street Journal,* July 5, 2007. https://www.wsj.com/articles/SB118358476840657463.

15. Zaslow J. The most praised generation goes to work. *Wall Street Journal,* April 20, 2007. https://www.wsj.com/articles/SB117702894815776259.

16. Heifetz R, Grashow A, Linsky M. Leadership in a (permanent) crisis. *Harv Bus Rev.* 2009;87(7–8):62–69, 153.

17. Heifetz RA, Grashow A, Linsky M. *The Practice of Adaptive Leadership: Tools and Tactics for Changing Your Organization and the World.* Boston, MA: Harvard Business Press; 2009.

CHAPTER 4

Ethical Leadership
Making Morally Defensible Choices

■■ OBJECTIVES

- ▪ Define ethics and ethical leadership.
- ▪ Describe frameworks for guiding ethical behavior.
- ▪ Compare and contrast ethical decision-making frameworks.
- ▪ Present guiding principles for ethical leadership.

Ethics is knowing the difference between what you have a right to do and what is right to do.

—Potter Stewart

◼ ● INTRODUCTION

Leadership was defined in Chapter 1 of this book as a process through which an individual attempts to intentionally influence another person or a group to accomplish a goal. This definition is silent on *how* leadership should be practiced or *how* the goal should be accomplished. Without further guidance, the definition suggests that anything is acceptable when influencing others: leaders can be manipulative, deceitful, unfair, abusive, and disrespectful of the people they lead and the individuals affected in pursuit of a goal. And any goal can be pursued, including selfish personal gain, retaliation against others, or capricious desires. However, one must question whether the following behavior by leaders is acceptable:

- Coercing others with threats and other forms of pressure

- Putting an individual's interests (including one's own) ahead of the group

- Putting the interests of one group ahead of another's

- Deceiving colleagues or the people the leader serves

- Restricting the rights of others

- Being inconsistent in the treatment of others

- Failing to hold oneself and one's colleagues to the highest principles of conduct

One might argue that the legal system and governance processes of organizations prevent leaders from acting inappropriately to meet malicious or selfish objectives. Yet laws, rules, policies, and procedures do not prevent leaders from acting badly. Often, laws are vague and poorly enforced. In addition, the good or bad quality of many leadership behaviors depends on the circumstances.[1] Actions might be highly unethical in some instances and ethically defensible in others.

In many instances, there is no clear ethical choice when influencing change.[2] Leaders need guidance from more than just the law or organizational policies and procedures. They need a moral framework to steer themselves through the gray areas of right and wrong.

Ethics provides that framework for leaders.[3-5] *Ethics* is a way of understanding and choosing between what is morally right and wrong. It employs ethical principles to achieve morally defensible outcomes. Thus, *ethical leadership* can be defined as the process through which leaders attempt to accomplish morally defensible goals in a morally defensible manner.

What does "morally defensible" mean? First, it means avoiding clearly immoral actions that are contrary to codes of behavior expected of pharmacists. One of the codes of conduct for pharmacists is the Oath of a Pharmacist, which was discussed in Chapter 1 of this book. Box 4.1 provides the complete Code of Ethics for Pharmacists.[6]

The Code of Ethics for Pharmacists establishes a set of principles for pharmacists to follow in their professional settings. A pharmacist who fails to behave in accordance with the code is likely to be seen and judged as unethical. Consequently, ethical pharmacist leaders should not take the following actions:

- Put their own interests before those of patients and others

- Skip opportunities to advocate for the welfare of patients

- Share the confidential information of any individual or group

- Be dishonest

- Forsake lifelong learning

- Show disrespect

- Fail to seek fair distribution of health resources

The problem is that the code's general guidelines are ambiguous when principles conflict. For example, how does one choose between being honest and hurting someone with that honesty? Similarly, what if respecting a person's autonomy will cause him or her harm or break the trust of a third individual? How does one choose among being honest, preventing harm, providing benefit, meeting one's responsibility to both a profession and an employer, or any other dilemma faced by pharmacists every day? Box 4.2 describes an ethical problem faced by leaders in the CVS pharmacy chain. The answers to ethical problems can be found by using ethical frameworks and processes to deal with morally ambiguous problems and situations.

⬛ ⬤ ETHICAL FRAMEWORKS

Ethical frameworks are structures for guiding moral decisions. They help leaders answer the question, "What does it mean to be ethical in this situation?" Ethical frameworks assume that decisions about "right" and "wrong" involve difficult choices and tradeoffs and that they rarely result in one best outcome. Instead,

BOX 4.1 Code of Ethics for Pharmacists[a]

The Code of Ethics for Pharmacists provides as follows:

PREAMBLE
Pharmacists are health professionals who assist individuals in making the best use of medications. This Code, prepared and supported by pharmacists, is intended to state publicly the principles that form the fundamental basis of the roles and responsibilities of pharmacists. These principles, based on moral obligations and virtues, are established to guide pharmacists in relationships with patients, health professionals, and society.

I. A pharmacist respects the covenantal relationship between the patient and pharmacist.
Considering the patient–pharmacist relationship as a covenant means that a pharmacist has moral obligations in response to the gift of trust received from society. In return for this gift, a pharmacist promises to help individuals achieve optimum benefit from their medications, to be committed to their welfare, and to maintain their trust.

II. A pharmacist promotes the good of every patient in a caring, compassionate, and confidential manner.
A pharmacist places concern for the well-being of the patient at the center of professional practice. In doing so, a pharmacist considers needs stated by the patient as well as those defined by health science. A pharmacist is dedicated to protecting the dignity of the patient. With a caring attitude and a compassionate spirit, a pharmacist focuses on serving the patient in a private and confidential manner.

III. A pharmacist respects the autonomy and dignity of each patient.
A pharmacist promotes the right of self-determination and recognizes individual self-worth by encouraging patients to participate in decisions about their health. A pharmacist communicates with patients in terms that are understandable. In all cases, a pharmacist respects personal and cultural differences among patients.

IV. A pharmacist acts with honesty and integrity in professional relationships.
A pharmacist has a duty to tell the truth and to act with conviction of conscience. A pharmacist avoids discriminatory practices, behavior or work conditions that impair professional judgment, and actions that compromise dedication to the best interests of patients.

V. A pharmacist maintains professional competence.
A pharmacist has a duty to maintain knowledge and abilities as new medications, devices, and technologies become available and as health information advances.

VI. A pharmacist respects the values and abilities of colleagues and other health professionals.
When appropriate, a pharmacist asks for the consultation of colleagues or other health professionals or refers the patient. A pharmacist acknowledges that colleagues and other health professionals may differ in the beliefs and values they apply to the care of the patient.

VII. A pharmacist serves individual, community, and societal needs.
The primary obligation of a pharmacist is to individual patients. However, the obligations of a pharmacist may at times extend beyond the individual to the community and society. In these situations, the pharmacist recognizes the responsibilities that accompany these obligations and acts accordingly.

VIII. A pharmacist seeks justice in the distribution of health resources.
When health resources are allocated, a pharmacist is fair and equitable, balancing the needs of patients and society.

a. See reference 6.

BOX 4.2 Leadership in Action: CVS Forces Workers to Reveal Weight or Pay Up[a]

Many employers, including pharmacies, are attempting to keep health care costs and insurance premiums low by encouraging employees to get healthy. Some employers pay for gym memberships, offer disease management programs, or hold exercise classes.

The CVS pharmacy chain decided to offer a wellness program that required workers to disclose their weight and other health metrics or pay more in health insurance—$600 more.

Questions

1. Is this program ethical from a utilitarian viewpoint? What are the benefits and potential costs of the program?

2. What ethical values are in conflict with such a program?

3. The program is said to be voluntary. Is it really voluntary? Is there greater pressure for some pharmacy employees to participate than others?

4. What are the potential abuses of the program? What concerns would you have with the program?

a. See reference 7.

frameworks help make those tradeoffs explicit and thoughtful, and they offer ways of judging the morality of the process and the outcomes.

Ethical frameworks fall into three major categories: (1) *virtue frameworks*, which are concerned with what type of person a leader is or wants to be; (2) *deontological frameworks*, which address the moral duties of leaders; and (3) *teleological frameworks*, which deal with the ethical consequences of a leader's actions. Each of these categories emphasizes a different part of the moral decision and asks different questions to judge the ethics of a decision (Table 4.1).

▣ *Virtue Framework*

Virtue frameworks are based on the principle that an individual's actions should be consistent with ideal human virtues. Virtues are the character traits and

TABLE 4.1 Ethical Frameworks for Decisions

Frameworks	Emphasis	Primary ethical question
Virtue	Moral character	"What kind of person should I strive to be as a leader?"
Deontological	Moral duty	"What behaviors are consistent with my duty as a leader?"
Teleological	Moral consequences	"What choices lead to the greatest benefit?"

characteristics acquired and learned from family, friends, faith, and experience. A person with good character is one who has attained ideal virtues. Individuals who seek to achieve and live these virtues are considered ethical.

Virtue frameworks emphasize what a person should be, instead of the way a person should act (i.e., duty) or the outcome of actions (e.g., consequences). Virtue frameworks are similar to trait theories of leadership because they focus on the traits and characteristics of ethical leaders. Virtues or traits commonly associated with ethical leaders include courage, integrity, honor, honesty, grit, humility, selflessness, compassion, and benevolence. Leaders who strive to achieve these virtues through training and experience are typically judged as ethical.

Virtues of pharmacy leaders are established in formal statements such as the pharmacist's Code of Ethics. Therefore, ethical pharmacy leaders should strive to accomplish the following:

- Respect the patient, colleagues, and the patient–pharmacist relationship.
- Put the interests of others before their own.
- Be fair in the way they treat others and in the distribution of health resources.
- Continually learn and set high expectations for themselves and others.
- Act with honesty and integrity.
- Build community.

Several problems are associated with the use of virtue frameworks in guiding leaders. First, virtues are not always associated with ethical behavior. Virtues such as courage, honesty, generosity, and compassion can be faults in some situations. For example, generosity can be used to exert power over others or to demean the lower status of individuals. Extravagant gifts may be seen by the giver as generous, but perceived by the receiver as a sign of disrespect.

Second, virtues are often seen in terms of black and white instead of shades of gray (i.e., matters of degree). Few people exhibit purity of virtue. Those who try are called "moral absolutists." People who are moral absolutists do not see shades of gray with respect to virtuous behavior, and this outlook often creates difficulty with coworkers. For example, pharmacists who are always honest with patients and coworkers can be seen as rude, culturally insensitive, and self-righteous. Moral absolutists' strident opinions may appear to devalue others' diversity of beliefs and backgrounds. Moral absolutism can cause conflict in workplaces, cultures, and societies.

Negotiating the line between virtue and vice is difficult. Indeed, the seven deadly sins of gluttony, greed, sloth, wrath, envy, lust, and pride can be seen as virtues when practiced in moderation. For example, greed by some people might be seen as healthy self-interest by others. Therefore, other ethical frameworks can help guide pharmacy leaders.

■ Deontology Framework

"Deonto" means obligation or duty, and deontology frames the duties associated with moral behavior. Rather than focusing on an individual's virtues or the outcomes of actions, deontology emphasizes the importance of a leader's actions or duties to the people being served. Pharmacy leaders who act according to their duties are judged as morally correct independent of the outcome generated.

For example, a pharmacist has obligations he or she must fulfill when treating patients. These obligations include doing no harm and ensuring the safety of patients' health and their confidential information. A pharmacist leader has the same duties plus the additional duties associated with leading people.

With the deontology framework, the pharmacist leader's actions are judged as ethical by the moral intentions of those actions rather than their consequences. The idea is that moral actions may not always lead to the best outcome in the short run, but over time, the accumulation of moral acts will lead to good consequences.

This idea can be illustrated by the example of a pharmacist leader who is tempted to ask team members, just this one time, to cut corners when serving patients. Although the consequence might be defensible in the short run as being in the best interests of patients (i.e., their prescriptions are filled in a timely manner), the act itself might be seen as morally doubtful by short-changing the medication management process and putting the patient at greater risk. Furthermore, the long-term consequence might be negative for patients (i.e., cutting corners might become the standard of care) and for the team–leader relationship because this action emphasizes the message that, "We act morally only when it is convenient or when we are not too busy."

■ Teleology Framework

"Telos" means end, and teleology (also called "consequentialist ethics") focuses on the consequences or results of actions as a measure of moral behavior. In this framework, morality is judged by the result of decisions made and actions taken. Utilitarianism is a doctrine that falls into this category, and it argues that a leader's actions are good or bad depending on how much overall utility (i.e., value) they provide to the most people. Thus, leadership is ethical if it promotes the greatest benefit to the most people.

The teleology framework is consistent with economic theory, which attempts to maximize utility in economic choices. In pharmacy leadership, this framework is associated with individuals who consider the effect their actions will have on patients, coworkers, employers, other professionals, the health care system, and more. Although laudable, this framework can lead to some problems in leadership.

First, the framework requires leaders to reliably forecast the future. It assumes that leaders have a deep understanding of how people will react when a change is made, when the truth is that people are complex and their responses are highly unpredictable. For instance, a leader may think that implementing a pay-for-performance plan will motivate individuals to be more productive, but such plans often have the opposite effect on productivity. Leaders may mean well, but best intentions can often lead to bad outcomes.

Second, the human capacity for perceptual biases can cloud the ability to predict the consequences of actions. Leaders often use motivated reasoning to justify immoral actions to help them feel better about the pain and suffering they inflict on others. Leaders can justify narcissism, cruelty, disrespect, insults, selfishness, and any other immoral action when these actions are in support of some promised outcome (e.g., being the best, maximizing shareholder value). In fact, many organizations enable this self-deception by overlooking some immoral behavior in leadership if the outcomes are justified.

Nevertheless, leaders making ethical decisions should consider the consequences of any choice. When leaders develop a track record for making decisions that show clear and measurable benefits for the most people over time, the case can be made that these leaders are ethical and acting morally.

Summary

Ultimately, all three frameworks attempt to achieve moral goodness. The virtue framework considers leaders to be ethical when they strive to be virtuous in the way they treat others and the outcomes they pursue. The deontology framework judges the ethical behavior of a leader's actions in both the short run and the long run. The teleological framework sees leadership as influencing change through people in a way that maximizes the benefit of the outcomes achieved.

Whether one framework is better than any other is a matter of debate. One might expect any framework to guide leaders to make morally defensible decisions. A person who attempts to be virtuous tries to act ethically and achieve good outcomes. Similarly, a person who acts ethically will be judged virtuous and attain morally good outcomes. Further, a leader who seeks moral goodness will be more likely do good and be seen as doing good. The key is that leaders use at least some moral framework to guide their decisions. All leaders should ask themselves the following:

- Is this action consistent with my values and the person I want to be?

- Would I feel good about my actions if they were being judged by my parents, peers, or an individual whom I highly respect?

- What are the potential consequences, both intended and unintended, of my actions?

If leaders answer these questions truthfully and with minimal bias, they will likely be seen as virtuous, acting according to their duties as pharmacists and leaders and achieving morally good consequences. Without a process for ethical inquiry, individuals will be more likely to act unethically using a variety of excuses, including those noted in Box 4.3.

BOX 4.3 Rationalizations for Unethical Behavior

People often justify unethical acts by rationalizing their behavior. The following are some common rationalizations for not acting ethically:

- *I might get sued.* Fear of legal action is often exaggerated to avoid acting in a morally correct manner.
- *It is against the law.* Fear of the law is often used to justify not acting in a person's best interest.
- *If it is not against the law, it is ethical.* Just because something is legal does not make it right.
- *It is not our policy.* Policies are weak excuses for inaction.
- *No harm, no foul.* Unethical actions are often justified when they do not cause any harm.
- *Everyone else does it.* Standards of practice or bad habits are never a reason for unethical behavior.
- *He is not like other people.* Individuals such as politicians and celebrities are often not held to the same norms as the masses.
- *It is a slippery slope.* Unethical actions are rationalized if they might cause a precedent that leads to a cascade of events.
- *It's for a good cause.* This is often used to support tribalism, that is, if it helps our tribe, any behavior is acceptable.
- *I have earned this.* Some people try to justify occasional current lapses in ethics with positive past ethical actions.

◼ ◼ ETHICAL DECISION-MAKING PROCESS

The process of ethical decision making follows many of the same steps as clinical, managerial, economic, and legal decision making.[8] These steps include identifying and defining the problem, suggesting and weighing solutions, making a choice, and assessing the results of the choice. A major difference is the intended result of the decision. The goal of ethical decision making is to do one's ethical duty in a way that achieves the most good.[2] The goals of other decision frameworks might focus on health outcomes, legal liability, organizational effectiveness, or cost-benefit.

◼ *Step 1: Gather the Facts*

Ethical decisions, like any other decision, should be based on facts. Although one might be tempted to rely on one's intuition or feelings in decision making, that approach has a greater potential for cognitive biases to lead to bad choices. For instance, a leader might assume that a trusted team member's account of a situation is fact without verifying it with other members of the team.

The facts to be gathered revolve around who, what, where, when, how, and why. Who are the individuals or groups involved and the affected parties? What is the problem and the potential consequences associated with the problem? Where is the location of the problem? When is the problem and over what time period? How has the problem arisen and why?

In many circumstances, facts will be missing or unattainable and assumptions will need to be made. In these situations, people might be overly confident that their assumptions are correct. Alternatively, some people might be tempted to delay making tough decisions because they lack all of the details.

One should realize the following realities in decision making. First, leaders never have all of the facts when making a decision. Second, sometimes it is better to make an acceptable quick decision instead of putting off a decision until the situation is perfect. Finally, assumptions are simply guesses based on inadequate information. Leaders should clarify any assumptions being made and continually challenge them as new facts are obtained.

◼ *Step 2: Identify Type of Ethical Problem*

The type of ethical problem being faced will help clarify the associated ethical issues.[2] An ethical problem is a situation that an individual believes presents a serious threat or challenge to his or her essential moral values and duties as a leader. It is a situation that requires reflection regarding the type of action to take and the potential consequences of the action. This type of decision contrasts with decisions made on the basis of one's intuition, which demand little thought.

There are several types of ethical problems faced by pharmacist leaders. The three primary ones are ethical distress, ethical dilemma, and locus of authority problem.

Ethical Distress

Ethical distress is a problem in which a leader faces a challenge about how to maintain his or her professional integrity or the integrity of the pharmacy profession.[9] It generally refers to a circumstance in which the pharmacist knows the proper course of action but hesitates to take that action because of outside pressures or concerns. Ethical distress is further divided into Type A, in which there is a clear barrier preventing an individual from doing what is right, and Type B, in which there is something wrong with a choice but discerning what is getting in the way of doing what is right is unclear. Examples of ethical distress include the following:

- The distress caused by having to choose between filling prescriptions quickly in a busy pharmacy or providing personalized care for patient-related needs

- The distress associated with charging a patient for a medication that he or she cannot afford and staying in business

- The distress resulting from the decision to lay off an unproductive employee who is one paycheck away from being homeless

The solution to dealing with ethical distress is to identify the source of distress and then take actions that are defensible to the parties involved, including oneself. Pharmacists know that patients' needs should take priority, but they also know that giving away pharmacist services and medications can cause a pharmacy to go out of business. In many cases, pharmacists will blame their distress on external sources such as a demanding employer or a health care system that does not adequately value pharmacists. Pharmacists may throw up their hands and say, "There's nothing I can do about it." Rather than take action, they become immune to the moral distress or rationalize it away.

A more morally responsible course of action is to act—act in any way that might help the needs of patients and the health care system. This type of action might include developing additional revenue sources to support clinical pharmacy services for those who need it or identifying strategies to help people with low financial means gain access to needed medications. Even if they fail, pharmacists who try to make a difference are more ethical and more faithful to their professional duty than those who do nothing. Also, doing nothing will never relieve the ethical stress they feel.

Ethical Dilemma

An *ethical dilemma* is a problem in which an individual faces a choice between two or more morally defensible courses of action.[10] No choice is clearly superior or inferior to any other choice, that is, they are just different. The dilemma lies in how to judge the differences and make the right choice.

Ethical dilemmas frequently occur when elements of moral codes or value systems conflict. Examples include dilemmas associated with counseling patients effectively in the face of severe time constraints, maintaining the confidentiality of a patient's intent to commit suicide, providing drug information for questionable uses, distributing soon-to-expire medications, using drugs for unapproved indications, and informing patients about diagnoses.[1] Pharmacists are supposed to respect an individual's autonomy, be honest, and also do good, but some values might take precedence over others in a given situation. Pharmacists are also supposed to act in the best interests of patients, coworkers, their employer, other health care professionals, and society. In many circumstances, the interests of some parties override the interests of others.

The solution to solving ethical dilemmas is to clearly understand the problem and the various choices. This solution includes understanding who is involved, seeing details from their perspective, and recognizing the conflicting moral choices to be made. For instance, an ethical dilemma relating to drug affordability might involve the patient, the insurer, the patient's employer, and the pharmacist. The conflicting moral choices might be between doing good, preventing harm, being honest, and using fairness. The solution lies in working through the moral problem and coming up with a solution that is best according to the pharmacist's best judgement.

Locus of Authority Problem

The *locus of authority problem* occurs when pharmacists must decide who should be the primary decision maker in a situation.[2] In this problem, two or more individuals in positions of authority have their own unique ideas for addressing a problem. This situation is common in pharmacy because a pharmacist's professional role is not clearly understood by the public, the health care system, and even pharmacists themselves. The conflict might be between the pharmacist and a physician, nurse, pharmacy benefit manager, or other entity involved in the medication use process.

The question in the locus of authority problem is, "Who is the rightful agent to make an important moral decision or determine a course of action?" For pharmacists, it typically arises from role ambiguities in medication use and financing.

The solution is to clarify the rightful agent to make a decision and ensure that there is a shared understanding about the locus of authority. The locus of authority might be based on an agent's formal authority, professional expertise, experience, or other source. Any conflict in shared understanding needs to be addressed with advocacy and negotiation. Establishing and maintaining a pharmacist's locus of authority in decisions requires him or her to demonstrate a sustained track record of good decisions and professional behavior.

■ Step 3: Analyze the Problem

Good moral judgments cannot be snap decisions. They involve careful thought and investigation; otherwise, good decisions are the result of luck more than judgment. Decisions can be challenging because they are frequently made using incomplete information, multiple viewpoints, and different approaches. They require attention to details such as an understanding of the available options, the parties affected by those options, and the potential consequences of various courses of action.

Identify the Parties Involved

Identifying the parties affected by the decision is important because they bear the consequences of the decision. This approach involves identifying everyone who has some direct or indirect stake in the decision and the reason they might care. Identifying the parties is also needed to understand their perspective. If the perspective is not clear, asking for parties' viewpoints may be necessary.

Understand the Consequences

Once the parties are identified, the potential positive and negative consequences of the decision need to be understood. Consequences should be studied from the multiple perspectives of the parties involved because the perspectives will form the basis of whether a decision is good or bad. If there are many perspectives, focusing on only the most important ones may be necessary to simplify the analysis. Answers to the following questions should be sought:

1. What is the time period under consideration? How might a focus on the short-term or long-term consequences make a difference in the decision?

2. Who is perceived to win and who is perceived to lose in the decision? Are those perceptions accurate or misinterpretations of fact?

3. What is the symbolic consequence of any decision? What does the decision say about which values and perspectives are prized over others?

4. How might cognitive biases influence an understanding of the consequences? Have the cognitive biases, such as motivated thinking, that might get in the way of a good choice been identified?

Identify the Values and Issues Involved

Some core ethical values are commonly associated with ethical decisions[2] (Table 4.2). These ethical values must be explicit to identify conflicting issues, tradeoffs, and priorities associated with the values.

TABLE 4.2 Ethical Values Associated with Common Decisions

Value	Description
Nonmaleficence	Maleficence is the act of committing harm or evil. Therefore, nonmaleficence is the principle of doing no harm. Decisions based on nonmaleficence seek to follow the medical principle of do no harm.
Beneficence	Beneficence is the value of attempting to bring about good or preventing harm. Decisions founded on beneficence seek to maximize the utility of consequences.
Autonomy	Autonomy is the principle of self-determination in which individuals have a right to make their own choice about things that affect them. Decisions based on autonomy give people freedom of choice and action.
Fidelity	Fidelity is the principle of being faithful to one's duty. It entails showing basic respect for individuals, being competent in one's expected roles, adhering to one's professional code of ethics or other guidelines of behavior, and keeping promises. Respect for fidelity in decisions means doing one's duty.
Veracity	Veracity is the value of truthfulness. It means not lying or being deceptive in dealing with others. It also deals with being consciously ignorant about issues and self-deception. Decisions founded on veracity seek truth and honesty.
Justice	Justice is the principle of being just and fair. It deals with distributive equity (i.e., how limited resources are allocated) and procedural equity (i.e., development and application of rules of behavior). Decisions based on seeking justice attempt to achieve fair outcomes using fair processes.

■ Step 4: Explore Practical Alternatives

When exploring practical alternatives, one should think creatively for additional solutions to the problem. If the answer is obvious, an individual should take a moment to explore less obvious solutions that might be more just, resulting in greater utility; that might be more consistent with duty; or that might improve moral good along with any other criteria. When the solution is obvious, individuals should challenge themselves to consider other alternatives.

When exploring alternatives, one should examine them in terms of their outcomes (i.e., moral consequences), one's obligations (i.e., moral duty), and the way they reflect on the individual (i.e., moral virtue). Although individuals may be tempted to emphasize a consequentialist approach to frame the problem, they should consider using their moral virtue and duty perspectives to remove any bias in making their final decisions. They should ask themselves if they can achieve their moral duty and virtue while still maximizing the overall good they can do.

■ Step 5: Make a Choice, and Act

This step might seem obvious, but people often put off making difficult moral choices. They do so for a variety of reasons including fear of conflict, waiting for someone else to make a decision, or just bad habit. The problem is that the failure to act is a choice. It is a choice to avoid one's moral responsibility. It is a choice to not influence a situation until later or not at all.

That is not to say that inaction is immoral. Often, conscious inaction is the best moral path to take. For instance, a leader may deliberately choose not to engage in a situation if doing so is likely to worsen the situation or if the problem is expected to resolve on its own. The key is to consciously decide on the proper ethical action based up the available facts. By doing so, a leader is prepared to justify the moral good of the choice and deal with any criticism regarding that choice.

■ Step 6: Evaluate the Process and Outcome

If pharmacists wish to learn and grow as professionals, they need to systematically reflect on their leadership experiences, evaluating both the way they acted and the results of that action. After making a difficult decision, they need to contemplate the following questions:

1. Would I be embarrassed to describe my actions to friends, family members, or professional colleagues?

2. How would I feel if a person acted in a similar manner toward me?

3. How would an objective jury of my peers judge my actions?

4. Does the choice benefit my stakeholders less than, as much as, or more than it benefits me?

5. Is the alternative consistent with my mission and ethical code?

6. Am I taking advantage of others who are vulnerable because of age, education, income, language, or other factor?

Their answers to these questions will help pharmacists decide whether the final choice was consistent with their ethical code and a positive reflection of their personal values. If the answers suggest room for improvement, pharmacists need to ask themselves what they might have done differently and whether that might have resulted in different outcomes. Finally, no matter how the problem was resolved, one should ask oneself, "What did I learn?"

Sometimes, ethical leaders unintentionally encourage immoral behavior by the way they manage their team. In essence, they make unethical behavior more likely in ways described in Box 4.4.

■■ CONCLUSION

At the beginning of this chapter, we define ethical leadership and summarize the qualities of an ethical leader. Ethical leadership is complex and consists of more than just influencing change. Ethical leaders commit to making ethics a priority in their lives and in their expectations of others. They regularly ponder the morality of their choices and of the resulting outcomes on the people they serve. Furthermore, they accept responsibility for the effects of their actions on others. Ethical leaders may not always be right, but they try to be.

■■ KEY TERMS AND CONCEPTS

■ Ethics

■ Ethical leadership

■ Morally defensible

BOX 4.4 Four Ways That Leadership May Be Encouraging Unethical Behavior[a]

Are upstanding, morally acting leaders really ethical if they encourage corrupt and unethical behavior in their followers? Many leaders might be surprised to discover that their management and leadership practices are inadvertently promoting ethical misconduct in organizations.

Some of the ways that leaders unintentionally encourage unethical conduct are as follows:

- *Leaders make coworkers and others feel psychologically unsafe to speak up.* They may say that they have an open-door policy, but many managers discourage dissent or discussion of controversial issues. When ethical concerns arise, people may not be comfortable speaking up. This leads to a culture in which people avoid talking about problems or addressing them until they are a much bigger issue. People may believe that speaking up is not worth the effort because it can cause leaders to become irritated or angry.
- *Leaders apply excessive pressure to reach unrealistic performance targets.* When people are asked to achieve impossible goals, they either fail, cut corners, or cheat. They are encouraged to "play" the system or lie when reporting their achievements. When given unrealistic goals, individuals respond with, "If my boss wants to set impossible objectives, it won't be my fault when things turn out bad." People will be compelled to manipulate performance metrics to give the appearance of meeting these goals, rather than actually achieving the desired outcomes.
- *Leaders do not make ethical behavior and integrity a routine conversation.* Leaders often assume ethical behavior is a given and fail to talk about it until a problem occurs. After scandals, everyone is asked to attend an ethics training session to receive a dose of ethics. Unless ethical behavior becomes a routine concern and discussion in an organization, the work environment will remain status quo.
- *Leaders do not set a good example.* Leaders who gossip, tell white lies, take unfair advantage of others, or engage in any other unethical act encourage similar behavior in others. In reality, leaders must be held to higher ethical standards than their followers. There is no justification for leading in a "do as I say, not as I do" manner. Leaders need to model ethical behavior through their own actions. Hypocrisy is not acceptable.

a. See reference 11.

- Code of Ethics
- Ethical frameworks
- Virtue framework
- Deontological framework
- Teleological framework
- Ethical distress
- Ethical dilemma
- Locus of authority problem
- Nonmaleficence

- Beneficence

- Autonomy

- Fidelity

- Veracity

- Justice

◼ ● DISCUSSION AND REVIEW QUESTIONS

1. List unethical behaviors inconsistent with the pharmacist's code of ethics. What areas in the code are ambiguous with regard to a pharmacist's ethical responsibility concerning the tradeoffs between serving patients and generating profits for an employer and the choices between home life and work life?

2. Do the ends always justify the means?

3. Can a moral person do immoral actions?

4. If a virtuous pharmacist does his or her moral duty but the results are a disaster for the patient, is the pharmacist ethical?

5. Compare and contrast moral distress and moral dilemmas. What is the major difference between the two?

6. When does following the rules become unethical?

● ● REFERENCES

1. Latif DA. The link between moral reasoning scores, social desirability, and patient care performance scores: empirical evidence from the retail pharmacy setting. *J Bus Ethics*. 2000;25(3):255–269. doi:10.1023/A:1006049605298.

2. Veatch RM, Haddad AM, Last EJ. *Case Studies in Pharmacy Ethics*. New York, NY: Oxford University Press; 2017.

3. Brown ME, Treviño LK. Ethical leadership: a review and future directions. *Leadersh Q*. 2006;17:595–616. doi:10.1016/j.leaqua.2006.10.004.

4. Thoms JC. Ethical integrity in leadership and organizational moral culture. *Leadersh*. 2008;4(4):419–442. doi:10.1177/1742715008095189.

5. Northouse PG. Leadership ethics. In: *Leadership: Theory and Practice*. 7th ed. Thousand Oaks, CA: Sage Publications; 2016: 329–362.

6. American Pharmacists Association. Code of Ethics for Pharmacists. https://www.pharmacist.com/code-ethics. Accessed October 4, 2018.

7. Garrison M. CVS forces workers to reveal weight or pay up. March 20, 2013. Marketplace. https://www.marketplace.org/2013/03/20/health-care/cvs-forces -workers-reveal-weight-or-pay. Accessed May 29, 2018.

8. Martin LC, Donohoe KL, Holdford DA. Decision-making and problem-solving approaches in pharmacy education. *Am J Pharm Educ.* 2016;80(3). doi:10.5688 /ajpe80352.

9. Sporrong SK, Höglund AT, Arnetz B. Measuring moral distress in pharmacy and clinical practice. *Nurs Ethics.* 2006;13(4):416–427. doi:10.1191/0969733006ne880oa.

10. Lowenthal W. Ethical dilemmas in pharmacy. *J Med Ethics.* 1988;14(1):31–34. doi:10.1136/jme.14.1.31.

11. Carucci R. Four ways your leadership may be encouraging unethical behavior. June 14, 2016. Forbes. https://www.forbes.com/sites/roncarucci/2016/06/14 /four-ways-your-leadership-may-be-encouraging-unethical-behavior/#75753f4455c0. Accessed May 29, 2018.

SECTION II

FOUNDATIONS OF LEADERSHIP

CHAPTER 5

Advocacy for Pharmacists
Advocating for Patients and the Profession

■ ■ OBJECTIVES

- ■ Define advocacy, and describe why it is an important part of being a professional.

- ■ Discuss the three types of advocacy.

- ■ Identify strategies for advocating for policy, the profession, and patients.

- ■ Learn how to develop messages that "stick."

I will embrace and advocate changes that improve patient care.

—Oath of the Pharmacist

⬛⬤ INTRODUCTION

Advocacy is an important part of being a pharmacy professional. Along with leadership, it is a skill pharmacists need to create positive change in their practice. This chapter introduces the topic of advocacy and describes how pharmacists can advocate for change.

Advocacy is "the act or process of supporting a cause or proposal: the act or process of advocating something."[1] It is a form of leadership that attempts to bring about change through education and persuasion.

Advocacy is an inherent part of being a professional. The word "profession" originates from the verb "to profess," which means to claim or declare openly on behalf of something or someone else, never in self-interest. Therefore, to be a professional is to promote things in which one believes—either as an individual or as part of a group.

The pharmacy profession supports the importance of advocacy. It is explicit in the oath of a pharmacist.[2] It is also a recommended competency of all graduating pharmacists.[3,4] The profession has been advocating for patients and the profession for decades, calling for greater responsibility in managing medication use to improve patient health outcomes.

These advocacy efforts have been hampered because many individual pharmacists have been ineffective advocates. Some pharmacists are simply reluctant to accept their role as patient advocates outside of a limited scope of practice. Many believe that a pharmacist's responsibility begins and ends at the pharmacy's front door. Other pharmacists are ineffective advocates because they do not believe that advocacy is important when compared with other professional tasks, such as filling prescriptions and providing clinical advice. Also, many pharmacists do not know how to advocate for others.

⬛⬤ TYPES OF ADVOCACY

Advocacy in pharmacy can be distilled into three primary categories: (1) political advocacy, regarding legislative and regulatory issues; (2) professional advocacy, regarding the role of pharmacists in health care; and (3) patient advocacy, concerning patients' medication-related needs.

⬛ Political Advocacy

When pharmacists speak of advocacy, they are typically referring to *political advocacy*, which consists of campaigning for political or social causes with legislators and governmental officials in state and federal government. This political advocacy might include lobbying one's elected official, communicating with regulators (e.g., U.S. Food and Drug Administration), testifying as an expert witness at a legislative committee, attending a state board of pharmacy meeting, donating money to a candidate's campaign or an association's political action committee, speaking with nongovernmental organizations (e.g., Joint Commission), or holding events such as Pharmacy Day at the Statehouse.

Political advocacy is critical for pharmacists because many professional activities are regulated by the government. Most pharmacy associations' Web sites provide directions and resources to assist members in advocating for specific issues of interest to legislators. Many of these associations help train political advocates and provide them talking points to guide their discussions in ways that provide coherent, consistent messages. In addition, they periodically bring political advocates together to blanket legislators with a united message on pressing professional issues. Readers who wish to learn more about political advocacy are directed to the book *Leadership and Advocacy for Pharmacy*[5] and to the advocacy pages available on most major pharmacy professional association Web sites.

Professional Advocacy

Professional advocacy is the process of advocating for the role of professionals in health care. Today, there are almost 200,000 pharmacists working in the United States who could be (but often are not) advocating for the profession. Pharmacists can advocate for the profession in many ways, including the following:

- Joining and actively participating in local and national professional associations

- Giving voice to medication-related issues within pharmacy chains, hospitals, and other large organizations that employ pharmacists

- Participating in organizations unrelated to health care, such as neighborhood associations, school boards, local and state government, and special interest groups

- Cultivating relationships as credible experts with local and national media

- Using social media to speak with authority about medication-related topics and pharmacy topics

- Engaging in day-to-day personal conversations with patients, health care professionals, and the general public

Professional advocacy consists of coaxing others to accept the roles that pharmacists have defined for themselves. These roles generally consist of activities associated with medication use, including prescribing, purchasing, preparing, dispensing, administering, and monitoring.

However, role conflicts occur when other members of other professions feel that pharmacists are encroaching on their professional domain. For example, physicians often resist the desire of pharmacists to influence medication prescribing and nurses can reject the pharmacist's role in medication administration.

In addition to disputes with members of other professions, pharmacists often face patients' biased perceptions of their professional roles. Studies show that patients believe that a pharmacist's role is limited to providing little more than basic dispensing services[5-7] and that many medication therapy management tasks are the responsibility of their physicians.

Even within pharmacists' own work setting, their nonpharmacist colleagues may not be aware of or appreciate the professional capabilities of pharmacists. Consequently, pharmacists must become expert salespeople within health care organizations and among the public—reaching out to inform, persuade, and remind others about the profession.

Patient Advocacy

There is no consensus on what comprises patient advocacy,[4,6] but a useful working definition is the process of representing and defending patients' rights and best interests within the health care system. Patient advocacy includes three broad core actions: (1) safeguarding patients' autonomy, (2) acting on behalf of patients, and (3) championing social justice in the provision of health care.[6]

In the pharmacy profession, patient advocacy includes the following activities:

- Taking extra steps to ensure that patients have everything they need to achieve desired outcomes with their medications

- Working with insurance and pharmaceutical companies to make medications affordable

- Guarding patient safety by monitoring the prescribing and administration of medications

- Fighting for good systems of medication-use management

- Protecting patient autonomy and confidentiality

Patient advocates safeguard patients' autonomy by helping them make the best decisions for their personal lives. For pharmacists, this approach requires respect for patient choices even if the choices might not match professional guidelines or personal preferences (e.g., tamping down their own professional opinions about patients' desires to take unproven therapies such as homeopathy or other complementary medicines). As long as the patient is fully informed and there is no health or other form of risk, pharmacists should respect a patient's right to choose.

Patient advocacy requires protecting the rights and safety of patients throughout the entire medication-use process. This type of advocacy includes taking responsibility for tasks that other professionals may believe are outside of a pharmacist's scope of practice. If a physician prescribes an unsafe or ineffective drug dose, a pharmacist is professionally bound to advocate for an alternative, even if the physician feels otherwise. If a pattern of medication-administration errors is identified within a hospital, a pharmacist is obligated to ensure that the causes are identified and mitigated. If patients have difficulty taking their medications appropriately as they transition from a hospital stay to care at home, pharmacists must provide a solution to help with the transition. Refusal to engage on the behalf of patients at any stage of the medication-use process is a failure of professional responsibility. Box 5.1 describes patient advocacy by pharmacy students at Ohio State University.

Patient advocacy also means championing the needs of underserved and disadvantaged patients such as the poor, the homeless, non-U.S. citizens, and non-English-speaking individuals. Pharmacists must be culturally sensitive to these patients' needs and treat them as well as they treat the wealthy and more advantaged patients.

Pharmacists have a unique perspective and responsibility to act as advocates for patients. As medication experts, pharmacists' expertise allows them to effectively identify and explain information about appropriate drug use to patients, family members, and other health care professionals. Pharmacists are still highly trusted, and being a part of the most accessible health care profession gives them multiple opportunities to advocate.

Occasionally, pharmacists might disagree with other health care professionals on a course of action regarding a patient's treatment (e.g., using antibiotics to treat viral infections) or an enacted policy (e.g., a formulary restriction). As professionals advocating for patients, pharmacists must strongly but respectfully present their position on the matter. Pharmacists' professional responsibility is

Box 5.1 Leadership in Action: Pharmacy Students Help Immigrants Navigate U.S. Pharmacy System[a]

In 2013, pharmacy students at Ohio State University and partners saw a need to help first-generation immigrants navigate the U.S. health care system. They initiated Pharmacy Ambassadors, a program that provides educational sessions about the U.S. health care and pharmacy systems for newly resettled refugees in the Columbus, Ohio, area.

Working with local resettlement agencies and community pharmacies, pharmacy students work with approximately 200 immigrants per year to provide education about navigating the U.S. pharmacy and health care system and to familiarize the immigrants with pharmacists and the services they provide as part of the health care team.

With the help of an interpreter if necessary, the attendees learn about a variety of topics such as understanding the difference between over-the-counter and prescription medications, refills, and the medication labels. The Pharmacy Ambassadors program provides an opportunity for participants to tour a pharmacy and feel more comfortable interacting with the pharmacy team through engagement with pharmacy students and community pharmacy staff. Additionally, students and pharmacy partners are able to learn about different cultures and the needs of members of their community.

Many pharmacy students became involved because of the difficulties faced by family members and the community. One student described her engagement in the following statement, "My parents are first-generation immigrants, so I really related to people who struggled with learning about how the U.S. health care system works. So, it was really important to me, and it was something I was passionate about."

Questions

1. What type of advocacy are students in the Pharmacy Ambassadors program doing—political, professional, or patient?

2. What are additional benefits of the Pharmacy Ambassadors program to the school and the pharmacy profession?

a. See references 7 and 8.

to use their power to influence care. Failure to advocate for the patient can cause patient suffering and even (avoidable) death.

Strategies for Advocating

Political, professional, and patient advocacy involve communicating with and persuading different audiences. The messaging and tactics will vary depending on the audience. However, several common strategies are used in advocacy.

Identify and Influence Key Opinion Leaders

Key opinion leaders (KOLs) are people who influence thoughts, ideas, and initiatives within organizations and in the public. KOLs, also called "thought leaders," are influential people. They have influence with others because of their expertise or credibility. KOLs are socially well-connected, and they are knowledgeable and often sought out for advice.[9] Their social and professional connections aid their ability to influence thinking and perceptions.

KOLs vary in their ability to influence.[9] When matched with formal authority (e.g., chief executive officer [CEO] of a pharmacy chain), KOLs can be quite influential. Swaying these influencers can have an outsized effect on a cause. Think about the effect that pharmacists might have on professional perceptions if they could enlist the support of major opinion leaders such as media giant Oprah Winfrey or Microsoft's Bill Gates in promoting the value of pharmacists.

However, even average individuals within organizations, such as staff pharmacists and technicians, have connections that can spread ideas. Those ideas might reach major influencers through only a few degrees of separation.

Network with Your Tribe

Usually, individuals are not alone in their interests. In the pharmacy and health care professions, many people share your passion for advocating for pharmacists. You just need to find them and engage with them.

Seth Godin, popular author and entrepreneur, calls these people your "tribe."[10] *Tribes* are like-minded individuals who have always coalesced into groups known by a variety of names: clubs, associations, and even cults. Tribes are groups of people connected to an idea, a leader, and one another. When you find your tribe, you can lead the tribe to advocate for change.

To advocate, connecting with key influencers in your tribe is important. If you cannot find a tribe to join, you might need to form one. When enough like-minded people form into a critical mass, there is greater potential to influence and spread ideas.

Advocating outside of your tribe is also important. Otherwise, you are just preaching to believers. Box 5.2 suggests ways for you to talk to someone outside of your tribe.

Take Advantage of Opportunities

Advocates need to be ready at all times to take advantage of opportunities to influence. Effective advocates always have an elevator speech ready to give at a moment's notice.

An *elevator speech* is a short, scripted discourse designed to promote a message in the time needed to ride an elevator. The idea behind the speech is to be prepared with a memorized, practiced message that powerfully conveys your ideas in a few words. A good elevator speech can concisely communicate an idea

Box 5.2 How to Talk to Someone Outside of Your Tribe

Effective advocacy often requires talking to people outside of your tribe—people who do not have the same beliefs as you. Indeed, your tribe is usually supportive of your cause. Most change comes from engaging with people who do not share your opinions.

Talking with people who do not share your viewpoints regarding the role of government in health care, the importance of education, or the value of pharmacists can be frustrating. Still, it must be done to influence change. Some hints for advocating to people who do not share your views are as follows:

- *Look at the situation from their viewpoint, not yours. Tailor your message to their viewpoint, not yours.* One of the biggest mistakes in advocacy is assuming that others care about what we care about. We assume that they will respond to the same ideas that excited us about an issue, and we get frustrated when they fail to see the light.

   Rather than pounding away with arguments you find persuasive, try to find arguments that might be persuasive to their viewpoint. This requires more listening than talking and more questions than answers. Find areas of common interest, and craft your message to their concerns.

- *Share your personal concerns about the issue.* People are more likely to respond to a personal story than to facts and arguments about an issue. Stories are more meaningful and easier to remember. People have been using stories for thousands of years to convey ideas because it works.

   Another advantage is that people can argue with facts but not with your story. Your personal tale expresses your concerns about a matter. Disputing your beliefs about an issue is difficult.

- *Encourage small acts toward your goal.* If you want to recruit people to your cause, do not give them something big to do. Big tasks are overwhelming, and even motivated people might hesitate to get involved. Instead, give them a small task—show up to a meeting, attend an event, read a short position piece, sign up for a newsletter, or respond to a blog post.

   Small acts can accumulate into big changes over time. They can also lead to bigger acts by individuals as their interest in a concern blossoms and their advocacy grows.

---

whenever an audience is available for a short time period. It is used to take advantage of chance encounters in public settings, social events, or any place where people meet.

For example, think about how people respond to the question, "What do you do for a living?" If a person responds, "I'm a pharmacist," the conversation often results in a stereotypical statement about pharmacists and then quickly trails off. This is a lost opportunity!

Instead, a pharmacist advocate might reply, "I'm a pharmacist who works with patients to control their medical conditions. I have a medication therapy clinic at Smith's Pharmacy. If you or anyone you know wants to talk about any drug or health issues, here is my card. Call that number, and ask for me." Responses such as this can generate interest for a pharmacist's practice and create a positive professional image for him or her and the profession.

██ ██ HOW TO ADVOCATE FOR THE PROFESSION AND PATIENTS

Advocacy is about communicating with individuals, and effective advocacy follows basic principles of communication and relationship building. These basic principles consist of the following steps.

██ *Step 1: Identify an Idea or Cause That Is Important to You*

It can be any topic as long as it is something that you care about. Caring is necessary to generate the passion needed to convince others to care. If you cannot think of anything for which to advocate, review your personal mission statement. Are there any barriers to achieving your professional mission? For instance, if you are committed to patient-medication management in community settings, you may choose to advocate for populations who cannot afford medication, for underserved populations who do not have access to drugs, for medication reconciliation for patients who suffer unnecessary drug-related problems as they transition from institutions to the community, or for any other issue related to barriers in patient-medication management in the community.

Many causes for advocacy come from personal experiences or observations of other people's personal experiences. Your interest may come when you see an injustice or something that irritates you. A cause does not have to be of vital importance. It just needs to be something you want to change.

Sometimes, you can identify personal passions and link them to the profession. Perhaps you have always been passionate about the environment and sustainability—you might extend your passion to medication management by advocating for proper medication disposal. Pharmacists with interests in music, art, dance, social justice, or another passion can find a way to link these interests to professional advocacy.

██ *Step 2: Find Your Tribe*

Your tribe can be any group of people connected to the cause you identified in step 1. Pharmacists and pharmacy students can be considered tribes.

If you are a pharmacy student, you can start the search by attending pharmacy student association meetings. Student associations typically advocate for their members' causes. This membership can lead to meeting fellow advocates at national association meetings—a highly recommended approach for any individual interested in the profession. Alternatively, you may search for your tribe on the Internet. Key-word searches on almost any topic will yield results for groups of like-minded individuals with whom you can connect.

Step 3: Develop Goals

Advocacy succeeds best with planning, and goal setting is an essential part of planning. A goal is a general outcome to be achieved. Examples of goals for pharmacists include the following:

- Enhance the image of pharmacists.

- Improve compensation to pharmacists for patient care services.

- Give pharmacists formal provider status.

- Expand the availability of residency training for pharmacists.

- Maintain patients' right to choose their personal pharmacist.

- Offer options for debt forgiveness to new pharmacy school graduates who practice in underserved areas.

- Encourage the use of evidence-based medication in the selection of therapies.

Part of goal setting in advocacy is to identify the audience you want to influence. KOLs are a typical audience because they are more likely to spread an advocate's message. The influence of KOLs depends on the size of their opinion network (e.g., Twitter follower). Normal opinion leaders are friends, family members, and acquaintances who might spread your idea via everyday word-of-mouth conversations with their friends, family members, and acquaintances. Highly influential opinion leaders are individuals in positions of power in media, government, entertainment, or business who can pass your message on to large audiences or individuals who can influence change.

The most influential thought leaders are celebrities such as Beyoncé, elected officials such as the president of the United States, and business leaders such as Amazon CEO Jeff Bezos. Influencing these individuals would be considerably advantageous, but they may be difficult to contact and influence. More accessible thought leaders are local elected officials, professional association leaders, university officials, local celebrities, and local business leaders.

Step 4: Turn Your Goals into SMART Objectives

A *SMART objective* is one that is **s**pecific, **m**easurable, **a**ttainable, **r**elevant, and time bound. For example, an objective in achieving the goal of "enhancing the image of pharmacists" might be to develop an elevator speech within a week's time about your training to be a pharmacist and to use that speech five times in the next month. This objective is SMART because it states specifically what will be done, it can be counted, it is not too difficult to achieve, it is relevant to enhancing pharmacists' image, and there is a deadline for it to be completed.

■ Step 5: Develop an Advocacy Message That You Can Deliver Well and Concisely

Advocacy requires the use of persuasion and education to change people's minds. When advocating for the pharmacy profession, you may want to work some of the following themes into your messages:

- Pharmacy has expanded its role within health care from a profession focusing on preparing and dispensing medications to one emphasizing a wide range of patient-oriented services designed to maximize the effectiveness of medications.

- Pharmacy is practiced in a broad range of settings: independent and chain community pharmacies, hospitals, long-term care facilities, pharmaceutical industry, mail service, academia, managed care, and government.

- Medications have the power to heal when taken correctly but can cause serious harm when used inappropriately. The pharmacist's role is to help patients achieve the benefits of drugs and avoid harm.

- Pharmacists have extensive education about drugs and the diseases treated with these drugs. They are the best health care professionals to assist patients with their medications.

- Patients should choose a pharmacist they trust and develop a partnership for good health. A pharmacist who knows a patient and the patient's health needs can best help the patient avoid harmful drug interactions, avoid allergic reactions, save money on drugs, and take drugs in the most effective manner.

Good messages are often *sticky*, or memorable. They incorporate strategies recommended by Dan and Chip Heath in their book *Made to Stick*.[11] Dan and Chip Heath convincingly argue that ideas are more likely to survive and be communicated to others when they follow the SUCCESs (simple, unexpected, concrete, credible, emotional stories) principle described in Table 5.1.

■ Step 6: Multiply Your Message

Messages that are repeated in multiple venues are more likely to be noticed, understood, and remembered. Whenever possible, seek to multiply your message by repeating and referring to it in different venues. Marketers call this approach "integrated marketing communications"—using a blend of old school

TABLE 5.1 Characteristics of Sticky Messages[a]

Sticky characteristic	Description
S—Simple	Ideas that are simple are easy to comprehend and remember. To make ideas simple, strip them down to their basics. This can be done by finding a one-sentence statement that conveys your core idea: "Hi! I help people with their medications."
U—Unexpected	Messages that are unexpected grab attention and generate surprise, interest, and curiosity: "Did you know that for every dollar spent on drugs, another dollar is spent treating the adverse effects of drugs!"
C—Concrete	Use concrete examples ("Twenty independent pharmacies went out of business in our state in the past year") instead of general ones ("Many independents are going out of business every year"). Concrete examples are easier to comprehend and remember.
C—Credible	Make certain that your idea is believable and trustworthy. Choose details about your message and its messenger with care. For example, a pharmacy student speaking about the effect of the high cost of college tuition has more credibility than a faculty member.
E—Emotional	Sticky messages tend to make people feel something—anger, sorrow, disgust. Simple changes in wording can make the difference. For example, Republicans opposed to estate taxes renamed them "death taxes." Although the word "taxes" already can generate powerful emotions in people, the term "death taxes" causes an even more powerful response.
S—Stories	Illustrate your point with stories. Storytelling is a powerful tool for building meaning through situations or examples. Stories can be told in engaging, entertaining ways.

a. See reference 11.

techniques such as advertising with newer methods such as social media marketing. Figure 5.1 shows how pharmacy students might multiply their message about a visit to see their congressional representatives.

■ Step 7: Assess Your Success

If you have defined a quantifiable objective to measure success, you will know if you achieved your objective or not. You may consider yourself successful if you talked to five people in a month about your issue, were interviewed for the school newspaper last month, or conducted several legislative visits with members of your state legislature. You should share the successes with other advocates, and your results should be used to inform your future actions.

■■ CONCLUSION

Advocacy is a professional responsibility of pharmacists. With experience, it can be done effectively and can benefit patients and the profession. Advocacy is built on trust, and all efforts should try to project an image of honesty, openness, and public benefit. This chapter provides guidance on how pharmacists can advocate for their causes.

Figure 5.1 Multiplying the Message about a Capitol Hill Visit

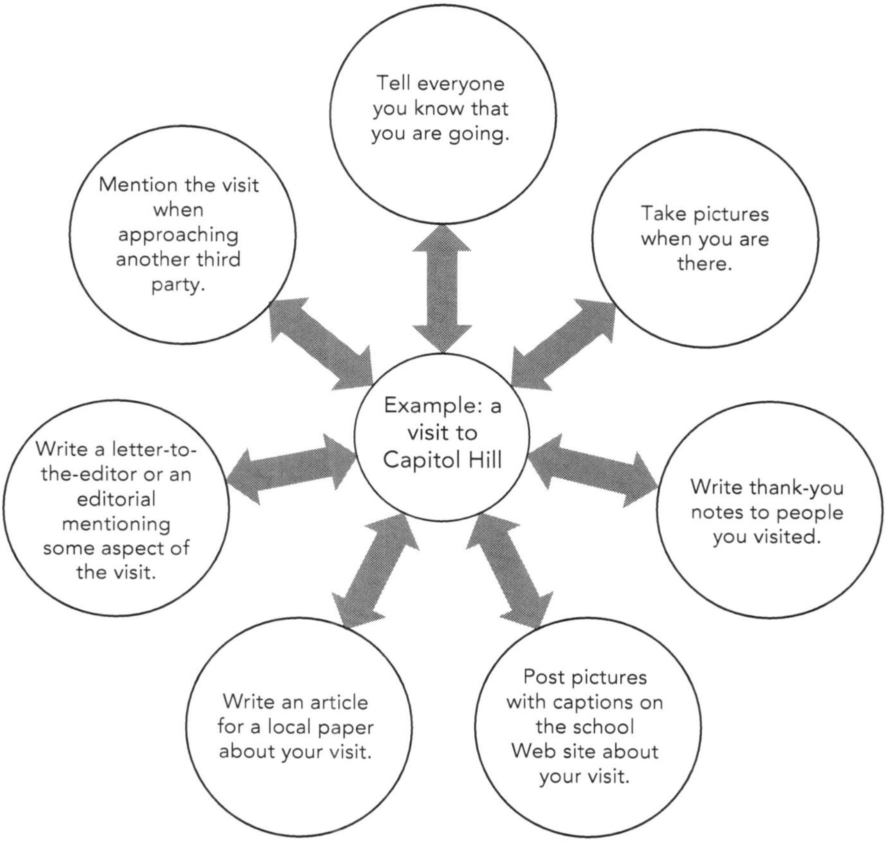

Tell everyone you know that you are going.

Mention the visit when approaching another third party.

Take pictures when you are there.

Example: a visit to Capitol Hill

Write a letter-to-the-editor or an editorial mentioning some aspect of the visit.

Write thank-you notes to people you visited.

Write an article for a local paper about your visit.

Post pictures with captions on the school Web site about your visit.

▰ ▰ KEY TERMS AND CONCEPTS

▰ Advocacy

▰ Political advocacy

▰ Professional advocacy

▰ Patient advocacy

▰ Key opinion leaders

▰ Tribes

▰ Elevator speech

- SMART objectives
- Sticky messages

⬛⬛ DISCUSSION AND REVIEW QUESTIONS

1. What aspects of health care, pharmacy, or the world bother you? Which of these aspects need to be changed? How might you advocate for change?

2. Have you ever discussed an interesting article, video, image, or social media post with someone else? What was interesting about it? What made it buzzworthy?

3. How can pharmacists make their work more buzzworthy?

4. List your tribes. What other tribes would you like to join?

5. What is tribalism?

6. How can passionate advocacy for a cause lead to bad solutions?

⬛⬛ REFERENCES

1. Oxford English Dictionary. http://www.oed.com/.
2. Oath of a Pharmacist. American Pharmacists Association. https://www.pharmacist.com/oath-pharmacist. Accessed May 15, 2018.
3. Boyle CJ. Advocacy: the essential competence. *J Am Pharm Assoc.* 2009;49(3): 364–366. doi:10.1331/JAPhA.2009.08135.
4. Bzowyckyj AS, Janke KK. A consensus definition and core competencies for being an advocate for pharmacy. *Am J Pharm Educ.* 2013;77(2):24. doi:10.5688/ajpe77224.
5. Boyle CJ, Beardsley RS, Holdford DA. *Leadership and Advocacy for Pharmacy.* Washington, DC: American Pharmacists Association; 2007.
6. Bu X, Jezewski MA. Developing a mid-range theory of patient advocacy through concept analysis. *J Adv Nurs.* 2007;57(1):101–110. doi:10.1111/j.1365-2648.2006.04096.x.
7. Ohio State University College of Pharmacy. Pharmacy Ambassadors program. https://pharmacy.osu.edu/pharmacy-ambassadors. Accessed May 28, 2018.
8. Gingerich L. Pharmacy students help immigrants navigate U.S. pharmacy system. The Lantern. February 2018. https://www.thelantern.com/2018/02/pharmacy-students-help-immigrants-navigate-u-s-pharmacy-system/. Accessed May 28, 2018.
9. Holdford DA. Using buzz marketing to promote ideas, services, and products. *J Am Pharm Assoc.* 2003;44(3):387–395. http://www.ncbi.nlm.nih.gov/pubmed/15191249. Accessed January 9, 2018.
10. Godin S. The tribes we lead. TED2009. February 2009. http://www.ted.com/talks/seth_godin_on_the_tribes_we_lead.html.
11. Heath C, Heath D. *Made to Stick: Why Some Ideas Survive and Others Die.* New York, NY: Random House; 2007.

CHAPTER 6

Managing Yourself
Before You Can Manage Others

▦ ▦ LEARNING OBJECTIVES

▪ Discuss why managing yourself is essential for leading change in pharmacy practice.

▪ Compare and contrast career planning and managing yourself.

▪ Describe the steps associated with self-management.

▪ Identify the role of a personal mission statement in managing yourself.

Let him that would move the world, first move himself.

—Socrates

⬛ ⬤ INTRODUCTION

Thousands of studies and numerous books have attempted to describe the perfect styles, characteristics, or traits of excellent leaders. None have provided a definitive answer, but almost all of them agree that individuals must manage themselves before they can successfully lead others. The ability to understand and manage your behaviors and habits is essential for dealing with conflict, managing professional relationships, inspiring trust, making difficult decisions, and sustaining a career through hardships and setbacks.

Pharmacists who want to lead change in pharmacy practice need to manage themselves, their careers, and their lives.[1] Changes in health care, technology, work, and society require all pharmacists to master the competencies of "self-awareness, innovation, leadership, and professionalism."[2,3] The expectation of self-management by pharmacists permeates the profession's pharmacy educational outcomes and professional standards.

Effective self-management is even more important for pharmacist leaders as illustrated in Box 6.1. The success of organizations, including pharmacies and pharmacy institutions, lies in the ability of leaders to manage themselves.[2,4-6] Leadership of organizations and teams is challenging and often frustrating. It requires dealing with complex human beings who are often working in high-pressure conditions. Leaders who cannot handle the stresses and strains of leading tired, distracted, emotional, or over-worked teams of people will struggle with success.

Hard work and intelligence are necessary but not sufficient.[7] Successful pharmacy leaders and managers must also have the following soft capabilities:

- **Communication:** the ability to listen to others, explain your ideas, write a coherent note in a patient chart or to a colleague, give a formal speech, write a research report, or advocate your point of view

- **Collaboration:** a talent for using team best practices to work with others to exceed what individuals can do on their own

- **Grit:** the perseverance and passion to push through barriers and disappointments

- **Problem solving:** the expertise in recognizing the presence of problems, analyzing their causes, coming up with solutions, and assessing their success over time

- **Conflict resolution:** knowledge of how to negotiate and resolve conflicts to achieve win-win solutions

- **Management of professional relationships:** the building and maintaining of commitment and trust in professional and interprofessional relationships

- **Motivation and leadership:** the use of sources of human influence to achieve results while respecting the rights and desires of others

BOX 6.1 Leadership in Action: The Importance of Self-Management

The ability to manage yourself is essential for building trust and commitment in others, two necessities for engaging people to actively support change. Leaders who cannot control their behaviors damage relationships with team members. The following anecdote illustrates the negative effect of a pharmacy district manager on people around him.

Emily Davidson, the pharmacist in charge at a successful store owned by a large pharmacy chain, was responsible for the day-to-day performance of the pharmacy department. "It was a busy, fast-paced working environment where employees would go home at night feeling drained but satisfied with their contributions," recounted Emily. That satisfaction went away when the pharmacy district manager appeared.

Joel, the pharmacy chain's district manager, was a challenging boss. He was a good manager of money and store resources, but he had a caustic style of interacting with people. He often spoke to pharmacy employees in a demeaning way, assuming the worst in peoples' motives and frequently accusing them of being lazy or not caring. He also tended to speak without thinking, claiming, "I just tell it like it is."

On a recent visit to a store, Joel inappropriately and not very quietly commented, "Business would really pick up if we could hire more hot pharmacy technicians." When met with uncomfortable looks by people within earshot, he responded, "Come on! I'm just joking! Don't be so sensitive!"

Deep down, Joel was a good person and excelled at managing things like money and paperwork. However, he struggled with self-awareness and did not appear to have much empathy for others. His behavior and words often offended coworkers and made them uncomfortable. People who showed visual discomfort around him were told by Joel to "relax" or "smile." But these comments typically achieved the opposite of their intentions, causing people to feel harassed and tense.

Employees started to dread his visits and minimized contact with him to avoid being offended. Communications between the store and Joel suffered. Tensions increased when Joel labeled the store "a problem" and started to speak badly about store employees to chain management. The situation escalated when an anonymous harassment complaint was filed with the corporate office regarding Joel's comment about hiring more "hot" technicians.

Shortly thereafter, Joel resigned from his position, but the damage was already done. Emily Davidson and most of the other store employees quit within a year to take positions at other pharmacies. Services at the pharmacy suffered because the store's damaged reputation ensured that only transient floater pharmacists would be willing to staff it. To this day, the pharmacy is ranked in the lowest performing quartile of the chain.

The outcome for Emily, Joel, and the other people involved could have been avoided if Joel had been able to recognize his shortcomings and develop strategies to prevent them from getting in the way of his job. Alternatively, Joel might have been able to recognize that he was the wrong person for the district manager position. But Joel was never one to analyze himself or his actions. He believed that only hard work and intelligence were needed for success in management. He was wrong.

(continues)

BOX 6.1 Leadership in Action: The Importance of Self-Management (*Continued*)

Questions

1. Why do you think Joel got his position as district manager? What were the expected competencies for a person in his position? How did Joel's boss fail him and the customers of the pharmacy chain?

2. If you were hiring a district manager, what questions would you ask to learn if Joel was right for the position?

3. What strategies could Joel use to better manage himself? How could he develop a self-assessment and personal learning system to become a better boss?

Effective pharmacist leaders, like all pharmacists, must exercise self-control over their immediate impulses and tendencies. Although they may want to speak plainly and act quickly, their impulsive actions can have unintended consequences. A frustrated pharmacy manager may want to publicly humiliate an employee for sloppy work, but public shaming often hurts the manager's reputation and can disrespect the entire team. A manager might want to "tell it like it is," but speaking without consideration can damage relationships with coworkers.

Acting without considering the potential consequences to the team is often counterproductive, especially in positions of authority. People are more sensitive to the words and actions of people who hold power over them. Every utterance, facial expression, and pose is observed for meaning. Good leaders understand that they are constantly being observed; therefore, they take great care in managing their personal emotions, choice of words, body language, and personal habits.

The desires and worries of leaders must take a back seat to the concerns of followers and the pharmacy operation. Leaders must balance their own desires with the demands of the people they serve and seek to influence.[7] Leaders must frequently put their own needs on hold to set an example for followers. A major change in attitude is often required of new leaders who may have never had to consider anyone but themselves when making decisions about what to do.

Pharmacists who accept responsibility for achieving goals and objectives are no longer free to do or say as they please, because doing so can hurt the success of the organization's mission (Box 6.2). A misplaced comment or a poorly articulated criticism by a leader can cause serious damage to the effectiveness and morale of a work team. Insufficient support for others or selfish actions by leaders can cause followers to disengage or actively resist initiatives.

BOX 6.2 Actions That Pharmacist Leaders Should Avoid

Leaders often give up more than they receive when taking a leadership position. Pharmacists who want to take leadership positions for selfish reasons should think twice before accepting a formal position. When pharmacists take a leadership role, they should no longer do any of the following:

* Speak without thinking
* Lack commitment to the pharmacy's success
* Be self-serving
* Fail to be aware of activities in the pharmacy
* Fail to care about coworkers
* Make bad decisions
* Be unclear when communicating to others
* Fail to embrace diversity
* Avoid conflicts
* Be disorganized
* Bring personal problems to work
* Be moody
* Be inconsistent with words and actions
* Fail to take responsibility for decisions
* Take revenge
* Gossip
* Fail to care about personal appearance and hygiene
* Fail to master the art of influence
* Ask people to do things that they would not do
* Expect to be liked by everyone
* Speak badly about one's boss
* Fail to adapt to the needs of the position
* Procrastinate on important tasks
* Goof off
* Show favoritism to individuals
* Fail to keep promises
* Push problems off on others
* Talk freely about fears and insecurities

■ ● CAREER PLANNING VERSUS MANAGING YOURSELF

Managing yourself is closely linked to career planning. Pharmacists who are excellent career planners are often good at managing themselves because both skills require introspection, awareness of surroundings, and planning. Still, climbing the career ladder while failing to manage other elements of one's life is possible.

Resumes are documents that outline a person's career history. They are summaries of meaningful personal and professional achievements, and they demonstrate a person's ability to succeed in future opportunities. However, resumes do not reveal everything about the person. They do not describe a person's character or emotional intelligence. They may provide hints, but a great resume can be compiled by someone who is a terrible coworker or boss.

Some resumes are built on a person's selfish pursuit of personal gains, while others are constructed in the service of customers and community. Further, learning much about a person's character or other trait that is not easily described in a written document is difficult. A person's character is better described by what other people say about that person.

The primary difference between career management and management of yourself is that the former is a process of pursuing personal advancement and the latter is about pursuing excellence in abilities and actions. Both describe a pharmacist's journey toward being a professional and his or her potential for future success, and both require conscious effort and planning. They are iterative processes in which challenges are faced, successes and failure lead to wisdom (or not), and wisdom leads to changes in personal and professional behavior. The key is to start planning now, at whatever stage of your career, for professional growth.

⬛⬛ STEPS TO MANAGING YOURSELF AND YOUR CAREER

Pharmacists who want to improve how they manage themselves, their lives, and their careers have plenty of self-help books and online resources available to them. Hundreds of thousands of self-help texts and even more articles are available for readers. One will notice, however, that after reading just a few of these resources, it becomes clear that they all coalesce into the steps laid out in this chapter.[1]

⬛ Step 1: Mentally Prepare for Change

Commit to Change

To change the world, you must first commit to developing whatever skills, habits, personal vision, and behaviors you need to do so.

Although change can occur at any career stage, it is easier to do earlier in one's pharmacy career. Immediately after graduation from pharmacy school, new pharmacists often have fewer competing commitments such as family or deeply entrenched bad habits to overcome. Unfortunately, many new pharmacists squander their early professional years drifting from job to job without committing to a career direction or goals. Without the day-to-day structure that they had as students, new pharmacists tend to slack off on personal and professional development, thereby missing opportunities.

The commitment to change can be small. In fact, most change is the result of a number of small actions taken over time. Even if pharmacists commit to taking baby steps in their personal and professional development, the results can be appreciable.

Accept Responsibility for Your Own Life

After making a commitment to change, taking personal responsibility for your choices and for any consequences of your actions is essential. This approach seems like common sense, but many pharmacists and students do not take personal responsibility in their careers and life.

Some people choose to be victims of the world, drifting through life with little direction and blaming others when events go poorly for them. In pharmacy school, they are often the students who blame their teacher for a bad grade rather than their own study habits. As pharmacists, they accuse their boss of holding them back or failing to recognize their contributions. By remaining victims, they are unable to learn from their failures or to prevent future ones because failures are never their fault. They have a "powerless" view of the world, believing that someone else—a parent, teacher, boss, spouse, family member, or even fate—is always the cause of their problems.

One reason some pharmacists play the victim is because many pharmacists' careers are stuck on autopilot. Many career paths in pharmacy are well-defined, and individuals do not have to put much thought into their choices: they are admitted to pharmacy school, go to classes and pass tests, graduate, pass the licensing exam, get a job, and go to work. They can get on the pharmacy career treadmill and take a high-paying job without taking responsibility for the success of their practice setting. A career on autopilot does not require a great deal of personal reflection or acceptance of personal responsibility for one's career.

A lack of personal responsibility can be compounded by perceptions of entitlement by some pharmacists. Entitlement is a learned behavior often reinforced in pharmacy school when students are taught to expect academic success without taking personal responsibility for achieving that success.[5] Entitled students feel that they are special and that simply showing up to class should be enough to receive good grades. When entitled students fail to perform, they blame others (e.g., a professor) instead of considering their own role in the failure. When these entitled students graduate, they can struggle in their careers.

Fear of failure is another reason that people in the pharmacy profession fail to take responsibility for achieving their dreams. Fear of failure often leads highly accomplished pharmacists to settle for the status quo and to avoid taking chances. This fear of failure might start in pharmacy school where students learn to avoid both challenging classes that might hurt their grade point average or advanced practice experiences that might expose gaps in their abilities. After graduation, this fear of failure may manifest itself when pharmacists refuse supervisory responsibilities that would stretch their capabilities, preferring to let others take responsibility for the pharmacy practice.

Until you take personal responsibility for your career and development, you can never grow as a professional. The price of doing so is that you can no longer blame others for your failure. The benefit is freedom for personal and professional growth.

Step 2: Know Yourself

Before you take any journey, even one of personal development, you need to know from where you are starting. This involves developing an idea of who you are in order to identify how to become the person you want to be. Knowing yourself is a lifelong task that is never completed. The key is to start the process.

This step is important to achieving a key dimension of emotional intelligence—self-awareness. *Self-awareness* is a person's ability to have a deep understanding of one's emotions, strengths, weaknesses, needs, and drives.[4] People who have a high degree of self-awareness can identify how their individual nature and behaviors can affect their lives. Thus, they are able to develop strategies and habits to adjust to their personal weaknesses and strengths. For instance, a self-aware manager might be able to better manage conflicts with subordinates because she understands both how her stress can cause those conflicts to escalate and how she can control her response to that stress.

Self-awareness includes an understanding of one's personal characteristics and priorities.[7] People who are highly self-aware can clearly understand what is important to them and why. This understanding helps in making difficult decisions, such as deciding to pursue a lucrative job offer that conflicts with personal principles. People who are self-aware are more able to make decisions without worrying or second-guessing themselves. With low self-awareness, managers and pharmacists have more difficulty choosing a path and then worry afterward whether they chose the proper path.

Self-Awareness and Authentic Leadership

Self-awareness is key to practicing authentic leadership. *Authentic leadership* is an emerging idea that proposes that leaders build legitimacy and commitment in followers through honesty about themselves and ethical professional relationships with others.[5,8] To live authentically, leaders need to be themselves and act in ways that align with their personal beliefs and personality.

The discomfort people feel about taking leadership positions often lies in their belief that they must be a different person in that role. They feel that they are living a lie in which people will eventually recognize them as imposters. In fact, this feeling is so common in accomplished people that it is labeled the *impostor syndrome*.[9] The imposter syndrome is a psychological pattern of behavior in which people can never feel joy in their successes because they have an unshakable, deep fear of being unmasked as a fraud.

In contrast, authentic leaders know who they are, what they want, and how they contribute.[5] They live their lives as their true selves, not as someone who is playing a role. Authentic leaders do not feel they need to project a specific image or fit into a specific mold. This view gives them the freedom to express their real feelings and perceptions as long as they respect others and take responsibility for the consequences of doing so. Self-awareness comes from self-reflection and feedback.

Self-Awareness and Personal Reflection

For personal reflection, you must remove all distractions, including turning off your mobile device, computer, or gaming device and stepping away from any other diversion, and reflect on your work, education, and daily activities. Analyze your daily activities, your choices, and the outcomes of your choices.[10] What do you like to do? What would you do if you did not have to worry about money? When were you happiest? What have you accomplished in life of which you are most proud? Taking time for personal reflection is a way for individuals to think seriously about their life and their future path. It also helps them consider alternatives to their current career paths.

Know your strengths

Personal reflection will help you understand your personal strengths. Most pharmacists believe they know their strengths, but they are probably wrong. Few have taken the time to systematically identify their capabilities. The typical pharmacist works in a job that, although busy and stressful, does not effectively challenge his or her capabilities. Many jobs do not test a pharmacist's creativity, ability to think strategically, writing skills, public speaking, sense of humor, or other capabilities.

To truly discover their strengths, pharmacists need to systematically challenge themselves with a difficult goal and assess their success in achieving that goal. When individuals continually challenge themselves professionally and assess their success, they learn about their strengths. In a similar vein, if they never place any real demands on their capabilities, they will never know what they can achieve.

The idea behind strength assessment is that career success is built on one's strengths.[11] Strengths positively differentiate an individual from others. Self-improvement gurus often recommend developing one's strengths. Thus, a pharmacist who is good at developing personal relationships might seek additional challenges to develop his or her capabilities through social entrepreneurship or leadership. Identifying their strengths can help people find a career that allows them to use those strengths to excel.

Know your weaknesses

Personal reflection also helps you recognize your personal weaknesses. If strengths help pharmacists succeed, weaknesses can cause them to fail. Therefore, individuals should also identify how personal weaknesses, such as poor time management or the inability to delegate, will hold them back in their professional life. If pharmacists find that their writing skills are not good enough for them to move up within a corporate environment, they may want to work with a writing coach to develop their writing capabilities. The objective is to improve sufficiently upon your weaknesses to prevent them from inhibiting progress toward career goals.

Understanding your own habits and tendencies is helpful. Your personal habits and tendencies are unconscious behaviors in the way you work and live.[9] They can help, hurt, or simply define you. Thus, they are important to understand and control. The majority of each person's day is spent in habitual, unconscious routines that communicate both desirable and undesirable messages to others.

Often, habitual behaviors say more to people than any words. Good habits save time by letting a person complete tasks with little conscious thought. Bad habits can reduce a person's effectiveness and even destroy a career.

Know your habits and tendencies

Understanding and changing bad habits is an important part of self-management. Bad habits can be unlearned if they are identified and consciously altered. Coworkers, friends, and family can help individuals identify and change their bad habits.

There are some well-established steps to breaking bad habits.[12] The first step is to identify a habit to change. For instance, a pharmacist may decide to address coworker complaints that he habitually dismisses new ideas without giving them much consideration. The second step might be to tell his coworkers about his intentions. This action will both reinforce his intention to change and allow coworkers to remind him whenever he regresses. The next step is to identify an alternative action to substitute for the undesired habitual behavior. To change the pharmacist's habit of brushing aside new ideas, he may decide to substitute only positive comments when faced with new ideas. The final step is to assess daily whether he successfully changed the habit, preferably by recording his success or failure on a daily calendar. At the end of each day, the pharmacist can ask himself if he was successful in changing the habitual behavior. If he succeeds in changing the behavior for a period of time (e.g., 21 days in a row), he is likely to have broken the bad habit. Then he can start working on changing another bad habit.

Personal tendencies involve the way an individual's nature affects his or her actions. They differ from habits because they are not learned. Instead, they are part of a person's makeup. Understanding a person's tendencies and their effect on perceptions and judgments is useful in managing oneself.

One strategy for personal reflection is to conduct a personal SWOT analysis. A *personal SWOT analysis* is a systematic assessment of your strengths (S) and weaknesses (W) as a potential pharmacist or leader and an evaluation of opportunities (O) and threats (T) in the pharmacy profession. Information from a personal SWOT analysis can help guide you in making career choices. The assessment of your strengths and weaknesses can be influenced by personal reflection and input from others as described earlier. The evaluation of opportunities and threats considers current conditions and future conditions that you will face after graduation. Figure 6.1 lists questions you should try to answer in a personal SWOT analysis.

FIGURE 6.1 Questions to Answer in a Personal SWOT Analysis

Your strengths	Your weaknesses
What do you do better than anybody else?	What type of work do you avoid because of a lack of confidence or preference?
What are your specific skills and knowledge (e.g., work experience, major accomplishments)?	What weaknesses do your peers, coworkers, and professors perceive in you?
What freedom do you have to act (e.g., no geographic ties, little debt)?	Which pharmacist skills do you feel least confident about (e.g., writing)?
What is your reputation among your peers, coworkers, and professors?	What are your bad habits (e.g., tardiness, speaking without thinking)?
What is your school's reputation among potential employers?	What strengths do your classmates and coworkers have that you do not?

Opportunities	Threats
Recent health care legislation is causing changes in the practice of pharmacy.	Residencies for pharmacists are becoming increasingly competitive.
The shortage of primary care physicians may open doors for ambitious pharmacists.	Job openings for pharmacists are less common.
Changes in technology may allow pharmacists to access more patient information in any work setting.	The number of graduates from pharmacy schools may be greater than the need in the health care market.

Solicit feedback from others

In addition to personal reflection, pharmacists can learn from the guidance of others. Ask successful people how they arrived at their current point, and most will tell you about a critical conversation they had with someone who put them on their path to success. That person may have been a parent, teacher, family friend, employer, or even a stranger who said the right thing, at the right time and in a way that crystalized a career path. In most cases, these conversations were random, but the resulting effect was life-changing. The key to effective self-assessment is to seek out these conversations and learn from them.

When seeking feedback, resist the urge to talk to only people who will tell you what you want to hear. Feedback is most useful when it challenges your beliefs and even makes you uncomfortable. Try to avoid arguing against criticisms, and be honest about your weaknesses.

Schedule informational interviews with people who have jobs that sound interesting to you. *Informational interviews*, which are scheduled meetings with knowledgeable people, allow you to seek advice regarding careers, industry opportunities, daily work life, and strategies for success. An informational interview differs from a job interview because it is conducted to gain insight, not a job. It also tends to be a low-stress conversation, not a critical assessment about your employment potential. Insight from informational interviews can lead to a future career path.

When soliciting feedback from others, listen to all advice but be selective. Many well-intentioned people offer terrible advice. The key to career success is to discriminate good advice from bad advice.

■ Step 3: Decide What You Want to Do

Life is much easier for pharmacists when they find their true purpose in the profession, often guided by a personal mission statement (Box 6.3). You can make better career choices when your career path aligns with your purpose. Make sure that career choices do not cause you to veer off course.

In addition to being able to guide their career choices, pharmacists who have a clear understanding of their purpose are better able to weather professional setbacks. In many cases, a professional setback can lead to unexpected opportunities.

BOX 6.3 How to Write a Personal Mission Statement

A *personal mission statement* is a broad and specific statement of direction. It is meant to guide a person's future actions. A personal mission might be as simple as "to leave the world in better condition than when I entered it," or the statement may be more complex.

There is no single way to write a mission statement, because it is personal. For some people, it can be as short as a single sentence in length: "To be the kind of person my dog thinks I am," "To live in the highest state of consciousness, the state of enlightenment," or "To raise a family and to give to others." One potential difficulty in a single-sentence mission statement is that it might not provide sufficient guidance for complex choices. For example, if you want to be the kind of person your dog thinks you are, how does that help you in choosing between a career in hospital pharmacy and a career in community practice? Your dog probably has no opinion on this.

Often, a personal mission statement is crafted after a detailed analysis of one's personal values, capabilities, and desires. Identifying one's core values is particularly important in developing a personal mission statement because the mission must be consistent with those values. If the personal values of honesty, contribution to society, and religion are important, they should be reflected explicitly or implicitly in the mission statement. Nevertheless, there are no wrong or right mission statements. The only requirement for yours is that it has significance to you. You are the only one who can judge its appropriateness.

■ *Step 4: Establish Goals and Objectives*

Once a person has completed a self-assessment and has clarified his or her mission statement, he or she should have a better idea of what needs to be done to achieve personal success. It may not be a perfect picture of the future, but it is a start. The next step is to start working toward achieving the life defined in the mission statement.

Achieving one's life mission takes goal setting. One suggestion is to limit oneself to three or four goals that are important and meaningful. Setting more than three or four goals can be overwhelming. For a pharmacy student, goal setting may include identifying a future employer, being elected to a student office, and enriching a personal relationship. For a practicing pharmacist, it might consist of making a career change, establishing financial independence, and spending more time with family.

Once major goals have been identified, individuals need to state the objectives for achieving each one. Objectives are specific declarations that establish precise, measurable outcomes to be achieved in a defined period of time. A goal for a pharmacist to "achieve financial independence" might be set into action by establishing an objective "to save 15 percent of my gross salary by the end of this year." At the end of the year, it will be obvious if this specific objective has been accomplished.

Writing the objectives on paper makes them more real and urgent than objectives that are left to float around vaguely in one's head. The process of writing your objectives also increases your commitment toward achieving them. You may want to identify short-term (weekly or monthly) and long-term (yearly) objectives. Short-term objectives drive immediate action, whereas long-term objectives encourage a strategic direction toward your final goals.

When developing objectives, asking yourself what skills, knowledge, and experience are needed to achieve your final goals is important. If you do not know, talk to people who have had success in achieving similar objectives. Then, prepare a list of objectives toward gaining those skills, knowledge, and experiences. For example, a pharmacist may decide to switch from a community pharmacy job to a job at a long-term care facility. To reach this goal, the pharmacist may set the following objectives: speak to three people about jobs in long-term care facilities, take a course in gerontology to help increase his or her skills, and plan to attend a meeting of the American Society of Consultant Pharmacists within the next year. The pharmacist will need to check his or her objectives periodically to see if he or she has achieved them.

Goal-directed behavior is useful because it continually moves individuals toward their final destination. Individuals who feel control over their future will also experience less stress. As long as they can see some progress toward their goals, they can more easily overlook everyday problems and aggravations. Focusing on one's mission, as illustrated in Box 6.4, can help individuals get through rough patches in their career.

◼ Step 5: Take Action

Pharmacists need to start working on their strategies for success — right now! They should not wait until next week or next year to start getting serious

BOX 6.4 Leadership in Action: Keeping an Eye on One's Mission

Don was a pharmacist in charge at a pharmacy owned by a national grocery store chain. His pharmacy was the most productive and profitable of all of the pharmacies in the chain. He loved his job because it was consistent with his mission "to change pharmacy practice through teamwork and patient-centered care."

When a district manager position opened up, Don applied for it. He thought he had a lock on the position because of his solid track record of success. After completing a series of interviews at the chain's corporate headquarters, he was even more convinced that he would get the district manager position.

Don was crushed when the position was filled by a pharmacist hired from outside of the chain. At first, Don felt betrayed because he believed his work record made him the ideal candidate for the position. In fact, he thought about immediately giving his two-week notice and quitting. But after contemplation, Don decided that he could continue serving his mission in his current position, while looking for new career challenges.

Three months later, Don's patience was rewarded when the corporate office of the chain offered him a newly designed position for training pharmacy department and store managers. A company vice president shared with Don that his passion for pharmacy practice and his team during the interview process helped corporate management realize that Don would be perfect for the new position. The position was actually a step above the district manager position, and it would allow him to better achieve his professional mission of changing pharmacy practice. After some negotiations, Don accepted the new position and has received much positive recognition for his work.

After his initial career setback, Don could have overreacted, quit, and missed out on a great opportunity. Instead, his sense of purpose gave him the patience to bide his time for the right position to emerge.

Questions

1. How do you think most pharmacists would have reacted to being overlooked for the district manager position?

2. Do you think professional missions are really necessary for the average pharmacist? Why?

3. How do you think Don would have reacted if his mission was "to become the CEO of a major pharmacy chain"? Is there a difference between a professional mission that focuses on selfish gains instead of making a difference in the lives of patients?

about their careers and work life. Today, they should ask themselves: "Where do I want to go?" "What skills and knowledge do I need to develop?" "What personal habits are holding me back?"

If this approach is overwhelming, and you do not know where to start, take small steps. Take five minutes to work on one action that moves you toward achieving your personal mission. If after five minutes, you do not feel like doing more, give yourself permission to stop. And if you want to keep going—press on!

Look at your resume, and ask yourself which of your listed accomplishments and skills stand out. When an employer sees your resume, which items clearly indicate that you will be a valuable and successful employee? Have your friends or coworkers provide feedback regarding your resume. Make it clear to them that you want an honest assessment of what they see. If there are gaps, take actions to fill them.

There is an entire industry employing people who can help you manage your life and career. Go to a bookstore, and browse the self-help section. Find a book that looks useful to you, and read it. Or attend a class. Many employers offer classes or will pay for them.

◼ ◼ CONCLUSION

The subject of managing yourself is not a new one. It has been covered extensively in the management and self-improvement literature. Whether you are a student or pharmacist, at the beginning of your career or in the middle, managing yourself is crucial.

To lead well within the profession takes skill. Individuals who have never managed people may think being a leader is easy, requiring just common sense. However, in high-pressure pharmacy practice conditions where pharmacy personnel might be tired, emotional, and overworked, managing is much more complex than it looks.

Managing is difficult, in part, because it requires pharmacy managers to balance their own desires and needs with the demands of the people they manage and the requirements of their employers. A pharmacist who accepts responsibility over others is no longer free to do or say whatever he or she wants, because doing so can hurt the productivity of the people whom he or she manages. A misplaced comment or a poorly articulated criticism can cause serious damage to the effectiveness and morale of a work team.

KEY TERMS AND CONCEPTS

- Career planning

- Managing yourself

- Self-awareness

- Authentic leadership

- Imposter syndrome

- Personal SWOT analysis

- Informational interviews

- Personal mission statement

DISCUSSION AND REVIEW QUESTIONS

1. Which do you think is most important for your future success: your strengths, your weaknesses, or your habits?

2. Why can having a mission statement reduce a person's stress about his or her career and life?

3. Which do you think is most important in pharmacy: mental intelligence (IQ) or emotional intelligence? Why?

4. How can informational interviews help people plan their careers?

5. How important are the grades one earns in pharmacy school in determining a pharmacist's future success?

6. Famous conservationist and scientist Jane Goodall once said, "What you do makes a difference, and you have to decide what kind of difference you want to make." What did she mean by this?

REFERENCES

1. Holdford DA. Managing oneself: an essential skill for managing others. *J Am Pharm Assoc.* 2009;49(3):436–43. doi:10.1331/JAPhA.2009.07066.
2. Nelson MH, Fierke KK, Sucher BJ, et al. Including emotional intelligence in pharmacy curricula to help achieve CAPE outcomes. *Am J Pharm Educ.* 2015;79(4):48. doi:10.5688/ajpe79448.

3. Medina MS, Plaza CM, Stowe CD, et al. *Center for the Advancement of Pharmacy Education 2013 Educational Outcomes*. Alexandria, VA: American Association of Colleges of Pharmacy; 2013. https://www.aacp.org/sites/default/files/2017-10/CAPEoutcomes2013.pdf.

4. Janke KK, Traynor AP, Boyle CJ. Competencies for student leadership development in doctor of pharmacy curricula to assist curriculum committees and leadership instructors. *Am J Pharm Educ*. 2013;77(10):222. doi:10.5688/ajpe7710222.

5. George B, Sims P, McLean AN, et al. Discovering your authentic leadership. *Harv Bus Rev*. 2007;85(2):129.

6. Maxwell JC. *The 21 Indispensable Qualities of a Leader: Becoming the Person Others Will Want to Follow*. Nashville, TN: Thomas Nelson; 1999.

7. Goleman D. What makes a leader? *Harv Bus Rev*. 1998;76(6):93–102. doi:10.4135/9781446213704.

8. Eriksen M. Authentic leadership. *J Manag Educ*. 2009;33(6):747–771. doi:10.1177/1052562909339307.

9. Lippman Z. Imposter syndrome. *Nature*. 2008;456(7220):418. doi:10.1038/nj7220-418c.

10. Kaplan RS. What to ask the person in the mirror. *Harv Bus Rev*. 2007;85(1):86–95. doi:10.1017/CBO9781107415324.004.

11. Rath T, Conchie B. *Strengths Based Leadership: Great Leaders, Teams, and Why People Follow*. New York, NY: Gallup Press; 2008.

12. Duhigg C. *The Power of Habit: Why We Do What We Do in Life and Business*. New York, NY: Random House Trade Paperbacks; 2014.

CHAPTER 7

Decision Making
Using a Systems Approach to Solve Problems

◼️◼️ OBJECTIVES

▪ Discuss different problem-solving and decision-making approaches.

▪ Identify barriers to good decision making.

▪ Delineate the steps in problem solving.

▪ Apply these steps to solve pharmacy managerial problems.

Thinking is the hardest work there is, which is the probable reason why so few engage in it.

—Henry Ford

⬛⬤ INTRODUCTION

Making decisions and solving problems are critical responsibilities of all pharmacists, whether they are managers or staff members. Pharmacists make numerous difficult, uncertain choices throughout the day. Pharmacy leaders do the same.

Making decisions and solving problems are processes that essentially describe the same concept. Decision making is the act of resolving questions or choosing between two or more options. Problem solving is the process of finding solutions to problems. These terms will be referred to interchangeably in this chapter and the following chapters.

Managerial problem solving, like any managerial skill, requires training and practice to master. Managerial or leadership problems are those that relate to achieving results through people. Few pharmacists receive formal training in problem solving, and typically they learn to make managerial decisions on the job.

On-the-job training in problem solving is a process of trial and error, where learning results (hopefully) after one makes mistakes. The trouble with trial and error is that it ensures that multiple errors will occur. Even worse, individuals may learn the wrong lessons from their mistakes. For example, a pharmacist who gets embroiled in a conflict between pharmacy technicians may learn to avoid conflicts altogether, when the better lesson would have been to learn that the approach just needs to be altered.

Managerial problem solving is just one of several approaches that pharmacists use to solve problems (Table 7.1). These approaches, which share many basic processes, should be mastered by all pharmacists.

TABLE 7.1 Types of Decisions Made by Pharmacists[a]

Approaches	Situations	Goal
Clinical	Need to choose between therapeutic alternatives	Maximize the therapeutic effect on patient health.
Ethical	Need to make a choice that may have important moral values and duties embedded in it	Make the most morally defensible choice.
Legal	Need to make a decision that may have legal consequences associated with it	Make the most legally defensible choice.
Managerial	Need to make a decision that is related to the business functions of an organization	Maximize the benefit toward achieving the organization's goals and mission.
Economic	Need to choose between options that may result in significant resource use	Make the most cost-effective choice.

a. See reference 1.

Poor decisions are common. Anyone with work or life experience will see and experience the consequences of poor decision making. The adoption of a formal process of problem solving can significantly improve the quality of managerial decisions.

▦ ▦ LINEAR AND SYSTEMS THINKING

How well problems are solved depends a great deal on the quality of the process employed and the way a problem is approached. There are two broad approaches to decision making: linear thinking and systems thinking.[2]

▦ Linear Thinking

Linear thinking is a simplistic approach to problem solving that, in its simplest form, assumes that (1) each problem has a single solution; (2) the solution will affect only the problem and nothing else; and (3) once implemented, a solution will remain "solved." A pharmacy manager might try to resolve a problem of lost revenue with the solution, "Fill more prescriptions." The manager might also say, "If we can double the number of prescriptions we fill at this pharmacy, my problem would be solved." On the face of it, this solution may appear obvious and appropriate, and further thought about the problem can seem unnecessary. But linear thinking such as this often results in ineffective solutions.

There are several difficulties associated with the solution "fill more prescriptions." Implementing the solution might require a broad mix of actions such as hiring additional technicians, using more technology, and isolating pharmacists from patients to reduce interruptions of the dispensing process. Each of these actions might lead to additional problems for the manager. Hiring additional technicians could complicate personnel management for the manager. Implementing technology or isolating the pharmacist would require employees to change the way they serve patients and would affect the patient–pharmacist relationship. Other unintended consequences might be fewer opportunities for pharmacists to have an effect on patient care, potential pharmacist job dissatisfaction, and the possible promotion of a negative public image of pharmacist services. Even when linear solutions resolve some problems in the short run, they can cause greater, more persistent problems in the long run.

▦ Issues with Linear Thinking

The first issue with linear thinking is that problems usually have multiple causes. For example, the problem of lost revenue originates from numerous sources. One stems from the structure of the health care system and its financing. Another comes from strategic choices made by pharmacy providers to focus on dispensing drugs rather than pursuing a service-focused or patient-focused pharmacy practice. Other causes include previous acceptance of small dispensing reimbursements, the refusal of many pharmacists to accept responsibility for patient outcomes, contradictory messages to payers from pharmacy leaders, and additional third-party involvement in paying for drugs. The solution "fill more prescriptions" does little to address many of the causes of lowered fees for pharmacists.

Linear thinking also ignores the fact that solutions have unintended consequences in addition to those intended. A well-known example of an unintended consequence in managed care pharmacy comes from a state Medicaid program that tried to reduce drug costs by implementing a three-drug limit per enrolled patient. A study of the program found that drug costs decreased, as intended. However, the program savings were more than offset by the additional unintended increase in nondrug costs as a result of increased nursing home admissions.[3]

Finally, linear thinking often makes the false assumption that once solutions are implemented, problems are solved and no further action is required. The problem with this assumption is that conditions change. An effective solution at one time may become ineffective in the future as circumstances and the world change.

People engage in linear thinking for the following reasons:

- *People are mentally lazy.* Some people do not want to expend the effort even when they are capable of doing so. Jumping to quick conclusions is easier than putting serious effort into problem solving.

- *People want quick and easy answers.* Having a problem that can be solved with a single unambiguous answer is much more comforting. That way, people can solve the problem and move on (although the problem may not really be "solved").

- *People need to manage their cognitive load.* Cognitive load refers to a person's working memory. Because people only have a limited capacity for information in their memory, they naturally try to simplify complex issues. Otherwise, life would be too complicated and overwhelm one's capacity to cope with it.

- *Linear thinking is often rewarded in life and work.* Voters elect politicians who give simplistic answers to complex problems in short sound bites. Television cable news shows profit by misstating facts, exaggerating circumstances, and jumping to foolish conclusions.

■ *People often do not learn from their mistakes made in linear thinking.* Sometimes, people do not recognize when a poor decision results in negative consequences. In other circumstances, linear thinkers do not suffer the consequences of their poor decisions. For example, managers who make a series of ill-advised changes in a pharmacy often get promoted before they have to deal with the fallout of those changes.

■ Systems Thinking

Systems thinking differs from linear thinking by its assumption that problems are complex and solutions can have both intended and unintended consequences.[2] Therefore, any solution from this approach should be evaluated for how well it solves the problem (i.e., intended results) with minimal negative, unintended results.

A systems approach considers the way that different systems are linked together instead of assuming that they exist as separate silos with no influence on each other. Thus, problems in pharmacy are affected by other parts of the health care system, health care financing, U.S. and world economies, politics, and a myriad of other systems. A systems approach further assumes that neither problems nor solutions remain constant, that is, situations change, problems change, and new solutions are constantly necessary.

A systems thinker approaches a problem by considering the interrelationships between different systems before implementing a solution. Before attempting to solve a problem, pharmacists who practice systems thinking always ask: "Who will be potentially affected by this problem and any possible solution, and how will they be affected?" "How will they react to potential solutions to the problem, and what can be done to increase acceptance and success of these solutions?" "How might things work out in an unexpected way, and how would this influence my decision?" Answers to these questions can help mitigate negative consequences and enhance positive ones.

■ ■ PROGRAMMED AND NONPROGRAMMED DECISIONS

Managerial decisions can be classified in many different ways. One classification separates them into (1) programmed and (2) nonprogrammed decisions.[4] Decisions fall into one or the other category depending on their degree of complexity, familiarity, and predictability.

Programmed decisions are those that are well understood, highly structured, routine, and repetitive and lend themselves to systematic procedures and rules. Examples of programmed decisions in pharmacy might include the following:

- What steps are involved in filling a prescription?

- How are narcotics records handled?

- What are pharmacists' responsibilities when a computerized drug interaction notice is received from a third-party insurance company?

These problems are not especially unique or complicated, and they can be resolved by developing written rules and procedures for dealing with them. Well-written and carefully considered rules and procedures help simplify decision making, allowing problems to be resolved more efficiently and quickly. This makes programmed decisions less stressful, less time consuming, and more consistent in their outcome.

In contrast, nonprogrammed decisions are those that are poorly understood, less structured, relatively unique, and less subject to routine or systematic procedures. Examples of nonprogrammed decisions might include the way to implement a new pharmacist service, the best way to motivate an employee, or the way to resolve a major career dilemma.

Many nonprogrammed problems become programmed over time as the problem becomes more familiar and solutions become routine. Indeed, standardizing complex decisions when possible with rules and procedures to deal with them more efficiently and effectively is often desirable. Tools used in pharmacy to standardize problems include critical pathways, service scripts, and policies and procedures.

However, some problems will never lend themselves to standardized, cookbook solutions. For example, designing a policy to effectively improve employee morale or motivation would be difficult. Solving these problems (and many other problems) requires judgment, intuition, and creativity.

● ● DECISIONS AND TIME MANAGEMENT

Good decision making requires knowing when decisions need to be made and how to prioritize them. One way to prioritize them is to rank them according to urgency and importance.[5]

Urgent and Important Problems

Problems that are urgent and important are also known as crises or emergencies (e.g., a surprise inspection by the U.S. Drug Enforcement Agency, an unexpected employee illness). They are placed at the top of the priority list because they demand immediate attention. Ignoring them or putting them off is not a reasonable option because doing so has negative consequences for the leader or the organization. Urgent and important decisions typically require an abbreviated problem-solving process because immediate solutions are needed.

Urgent but Not Important Problems

These types of problems demand our attention but are of minimal consequence to the leader or the organization. They typically have someone, often a boss or team member, insisting that they be addressed immediately, but the business will not fail or people will not die if the problems are not resolved. They are the routine problems and interruptions that demand an individual's attention and include routine meetings, completion of paperwork, and answering communications.

Not Urgent but Important Problems

These problems do not demand our attention but are vital to an organization's mission and long-term success. Also known as opportunities, they are often not recognized as problems and are frequently overlooked or ignored. If they are overlooked or put off for too long, they can turn into crises or emergencies. To find opportunities, you must look for them. An opportunity might appear with a complaint by an employee or a criticism by a customer. The key is to recognize complaints and criticisms as opportunities for improvement.

Neither Urgent nor Important Problems

These are problems that waste time and provide minimal positive result. Box 7.1 describes some problems that should be avoided.

Routine Problems versus Crises

Days are spent, for most pharmacists and managers, dealing with routine problems and crises. Addressing routine problems can burn up time without accomplishing much of importance at the end of the day. Nevertheless, managers often enjoy dealing with routine problems such as paper shuffling and busy work

---

BOX 7.1 Problems that Should be Avoided

Being sucked into problems that waste time and offer little benefit is easy. The key is to identify and avoid them. Problems that are neither urgent nor important include the following:

* *It is not your problem.* A leader has enough problems without spending time trying to solve the problems of others. People may try to embroil you in both their personal and work-related problems, but avoid these issues if they have little effect on the work of the organization.
* *The problem will probably correct itself.* Discriminating between this situation and one where the problem is simmering below the surface ready to explode is often difficult. Being able to differentiate between the two requires experience.
* *Interference will only make matters worse.* Sometimes, there is no good solution to a problem and any attempt to intervene may make a difficult situation impossible.

---

because they can give the impression that something is being accomplished and can make the time at work pass more quickly. Crises, in contrast, are critically important to the organization and need immediate attention. The problem with crises, however, is that many are unnecessary. They are often the result of someone's procrastination or inattention. For instance, a manager may delay dealing with personnel problems until employees quit or fist fights occur.

Problems in pharmacy would be more manageable if every manager and pharmacist spent more time identifying and taking advantage of opportunities and spent less time dealing with routine problems and crises. Time spent on opportunities could identify ways of preventing crises and reducing routine problems. Spending time on opportunities that reduce medication errors could lessen time spent on responding to them when they occur. The long-term payoffs could be significant.

●● MAKING GOOD DECISIONS

All complex managerial decisions consist of the following steps, although some steps may be considered only implicitly in the process.[6,7] In fact, experienced leaders may have internalized the process and may never need to consciously think of each individual step when making decisions. However, experienced individuals can find this systematic process valuable for important and complex decisions. Even experienced managers are prone to biases and bad habits that blind their thought processes. The systematic process described in the following steps helps managers make better decisions.

■ Step 1: Identify the Problem

To solve a problem, you must first be aware that it exists. This awareness can be difficult because many problems are the result of gradual change. Gradual change is more difficult to detect because humans are programmed through evolutionary processes to react to sudden dangers, such as an attack from a grizzly bear or mountain lion—threats that are rarely faced by modern humans.

Today, the primary threats to jobs and safety come not from sudden events but from slow, gradual processes.[8] Indeed, few pharmacists are fired from their jobs because of a single event. Most are fired because they made a series of blunders over time that led to their dismissal. In many cases, these blunders might have been prevented if the pharmacists were able and willing to recognize their problems and correct them. But human nature often prevents people from recognizing these gradual changes.

We recognize existing problems in several ways. One is by deviation from the past. Problems are often identified by people when they recognize that circumstances have changed. A pharmacist may declare that, "Dispensing errors are greater than usual" or "Patient complaints seem to be increasing." Individuals often rely on personal memory to detect deviations from the past, but memories can fade or distort reality. A more reliable method is to keep accurate records of key quality and productivity measures that can be followed over time. Any negative trends in these measures may indicate a problem.

Another way to identify problems is by recognizing a deviation from the plan (e.g., "We didn't expect so many people to show up for our cholesterol screenings"). Because memory can be faulty in identifying deviations from the plan, any new program or initiative must include a formal process to collect data that will indicate its success or failure.

Outside criticism is another way to learn about problems, and it is also the worst way to learn about problems. Problems are likely to be out of control by the time outsiders can recognize them and offer criticism. At that point, pharmacists are forced to deal with both the problem and the criticism. This issue is what happened to pharmacists in the Chicago area who had to respond to a series of articles in the *Chicago Tribune* regarding a failure to deal with dangerous drug interactions.[9] They had two problems: (1) they had to respond to the criticism and its effect on their reputations, and (2) they had to improve dispensing systems to address the issue of drug interactions. The key is to identify and solve the problem before an outsider raises it.

■ Step 2: Define and Frame the Problem

Albert Einstein famously said, "If I were given one hour to save the planet, I would spend 59 minutes defining the problem and 1 minute resolving it." However, defining the problem is often the step skipped in decision making. Sometimes, it is skipped because the problem appears obvious. Other times, it is skipped because people are pressed for time, and therefore, decision makers jump directly to potential solutions.

Skipping this step can be a problem because there is a lot of truth to the aphorism, "A problem well defined is half solved." Defining or framing a problem helps determine how it will be solved. If the problem is defined incorrectly, the proposed solution may solve the wrong problem.

Framing the Problem

Framing refers to how a question is set up to be answered. It considers issues such as the perspective taken, the elements of the problem to be considered, and the criteria used to choose one solution over another. Framing helps simplify the problem by including some information and excluding other information. When purchasing a car, you simplify your options by listing a limited number of key characteristics that you want (e.g., color, safety, gas mileage). Other characteristics you might ignore (e.g., type of spare tire, cleanliness of undercarriage). Think about how the following ways of framing the car-buying decision affect the final choice:

- "What American car should I choose?" versus "What car should I choose?"

- "Which car will result in the most affordable monthly payment?" versus "Which car can be purchased for the lowest price?"

- "Which is the best car for me?" versus "Which car will my family want for me?"

Poor solutions to problems result when managers make common framing errors. Errors in framing can result in poorly defined problems because they inappropriately hinder the assumptions involved in the decision. A pharmacist may frame a drug cost question as "How can we cut drug costs?" or "How can we provide more cost-effective drug therapy?" The first question narrows the frame by asking about influencing drug costs while the second question broadens the frame to include both costs and effectiveness. The two questions may result in completely different solutions. Table 7.2 lists common errors in framing that can lead to poor problem statements.

TABLE 7.2 Common Framing Errors When Defining the Problem

Framing error	Description	Examples
Defining problems with solutions	When individuals already have a solution in mind when defining a problem, blinding them to other potential solutions	"The problem with technician turnover is that we need to raise their pay." In this example, the choice of a solution shuts down consideration of any other solutions.
Confusing symptoms with problems	When symptoms are mistaken for the cause of a problem	"The problem at work is that too many people are complaining." Symptoms such as employee complaints and turnover often indicate the presence of an underlying problem—not necessarily the problem itself.
Seeing the world from a pharmacist's perspective	When your personal or professional identity blinds you to relevant information or limits your viewpoint to the boundaries of the pharmacist position	A pharmacist might frame a problem as "the patient is not compliant with his medication," while the patient frames it as "I am having trouble balancing the need to take my medication with my family and work responsibilities."

Developing Good Problem Statements

When defining a problem, writing a good statement of the problem is important. Good problem statements are concise and address the heart of an issue. Avoiding framing errors is also important. A first step in a good problem statement is to define the broad problem in a single short sentence to help provide focus and clarity.

One way of determining if you are addressing the real problem and not just a symptom is to ask yourself, "What would happen if the problem, as I defined it, was fixed?" For example, if you decided that poor morale was the result of low pay, then ask yourself if increasing pay will solve the morale problem. If not, you may need to redefine the problem.

Another way to reach the real problem is to repeatedly ask yourself, "Why?" If a problem is defined as "the employees are complaining," you should ask "Why?" The answer might be, "Because they are unhappy at work." "Why?" "Because they don't feel they are being paid enough." "Why?" "Because their friends working at other pharmacies claim that they are being paid more." "Aha!!!" The real morale problem might be the employees' perception, correct or incorrect, that their peers are being paid more for the same work. This insight provides a clearer path to defining effective solutions to the problem.

A single problem statement about a broad, complex problem often requires a series of subproblem statements that relate to the broad problem. The purpose of defining subproblems is to make the problem more manageable. Attacking a major problem (e.g., "How do we improve employee morale?") can be overwhelming. However, attacking subproblems one by one (e.g., "How much are our competitors paying?") can be easier to handle.

Explicitly stating the perspective of the decision maker in any problem statement is useful. The solution of a problem may differ depending on whether you define the problem from your personal perspective or from the perspective of your boss, coworkers, or patients. Ideally, any problem statement should be acceptable to all perspectives, but this is not always possible for people with competing interests. Box 7.2 discusses a situation in need of a good problem statement.

▇ Step 3: Identify Potential Solutions

The next step in making a final decision is to identify all potential solution options. In this phase, people often choose the first and most obvious solution and ignore better alternatives. They ignore better alternatives because of their overconfidence in their ability to choose the best solution.[10]

Overconfidence is a major cognitive bias that occurs when people are unjustifiably certain in their beliefs and abilities. In leadership, confidence can be useful because it helps prevent indecisiveness and doubt when making difficult choices. But when confidence is excessive, it can cause errors in judgment and bad decisions.

Overconfidence encourages bad decisions because it causes people to ignore their psychological biases. An excessive faith in their capabilities and judgment causes people to ignore their vulnerability to bias and error. Good decisions require humility and a willingness to challenge biases and assumptions about problems. In making good decisions, knowing what you do not know is often more important than knowing what you know.

Cognitive biases come from the use of heuristics (i.e., rules of thumb) to simplify thinking. *Heuristics* help people make quick decisions, but they also lead to systematic errors in thought that result in bad choices.

An example of a heuristic is the tendency to give more credence to information gained from personal experience than from other forms of evidence. This personal experience bias is often exploited by pharmaceutical companies when they give drug samples to physicians. The hope is that physicians will have good personal experience with a medication and continue to prescribe it despite any evidence to the contrary.

BOX 7.2 Leadership in Action: Ruth Ann's Opportunity

Ruth Ann Farthing has just moved to a new town to take a position as pharmacy supervisor for a 200-bed community hospital. The hospital caters to a fast-growing suburb of a southern city.

Ruth Ann's responsibility at the hospital is to take care of the day-to-day operations of the inpatient department and ambulatory care facility. She supervises more than 30 employees on the day and evening shifts. The pharmacy provides centralized pharmacy services (i.e., the pharmacists dispense from the main pharmacy instead of up on the floor in satellite units). The centralized pharmacy provides intravenous (IV) compounding services but few advanced clinical services. Ruth Ann hopes that decentralized clinical pharmacy services can be started soon. At first glance, the job seems to be a wonderful opportunity for her to gain management experience, which will permit her to reach her long-range goal of director of pharmacy.

However, things are never as simple as they first seem. Ruth Ann's boss (the pharmacy director) is (to put it nicely) not a people person. Some days, she is sullen, and other days, she rants and raves at pharmacy employees, nurses, or whoever crosses her path. She has been in the position for 20 years, and she will likely remain there until she retires. She hates the people in nursing administration, but she curries favor with the doctors so she is in no danger of losing her job. Also, she is good at keeping drug costs down, which makes the hospital administration very happy. Through discussions with the IV room supervisor and the clinical pharmacy coordinator, Ruth Ann has learned that her boss prides herself in being difficult and has on numerous occasions failed to support her employees and supervisors. The other supervisors have learned to deal with her by avoiding confrontations.

The employees are an equally sullen lot. They whine and complain constantly about the smallest problems. When slighted by another employee or customer, they are quick to anger. Two times in the past week, Ruth Ann has had to break up shouting matches between employees. The pharmacists show no initiative, and they order the technicians around as if they are slaves. Technicians bicker so much among themselves that they seem to enjoy it.

Relationships with nursing administration members and the staff nurses are very negative. Nursing administration members have complained to the director of pharmacy about slow service and inappropriate behavior on the part of pharmacy personnel. Pharmacists have been known to lose their temper with nurses during phone conversations and slam down the phone.

Despite the apparent hopelessness of the situation, Ruth Ann believes that she can turn the pharmacy around and make it an enjoyable, progressive place to work.

Questions

1. Define the problem faced by Ruth Ann using her perspective. Now define it from the perspective of the patients served by the pharmacy and the employees working there. How does the perspective change the problem definition?

2. What information is missing that would be useful to know? Can a decision be made with limited information?

3. What would happen if Ruth Ann ignored the problem? What are the advantages of doing so? What are the disadvantages?

When people are too sure of their assumptions and opinions, they can be blinded to the best solutions. The following are common cognitive biases that hamper decisions.[7,11]

- **Availability bias.** Individuals place greater emphasis on information that is easy to recall. This leads them to give more weight to information that is often repeated, more recent, or extreme in nature. For that reason, people tend to overemphasize risks reported in the news because the risks are vividly presented and foremost in their minds.

- **Confirmation bias.** People lean toward their initial judgments rather than look for disconfirming evidence. This is illustrated from the expression, "First impressions are lasting." This bias is aggravated by the fact that most individuals seek information that is consistent with their beliefs and discount information that differs from their beliefs.

- **Group think.** Peer pressure can cause individuals to conform to the opinions of a group and ignore contrary information. It is also known as the bandwagon effect, where people follow group norms instead of using independent thought.

- **Anchoring bias.** Anchoring describes the human tendency to rely too much on an initial piece of information to make decisions. The initial information, called the "anchor," sets an arbitrary focal point for discussing any future information. For instance, if a nurse asks a pharmacist, "Is this white pill an aspirin?" she has anchored the discussion to focus on whether the pill is an aspirin. She could avoid anchoring by asking, "What is this white pill?"

- **Affect heuristic.** This bias describes how people let their emotions influence their beliefs about the world. Politicians take advantage of this bias by playing to voters' emotions and fears instead of relying on objective, factual information.

- **Curse of knowledge.** Too much knowledge can be a curse when it hampers understanding and communicating with people who are less knowledgeable. The curse describes experts' difficulty in explaining information to others who are less informed. Experts like pharmacists take for granted that others will be able to grasp complex concepts and terminology that are second nature to them.

- **Attribution bias.** People tend to attribute their successes to personal performances but attribute their failures to bad luck. This bias increases the likelihood that they will not learn from their mistakes.

■ **Halo effect**. This bias occurs when people take a positive attribute or impression about a person or thing and associate it with everything else about that person or thing.

Several strategies can help control the negative effect of overconfidence on decision making. The first strategy is simple awareness. Knowing about overconfidence can help managers develop strategies to attenuate its effect on decisions. For instance, a manager may consciously choose to argue against the first and most obvious solution to important problems in favor of less obvious ones. Alternatively, the manager may dream up potential negative outcomes of an option in addition to the intended ones.

Another well-known strategy is to generate as many alternative solutions as possible in the beginning. A greater number of alternatives to select from can help ensure that the best alternative is considered. Brainstorming can be used to generate as many possible solutions to a problem. During brainstorming, be careful not to criticize any solutions that you or your team discover because even the most foolish solutions can lead to an innovative idea.

Recognition of self-interest or emotional attachments can also help diminish bias. Self-interest in the outcomes causes decision makers to rate options higher when they might benefit. Although financial benefits are an obvious form of self-interest, nonfinancial benefits can be just as important. A less-recognized bias is that associated with emotional attachments. People's bonds to others, places, and things are potential sources of bias in decision making. Pharmacists' professional identity tends to bias solutions that involve pharmacists or medications over those that do not. People also tend to choose solutions that benefit their team over other teams. Simple awareness of these biases can help in developing ways to overcome them.

Various strategies can be employed to counteract potential bias once people are alerted to its presence. One strategy is to include someone with a different viewpoint or background in the analysis. Adding a technician to a team of pharmacists or a non-health care professional to a team of health care providers can add diversity and help the group overcome biases such as the curse of knowledge, group think, and the affect heuristic. Another strategy is to allow some extra time in debating the options. Rather than rushing to a solution, slowing down the process allows decision makers to consider alternative solutions. This strategy can blunt the effect of confirmation bias and other heuristics that lead to a rush to judgment.

Finally, people can counteract bias by using feedback loops in their decisions.[12] A *feedback loop* occurs when people collect data to provide timely evidence about the consequences of their choices. Feedback loops provide objective data regarding behavior, and they can help people overcome predispositions to attribution bias, confirmation bias, and halo effect, among others. Keeping records of predictions and their final results is a way of gaining accurate assessments about the success of decisions. Without accurate feedback about decisions, learning from mistakes is impossible.

■ Step 4: Evaluate Alternative Options

The goal of this step is to identify the most favorable outcome with the least number of unintended negative effects. This approach requires that criteria be established to assess alternatives. These criteria can be absolute or differential.[13]

Absolute criteria are those for which strict limits are established for acceptable decisions. For example, absolute criteria for hiring a new hospital pharmacy manager could be the possession of a state pharmacy license, the completion of a residency accredited by the American Society of Health-System Pharmacists, and experience as a manager. Any individual not meeting all of these criteria would be an unacceptable candidate. Absolute criteria help screen out unacceptable options for further consideration.

Differential criteria distinguish preferences of one alternative over another. Differential criteria for choosing the new hospital pharmacy manager could be the number of years of managerial experience, technical managerial skills developed, the completion of a graduate degree, and the quality of professional references.

After unacceptable candidates are screened out using absolute criteria, differential criteria can be used to rank the remaining candidates. Ranking can be accomplished in a variety of ways such as listing the advantages and disadvantages of the options for each criterion and then ranking candidates. This ranking process may be refined using a form of weighting criteria that give emphasis to those that are especially important. In the choosing of a hospital pharmacy manager, the number of years of managerial experience might be emphasized over other criteria.

■ Step 5: Choose an Alternative

The final selection of an alternative solution to a problem is often obvious when the preceding steps of the decision-making process are effectively followed. Even so, the final choice can still significantly depend on who makes the final decision. Personal factors, such as decision makers' personal values, personality, and comfort with risk, can affect the final choice of solutions. The effect of personal perceptions of risk on decision making can be extremely important. For example, individuals' discomfort with risk can bias them toward solutions that are familiar and comfortable to them. Alternatively, a risk seeker may prefer to take chances. All managers need to understand their preferences for risk and the potential effect of risk perceptions on decisions. Knowing about their risk aversion can help managers develop the habit of examining the potential downside of "safe" alternatives.

Some people like to rely on their "gut" feelings when making a final decision. Gut feelings, or intuition, can be useful in making minor decisions. However, systematic and objective methods are preferred in the resolution of very important problems.

Intuition-based decisions are more affected by various forms of bias, fatigue, mood, boredom, and a broad range of other factors. Therefore, when the data and objective analysis suggest a course of action, intuition should not be used to override that choice. Intuition should be only one of many factors to consider when making a choice. If intuition is used as the primary basis for a decision, self-checking and feedback should be employed to ensure a manager is not blinded to the best option by emotions and bias.

Step 6: Implement the Decision

Poor implementation of decisions often ruins many good decision-making processes. The reasons for failure are many. Sometimes, people just fail to follow the planned solution. If people are not committed to it, their half-hearted efforts may lead to failure. In other cases, the situation changes or unexpected problems arise. For this reason, solutions need contingency plans and flexibility built into them. In many cases, solutions to problems must be permitted to evolve as circumstances demand. That approach is why people who are required to implement a solution should be included in the decision-making process from the beginning. Otherwise, a good solution on paper may not succeed in real life.

Step 7: Monitor and Assess the Consequences of the Decision

This final step is often overlooked, although it is a critical element of the problem-solving process. Systems thinkers recognize that a problem is never solved, so they develop monitoring mechanisms to provide feedback about decisions. One reason for such mechanisms is to determine if a decision was implemented as decided. Another reason is to identify correctable flaws in planning and implementation. Feedback also helps managers learn about their decision-making skills and identify ways to improve them.

Feedback typically starts early in the decision-making process when a manager answers the question, "How will I know if this decision is a success?" The answer usually requires that some measure of success be identified and collected. Collecting these quality measures may be a one-time event (e.g., the diabetes monitoring event had 150 patients) or persist over time (e.g., the monthly medication error rate has decreased since implementing the program). When measures are continually collected over time, a statistical test can be employed to identify if changes are significant. Statistical testing is an important element of most quality improvement programs.

Good managerial decisions require both feedback and accountability. Most managers know, "If it is not measured, it is not important." Therefore, when the consequences of their choices are never measured or assessed, there is no pressure on managers to improve the quality of their decisions. Managers and employees need to receive systematic feedback in order to learn from their mistakes.

■■ CONCLUSION

Many of today's problems come from yesterday's solutions.[5] This means that many of people's current problems are of their own making. However, it also means that improving the way people make decisions can avoid future problems. To do so requires an understanding of the process of decision making and practice in properly applying it.

Changes are also required in how pharmacists approach decisions. For example, pharmacist managers should understand the long-term consequences of their decisions. Although short-term solutions may appear to resolve problems, they are often ineffective over the long term. Capable decision makers must always be cognizant that poor solutions are often worse than the original problems.

■■ KEY TERMS AND CONCEPTS

- Linear thinking
- Systems thinking
- Programmed decisions
- Nonprogrammed decisions

- Framing
- Framing errors
- Overconfidence bias
- Heuristics
- Availability bias
- Confirmation bias
- Group think
- Anchoring bias
- Affect heuristic
- Curse of knowledge
- Attribution bias
- Halo effect
- Absolute decision-making criteria
- Differential decision-making criteria

■ ● DISCUSSION AND REVIEW QUESTIONS

1. How is linear thinking in your Internet and voting habits rewarded?

2. Why might you as a pharmacist be better served spending more time working on nonprogrammed decisions at work instead of programmed ones? How might working on nonprogrammed decisions be important for your long-term career?

3. What strategies do you use to reduce your cognitive load in keeping up with the news or pharmacy literature? How deep (or superficial) is your learning with these strategies?

4. What absolute criteria do you have for any job you accept? What differential criteria are most important? Least important?

5. Albert Einstein said, "We cannot solve our problems with the same thinking we used when we created them." What does he mean by this, and how can it apply to the way we change pharmacy practice?

●● REFERENCES

1. Martin LC, Donohoe KL, Holdford DA. Decision-making and problem-solving approaches in pharmacy education. *Am J Pharm Educ.* 2016;80(3). doi:10.5688/ajpe80352.

2. Senge PM, Sterman JD. Systems thinking and organizational learning: acting locally and thinking globally in the organization of the future. *Eur J Oper Res.* 1992;59(1):137–150. doi:10.1016/0377-2217(92)90011-W.

3. Soumerai SB, Ross-Degnan D, Avorn J, et al. Effects of Medicaid drug-payment limits on admission to hospitals and nursing homes. *N Engl J Med.* 1991;325(15):1072–1077. doi:10.1056/NEJM199110103251505.

4. Woehrle SL. Decision classification enhances case-based reasoning. *Int Bus Econ Res J.* 2011;1(4). https://www.researchgate.net/publication/268402440_Decision_Classification_Enhances_Case-Based_Reasoning/fulltext/55bacb6e08aec0e5f43ea4bc/268402440_Decision_Classification_Enhances_Case-Based_Reasoning.pdf. Accessed May 30, 2018.

5. Covey SR. *The 7 Habits of Highly Effective People.* New York, NY: Free Press; 2004. doi:10.1108/00251749810245309.

6. Roberto M. *The Art of Critical Decision Making.* New York, NY: The Teaching Company; 2009. doi:10.1037/e523602012-001.

7. Russo JE, Schoemaker PJH. *Decision Traps: Ten Barriers to Brilliant Decision-Making and How to Overcome Them.* New York, NY: Simon & Schuster; 1990.

8. Senge P. *The Fifth Discipline: The Art and Practice of Learning.* New York, NY: Doubleday; 1990.

9. Roe S, Long R, King K. Pharmacies miss half of dangerous drug combinations. *Chicago Tribune.* December 15, 2016. http://www.chicagotribune.com/news/watchdog/druginteractions/ct-drug-interactions-pharmacy-met-20161214-story.html. Accessed February 3, 2017.

10. Russo EJ, Shoemaker PJ. Managing overconfidence. *Sloan Manage Rev.* 1992;33(2):7–17. doi:10.3102/00346543067001043.

11. List of cognitive biases. Wikipedia. https://en.wikipedia.org/wiki/List_of_cognitive_biases. doi:10.1177/0146167295211011.

12. Goetz T. Harnessing the Power of Feedback Loops. *WIRED.* June 2011. https://www.wired.com/2011/06/ff_feedbackloop/. Accessed May 30, 2018.

13. Hammond JS, Keeney RL, Raiffa H. Even swaps: a rational method for making trade-offs. *Harv Bus Rev.* 1998;76(2).

CHAPTER 8

Motivation Principles and Theories
Why Do People Act as They Do?

■■ OBJECTIVES

- ▨ Describe the link between performance, morale, and motivation.
- ▨ Discuss the basic features of key motivation theories.
- ▨ Discuss practices that enhance motivation.
- ▨ Describe practices that demotivate.

Too many organizations are making their decisions, their policies about talent and people, based on assumptions that are outdated, unexamined, and rooted more in folklore than in science.

—Daniel Pink

⬛⬛ INTRODUCTION

Getting people to do their best work is one of the most important but difficult tasks of leaders. Despite extensive scientific literature about what motivates people, humans are complex and act in a variety of unpredictable ways. Furthermore, many leaders' ideas about motivation are based on outdated and incorrect views about what motivates people. They believe that just paying people a little more or that scaring them with a potential penalty will motivate them to apply greater effort and perform better. However, this assumption is based on simplistic and often incorrect notions about what drives people to perform.

To influence change in pharmacy practice and health care, pharmacists need a basic understanding of the theories of motivation. It is a fundamental fact that leaders must rely on others to achieve their goals, and unless followers engage, the leader fails. This fact can be one of the most frustrating *and* rewarding aspects of being a leader.

Effective leaders must recognize and use the levers of change available to them. Motivational levers are numerous and include charisma, coercion, and trading of favors—each having upsides and downsides depending on the individuals involved and the conditions at hand. Knowing the potential benefits and pitfalls of these and other levers will determine a pharmacist's success in influencing practice.

Evidence-based motivational practices are not common in pharmacy practice. Most pharmacists rely on their intuition, limited personal experiences, and common sense cultural beliefs to motivate themselves and others. However, this type of motivation rarely brings about the high performance needed to make meaningful change in pharmacy practice. If pharmacies are like most other industries, two-thirds of employees are functioning well below their capabilities.[1]

Indeed, many pharmacists do not know much about their personal motivational levers, let alone those of others. Many of people think that if they can just get that raise or promotion, then their lives will be better. Yet when they achieve their goals, they are still unsatisfied—perhaps because they are chasing the wrong things. Understanding motivation is a critical aspect of managing oneself. People need to understand their own motivational levers to make personal choices about what they really want out of their career and life. Otherwise, they may choose paths and make choices that drain their energy and lead to dissatisfaction.

The truth is that pharmacists and others who work in pharmacy organizations are capable of far higher motivation and performance levels than those seen in the average work setting. Good leaders realize the capacity of their employees to do better and challenge them to do their best.

Although motivation has been studied for centuries, there are still no comprehensive answers to what motivates humans. However, research has yielded potential rules to guide behaviors, provided people understand that many of these rules can be wrong when dealing with the complexity of human behavior.

◼◼ RELATIONSHIP BETWEEN MOTIVATION AND PERFORMANCE

Motivation is a force or influence that causes someone to do something.[2] That force can come from internal factors (e.g., self-motivation) or from external factors (e.g., a reward or the threat of punishment). Motivation is not a fixed state. It is constantly in flux in response to the influence of personal and situational factors.

Performance is the action or process of carrying out or accomplishing an action, task, or function.[2] Motivation is related to performance in that people who are motivated typically perform tasks better. However, motivation and performance are two distinct concepts that are not always correlated. For example, a person might be motivated to perform (e.g., play the piano) but lack other requirements needed to perform well (e.g., talent, time to practice). Motivation is only one of several requirements for the performance of tasks. Performance requires the following:

- **An environment that encourages performance.** Individuals may need specific tools, time, coworkers, and systems to perform well. For pharmacists to consistently perform well with regard to the dispensing of medications, they need a computerized patient records system with fast linkages to printers and other technology, well-trained technicians who can perform their roles in the dispensing process, sufficient staffing to complete the tasks in a timely manner, appropriate lighting to see, and so on.

- **Adequate training and experience.** To perform well, pharmacists must be trained to complete the task at hand. For dispensing medications, they must be up to date with current drug therapies, understand the roles of various individuals in the work flow, know where to find the medications on the shelf, and so on.

▓ **An individual's motivation.** People must be motivated to perform. Even well-trained pharmacists with a good work environment can perform poorly if they do not exert the effort needed.

The environment, training, and motivation are all necessary for performance. Consider the following case in Box 8.1, and decide whether the performance problem arises from the environment, the training, or the motivation, or from a combination of each.

People fail to perform tasks for a myriad of reasons (Table 8.1). Some reasons are within their control, such as motivation or training. Other reasons are outside their control and require outside help. A manager is responsible for understanding what people need for enhancing their performance and how to meet those needs.

▓▓ MOTIVATION AND JOB SATISFACTION

Generally, individuals who are satisfied with their jobs are more motivated to do their jobs. In general, this common knowledge is true; however, there are many exceptions because motivation and job satisfaction are distinctly different constructs.

BOX 8.1 Leadership in Action: Is This a Problem of Motivation?

Diane Messenger works for an independent pharmacy in a small Wisconsin town after recently graduating from the University of Wisconsin. For the past year, she has been working 12-hour days, 6 days per week, at the pharmacy.

Diane has had few days off since the owner, Art Alfred, had surgery to repair his fractured hip. Art has compensated Diane generously for her extra effort by helping pay off her school loans and making payments on her new car, a Mini Cooper. Unfortunately, Art has been receiving complaints from long-time customers that Diane has been rude to customers and sloppy in her work. Art was surprised because, in the past, Diane was always pleasant to customers and meticulous in her work habits.

Questions

1. What is the problem with Diane? Is it one of motivation? If not, what is it?

2. Some people are perfectly happy working 12-hour days, 6 days per week, if they are adequately compensated. Would doubling Diane's salary put her in a better mood? If so, how long would her good mood last?

3. If Diane used her extra money to hire people to take care of her housework, cooking, and errands, would this solve the problem? Would Diane better perform her tasks if she got more sleep, ate healthier food, and exercised?

4. What options are available to Art Alfred to solve this problem?

TABLE 8.1 Reasons That People Do Not Perform as Expected in Tasks

Reasons	Motivation, environment, lack of training or knowledge, or job fit
People do not know what tasks to perform.	Lack of training or knowledge
People do not know why they should perform tasks.	Lack of training or knowledge
People do not know how to perform tasks.	Lack of training or knowledge
People think that other tasks are more important.	Lack of training or knowledge
People lack the capability to perform the task as desired despite their aspiration.	Job fit
People put off the task because of procrastination.	Motivation
People do not want to perform the task.	Motivation
People are rewarded for not performing the task.	Motivation
People are not punished for failing to perform the task.	Motivation
People do not perform the task because they do not have the necessary tools.	Environment
Unexpected events get in the way of performing the task.	Environment
People have personal problems that get in the way.	Motivation or environment

Motivation is the desire to act. When a person has an unsatisfied need, the desire to fulfill it creates motivation. *Job satisfaction* comes from the pleasure of or contentment in a job, and it is based on individuals' perceptions of their work, colleagues, supervisors, and employers. In a pharmacy, highly satisfied employees are often motivated to work harder in their tasks.

However, what satisfies individuals sometimes contrasts with the needs of the pharmacy. For example, a pharmacy technician might be more interested in socializing with coworkers than in serving the customers; a pharmacist might be more content in a job that requires very little work from him or her; or a pharmacy manager might be more concerned about issues going on at home than about the day-to-day tasks at work.

When policies and practices that are best for the organization conflict with the wants of individuals in the organization, leaders need to put the organization first. The primary responsibility of leaders and managers is not to satisfy. It is to achieve the organization's mission. In most instances, increasing job satisfaction will facilitate employees' efforts to achieve the organization's mission. But in the few instances when they conflict, the mission comes first. Good leaders can typically balance the demands of an organization to achieve job satisfaction and the mission.

⬛ ⬛ MOTIVATION THEORIES

Understanding basic theories of motivation helps pharmacists explain and predict human behavior and allows them to predict how people might act in different circumstances. Theories present a systematic way of understanding events or situations based on the best evidence available. They can help pharmacists deal better with people and help them avoid misconceptions and missteps that result in avoidable conflict and wasted effort. The following section discusses the most common theories and their lessons for motivating behavior.

⬛ Expectancy Theory

Expectancy theory asserts that people's work effort is more intense depending on how much they perceive that the effort will result in a desired outcome (e.g., pay, time off).[3] The theory states that an individual's intensity of effort is governed by his or her expectancy, instrumentality, and preferences. *Expectancy* is defined as a belief that if individuals increase their level of effort toward a task, greater performance will result. *Instrumentality* describes individuals' perceptions that if they perform better, they will be rewarded for that performance. *Preference* is the degree to which any reward that results from work effort will be valued by the individual. Expectancy theory argues that individuals' expectancy, instrumentality, and preferences combine to determine their intensity of effort toward a task.

$$\text{Motivation} = \text{Expectancy} \times \text{Instrumentality} \times \text{Preference}$$

Expectancy theory asserts that all three conditions are necessary for rewards to motivate effort. Individuals will work harder to achieve a reward only if they (1) believe that greater effort will result in greater performance, (2) believe those higher levels of performance will be rewarded, and (3) believe the rewards will be worth the effort. If any of these conditions is not present, individuals will not be motivated.

The theory explains, for example, why a pharmacist might not work toward getting the employee-of-the-month award. The pharmacist may decide that extra effort on her part would not increase her performance enough to get a reward. She may also believe that higher performance would not result in receiving the award because of her perception that other employees are more deserving or that the process is unfair (e.g., a popularity contest). The pharmacist also may not value the award because it may bring undesired public attention to her or negative comments from jealous coworkers.

The theory also explains why many pharmacy students calculate how many points they need to receive on a final exam to get a certain grade. Professional education makes heavy use of rewards (i.e., grades) to motivate effort and performance,[4] so students rationally calculate the effort needed to achieve sufficient points on a test to receive those rewards. Using that calculation, students make choices on how to apportion their time and effort.

The problem is that the grading system in education can lack expectancy, instrumentality, and preference. Grades lack expectancy when students do not believe that more intense studying will result in better performance on exams or a higher final grade. Indeed, students frequently complain that the effort spent studying has little relationship with exam performance. Grades can also lack instrumentality if performance is defined as "deep learning" rather than "getting a high grade," because high grades do not always indicate mastery of a topic. Cramming for an exam is a frequent study technique of students that permits sufficient short-term retention of class material to pass an exam but inadequate long-term mastery of it. Finally, some students may not value high grades sufficiently to work for them. An average pharmacy student may decide after a mental cost-benefit analysis that a B or C grade is an adequate reward for his or her efforts.

Expectancy theory makes a case for developing an environment for workers that provides valued rewards for appropriate behavior. Leaders who understand the goals and aspirations of individuals can align reward systems to have expectancy and instrumentality according to each person's preferences. Expectancy theory emphasizes the carrot (i.e., reward) over the stick (i.e., punishment) to drive behavior. But in real-life work settings, sometimes the carrot is not enough to motivate, and the stick needs to be applied.

Reinforcement Theory

Reinforcement theory, also known as operant conditioning or behavior modification, states that the consequences of behavior will determine the future likelihood of that behavior.[5] Like expectancy theory, it assumes that humans are rational in their behavior and act in ways that will increase their overall utility—the basic foundation of economic theory.

Hence, reinforcement theory assumes that people will act in ways that result in good consequences and avoid acting in ways that result in bad consequences

FIGURE 8.1 Consequences of Behavior According to Reinforcement Theory

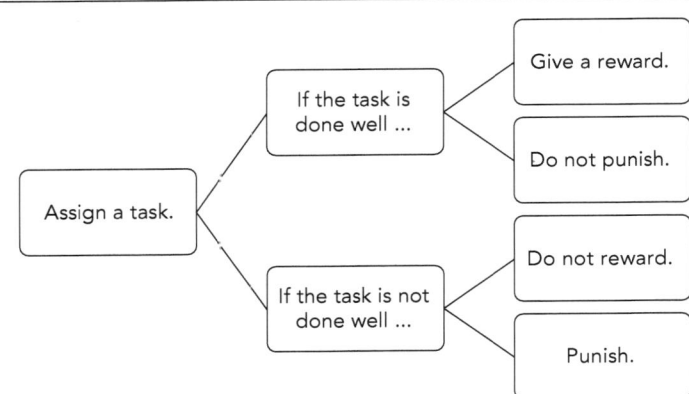

(Figure 8.1). According to the theory, there are four types of consequences of behavior: positive reinforcement (rewards), negative reinforcement (avoidance of punishment), extinction (withholding of rewards), and punishment. However, these consequences can be simplified into just two categories: rewards (i.e., good consequences) and punishments (i.e., bad consequences).

Reinforcement theory argues that people are motivated in an environment where desirable behaviors are rewarded and undesirable actions are punished. Most pharmacists and students understand and accept this motivational method because it is intuitive and is consistent with how most people were raised. The theory states that people who are capable of performing a desired task often do not do so because the incentives are wrong. For example, a pharmacist who acts unprofessionally with rude behavior toward coworkers may be rewarded with fewer interruptions and less work. For the pharmacist's behavior to change, the pharmacist would need to suffer penalties (e.g., a reprimand) when acting in a rude manner or positive consequences (e.g., a complement) when acting politely.

One of the limitations of both expectancy and reinforcement theories is that they incorrectly assume that humans act rationally and unemotionally.[6] Both theories assume away the effect of personal feelings in human motivation. Consequently, pharmacy managers who are unsophisticated in their use of these two transactional approaches (i.e., do this and you get that) often achieve unintentional and undesired results.

Many people see the heavy use of *carrots* and *sticks* as manipulative and unnecessary for motivating professionals and others who care about their work. The phrase *carrot and stick* is a metaphor for the combined use of rewards and punishments to motivate. It comes from the idea that donkeys can be motivated to carry heavy loads with rewards such as receiving carrots or with punishments such as being hit with a stick. The problem is that humans are not donkeys and they tend to resent manipulative reward systems. Consider how you might feel if after assigning each task to you, your boss said, "If you don't do it right, I will remember it when your annual evaluation comes around." Most people would feel insulted. However, a "do this or else" approach is exactly how most reward systems work. This type of reward system can get in the way of professional relationships.

Although use of the carrot and stick approach typically results in compliance with a task, it generates little energy and enthusiasm in individuals for doing so. Relationships founded on rewards and punishments deteriorate into a series of transactions in which the effort and the performance rarely occur without receipt of something in return. Each partner says, "You do this, and I will do that." An unspoken addition to that sentence is "And no more." Consequently, transactional motivation methods encourage only compliance; they do not encourage the higher levels of commitment needed to achieve excellent performance.

This situation occurs in our educational system, where many students do only what is necessary to achieve a grade, but no more. In fact, some students may even feel cheated if they mistakenly study harder for a test than what was needed. When grades are the primary motivational method, student interactions with faculty members are more likely to revolve around ways to improve grades rather than mastery of the material.

■ Maslow's Hierarchy of Needs

Maslow's hierarchy of needs states that human needs can be grouped into five categories: physiological, safety and security, social belonging, esteem, and self-actualization.[7] People typically attempt to meet these needs in a hierarchical fashion, from the most basic, low-order needs to the most complex, high-order needs (Figure 8.2).

When these needs categories are arranged in ascending order from the most basic to the most complex, research found that people usually tried to satisfy lower-level needs before attempting to meet higher-level needs. Maslow's theory is useful in explaining challenging motivational situations.

FIGURE 8.2 Maslow Need Categories and Descriptions[a]

Self-actualization: the need to fulfill full potential

Esteem needs: self-perceptions, feelings of achievement, respect given by others

Social belonging needs: love, friendships, intimacy, and family

Safety and security needs: personal and financial security, health and well-being, and safety against physical harm

Physiological needs: air, water, food, sleep, clothing, sex, and shelter

a. See reference 7.

For instance, a director of pharmacy in a health care system identifies one of her staff pharmacists as an excellent candidate for a clinical coordinator position. She invites the candidate into her office to offer the position. Surprisingly, the candidate turns down the opportunity, stating that he is happy being a staff pharmacist and has no interest in managing others or coordinating programs. Even when told about the generous salary increase accompanying the promotion, the pharmacist politely declines.

Maslow's hierarchy of needs offers reasons that pharmacists might willingly refuse job promotions or overtime pay opportunities. Maslow asserts that people's needs depend on what they have, that is, the wealthy are motivated by needs different from those of people who are less fortunate. He also states that humans are motivated only by unsatisfied needs. Therefore, pharmacists who have sufficient money to meet their needs may forgo a job promotion or overtime situation that takes them away from family time or leisurely pursuits. In contrast, pharmacists who are in a precarious financial situation may jump at the chance to make extra money.

Maslow's hierarchy of needs also helps explain why employees who are worried about layoffs, personal bankruptcy, and family problems tend to concentrate on those concerns instead of their assigned tasks. For example, when workers are worried about potential layoffs, they focus on dealing with the immediate threat to their financial safety and often take time out of their work day to focus on their resume, to make personal calls to identify who is hiring, or to simply worry about their situation. Until threats are reduced, workers will have difficulty focusing on the job at hand.

Understanding Maslow's hierarchy of needs can help when communicating with or counseling employees about performance. Managers often carelessly make explicit and implicit threats toward employees without understanding the potential harm in doing so. Threats may be perceived whenever a manager emphasizes rewards or punishments in motivating behaviors. Threats can be strongly worded, "Do this or you will be fired," or oblique, "If you don't meet the deadline, I don't know what we'll do." Rather than getting workers to focus on their job, such statements make them focus on the threat to their job. When workers feel threatened, they protect themselves in various ways—join unions, avoid the boss, withhold information, organize resistance among coworkers, or start looking for a new job.

Hence, threats should be avoided or de-emphasized whenever possible and replaced by more encouraging forms of communication such as a pat on the back for a job well done or a public recognition of good work. These positive techniques are more likely to enhance esteem and self-actualization in employees. When verbal or written warnings are made, they should be crafted in a way that informs workers how they can improve their behavior to remove the threat and start to focus again on higher-level needs.

Herzberg's Two-Factor Theory

Herzberg's two-factor theory addresses the effects of working conditions on worker satisfaction and motivation.[8] Herzberg discovered in interviews with a broad range of workers that dissatisfying job conditions often differ from those job conditions that satisfy individuals.

The job conditions that dissatisfy, or *maintenance factors*, tend to do so when they are *not* present in the workplace. In addition, these dissatisfying conditions reduce worker motivation. Herzberg found 10 dissatisfying conditions (or *dissatisfiers*): policies; supervision; interpersonal relationships with one's supervisor, peers, and subordinates; salary; job security; personal life; working conditions; and status. Whenever workers feel any of these conditions are wanting, job dissatisfaction and lowered motivation likely result.

Once maintenance factors are present in a sufficient amount to satisfy a worker, any increases tend to have little additional effect on satisfaction. Therefore, individuals who are generally satisfied with their salary or working conditions will feel little additional motivation to perform for factors such as higher pay or better conditions.

Other aspects of jobs, or *motivational factors*, have the contrasting effect of stimulating higher levels of job satisfaction and motivation when present, but causing minimal dissatisfaction when absent. There are six of these job characteristics: achievement, recognition, advancement, work itself, possibilities for personal growth, and responsibility. When these conditions (or *satisfiers*) are present, workers tend to achieve both greater satisfaction in their job and job motivation. However, when they are absent, workers are neither satisfied nor dissatisfied. Consider the motivational factor of personal recognition—workers might derive significant satisfaction when formally recognized for excellence, but they might not be significantly dissatisfied if they are not recognized for a job well done.

The distinction Herzberg makes between maintenance factors and motivating factors is similar to psychologists' premises of extrinsic and intrinsic motivators. *Extrinsic motivators* are rewards provided in exchange for working. They are furnished by employers as part of a verbal or written contract to motivate employees to complete tasks related to their job, but they have little effect on satisfaction with these job tasks or the job itself. Satisfaction results only when the extrinsic reward is received and then, only for a short time. Pay and working conditions are classic extrinsic motivators.

Intrinsic motivation, however, occurs by engaging in the task itself. It occurs when people engage in behavior purely for the joy of doing so or for the opportunity it presents to explore, learn, understand, develop, or challenge themselves. It is what drives children to play, amateur athletes to train, poor artists to continually create art that may not sell, and wealthy people to keep working.

Herzberg's and Maslow's theories are similar because they both focus on satisfying unmet needs. Herzberg's maintenance factors resemble the lower-level physical, safety, and social needs of Maslow. Motivational factors mirror the higher-level achievement and self-actualization needs.

Taken together, they can be used to explain why pharmacists may not be satisfied working in a job where they are well paid, comfortable, and safe or why pharmacists would gladly work in an inner-city clinic for significantly less pay. Many dissatisfied pharmacists find that pay, comfort, and safety are not enough to sustain them. High-paying jobs may dissatisfy if they lack challenge or feelings of accomplishment. In contrast, pharmacists can be greatly satisfied working in difficult surroundings for low pay if they feel needed and believe they are accomplishing important work.

Equity Theory

Equity theory revolves around the question of fairness in peoples' actions and choices. It argues that people are motivated to act to correct perceived instances of unfair treatment.[9] It asserts that each person keeps a mental tally of present and past experiences with others. The equity (i.e., fairness) of these experiences is judged by comparing what was received in the relationship versus what was contributed. If people judge a relationship to be equitable, they will be motivated to reciprocate with some fair level of response.

Evidence for equity theory has been demonstrated in the pharmacy literature. Ried and McGhan examined pharmacist job satisfaction and employers' compensation practices.[10] They found that low compensation (compared to that of other pharmacists) was the most important influence on job satisfaction.

In employee and employer relationships, workers who feel unfairly treated can act to correct the inequity by seeking fairer treatment; reducing their level of output to meet their perceived equitable amount; or seeking another, more equitable employer. One caveat should be noted—equity judgments are based on an individual's perceptions, which may have little to do with actual circumstances.

Not all responses to inequity seek to correct unfair treatment.[9] Retaliation is a common response. For example, if Bob, the pharmacy manager, is perceived by some workers to unfairly give another worker, Susan, a better work schedule, the injured parties will likely seek revenge on both the source (i.e., Bob) and the beneficiary (i.e., Susan) of the inequity. In fact, the desire for revenge often is so strong that it will cause individuals to act at cost to themselves. Economic models of motivation do not predict this behavior because they assume behavior is rational, and emotional impulses like the need to punish are irrational.

Nevertheless, emotions are a key element of human behavior and fundamental to perceptions of equity.

When considering the issue of equity, one must differentiate between two types of equity: distributive and procedural.[9] *Distributive equity* describes people's perceptions about how benefits and burdens are divided among any parties who are treated differently. It focuses on the outcomes (e.g., work schedule, raises, attention) of any situation. Pharmacy managers who emphasize achieving distributive equity in their interactions with employees are in an untenable situation because people tend to overestimate their contributions and underestimate the contributions of others. Therefore, someone is always likely to believe that he or she is receiving a raw deal despite the reality of a situation.

The other form of fairness, *procedural equity*, describes the manner in which outcomes are distributed. It describes due process—the fairness of policies and procedures for dealing with situations and the way those procedures are applied. Although people care about the distribution of outcomes, they also care about the process. For example, two pharmacists of equal performance and accomplishments work at the same pharmacy. One is offered a 5 percent raise in salary without any effort on his part. The other pharmacist must ask for the raise. After arguing her case, she is given a 5 percent raise also. Each pharmacist received the same outcome, but the second pharmacist will probably feel less fairly treated because of the process involved.

If the outcomes are perceived to be unfair, individuals are often willing to accept this temporary inequity if they believe fair procedures will balance the distribution of outcomes over time. Indeed, the willingness to emphasize procedural equity over distributive equity is the foundation of modern law and government. Citizens often willingly follow laws and regulations because they believe that societal equity will be maximized. They also realize that without rules and laws, anarchy and chaos often result.

Box 8.2 shows how perceptions of procedural equity can overcome inequity in distribution.

Pharmacy managers who want to ensure fairness try to show both forms of fairness.[11] To show distributive fairness, managers document good and bad behavior of workers and use objective measures to evaluate them and to fairly distribute rewards and punishments. To show procedural fairness, managers clearly set out procedures for rewards and punishment and apply them consistently. When exceptions are made, they are explained clearly and explicitly.

BOX 8.2 Leadership in Action: If I Do It for You, I Will Have to Do It for Everybody

One of the most common excuses given by managers for not accommodating an employee's request is, "If I do it for you, I will have to do it for everybody." However, the following situation describes how understanding the difference between distributive and procedural equity can help overcome this knee-jerk response to requests.

Linda, the best technician in a community hospital's pharmacy department, had a chronic problem arriving to work on time because of childcare issues. She asked for permission to arrive 30 minutes after the start of her shift. She stated that she would stay 30 minutes after everyone else left to make up the time lost and to help the technicians on the following shift get a jump on their workload.

Initially, her supervisor John thought to himself, "If I let you do it, then I will have to let everyone do it." He had learned through experience that this response was easiest because previous attempts to be fair had backfired. Plus, he was adamant that people be at work on time every day, and he did not want to be called a hypocrite.

Nevertheless, Linda was an exceptional employee in every other way. She was highly productive, and everyone enjoyed working with her. Her coworkers respected her, and the childcare problem was something beyond Linda's control. Still, he was worried about the response of others in the pharmacy department if he granted Linda's request. Fortunately, John found a solution by presenting a fair procedure that served everyone's needs.

First, John called the technicians together to lay out the situation. He explained Linda's circumstances and his concerns about granting her request. He argued that Linda faced an unavoidable conflict between her responsibilities as an employee and a mother, but he would permit the switch only if all of the technicians agreed to it.

Surprisingly, the technicians expressed support for accommodating Linda's request without complaint or comment because a clear and reasonable procedure was applied to her situation. First, the technicians respected Linda and realized that her situation was unique and required a unique solution. Second, John showed appreciation for Linda's situation and therefore demonstrated concern for all of the technicians. Third, he gave the impression that he would make similar exceptions for them under unique and unavoidable circumstances. Consequently, John's decision-making procedure was perceived as reasonable and equitable to all involved.

Once the solution was implemented, John was relieved to see that nothing changed in the daily work of the pharmacy and no one complained that the decision was unfair.

Questions

1. Why is this a fair solution when some people are receiving benefits that others are not?

2. What would have happened if John just accommodated Linda's request without talking it over with the technicians? Would he get the same results? Why?

3. Would this procedure work with regard to a technician who is less competent? With regard to one who is selfish and not well liked?

Furthermore, workers need to appreciate that procedures for dealing with situations may not be fair in the short run but will be fair over time. Their responsibility is to understand the policies, rules, and procedures under which they work. Otherwise, their ignorance might be the cause of unnecessary conflict.

⬛ ⬛ EMERGING THEORIES

Up to this point, motivational theories identify three primary drives that power peoples' behaviors. The first drive is biological needs, such as Maslow's lower-level needs for food, air, and shelter. The second is the drive to achieve extrinsic rewards and avoid punishments. The third is the drive to satisfy intrinsic desires such as achievement, recognition, and personal growth.

A complaint about intrinsic motivation as described by Herzberg is that it does not fully capture the complexity of how people's internal desires drive their behavior. Several theories of motivation have emerged in recent years that may help pharmacists understand their own motivations and the motivations of others. They focus on increasing the understanding of intrinsic motivation and the elements associated with self-motivation. The most prominent theory is self-determination theory.

⬛ Self-Determination Theory

Self-determination theory states that people are innately self-motivated toward personal growth, but that this self-motivation is often blocked by their immediate surroundings and situations.[12] The removal of these barriers will result in conditions that allow individuals to achieve their highest level of effort and performance. In fact, self-determination theory argues that many managerial systems that try to control and direct motivation can get in the way of self-motivation.

The theory states that motivation and engagement in tasks are influenced by individuals' needs to direct their own life (i.e., autonomy), control the outcome and develop mastery (i.e., competence), and connect with others and be a part of something greater than themselves (i.e., relatedness) (Table 8.2). *Autonomy* involves acting with free will and having the ability to make choices. When people do things autonomously, they do so without being directed in any way. Rather than acting to receive something, they engage in an activity because they deem it to be important or find it interesting. *Competence* refers to people's need to believe that they are good at doing things. Competence is associated with

TABLE 8.2 Relationship Between Self-Determination and Engagement

Self-determination	Engagement	Disengagement
Autonomy	Feeling in control	Feeling out of control
Competence (i.e., mastery)	Perceiving that one is on the path to self-actualization	Feeling inept, that personal growth is stagnant
Relatedness (i.e., purpose)	Feeling a part of a group, of contributing to something greater than oneself	Feeling alone, that one's actions have little meaning

perceptions of self-worth and social standing in that people derive satisfaction by being perceived as proficient at skills valued by others. Also, if people are able to overcome significant challenges through competence, their satisfaction is even greater. *Relatedness* refers to the basic desire to interact with and be connected to other people. The need for relatedness is associated with the need to belong and to feel a sense of purpose. A feeling of belonging gives people comfort and acceptance just as the feelings people experience when they are with family and friends. A sense of purpose gives a feeling of being something greater than oneself.

Self-determination theory suggests that environments that allow humans to have autonomy, competence, and relatedness will encourage engagement with tasks.[12] Engagement by workers is the emotional commitment to tasks and the goals underlying them. Environments that engage can be developed by setting expectations about the goal to be achieved but allowing workers to choose the path to achieving it. Engagement can be encouraged by actions such as permitting people to choose their team and the process used to achieve the tasks. As long as the desired results are achieved, the process used does not really matter. Giving people choices allows them not only to select tasks that they can master and work with people with whom they can establish a sense of relatedness, but also to gain a perception of control over their lives. Self-determination theory is the foundation for many modern management interventions designed to improve performance in professionals.

▇ *Theory of 16 Basic Desires*

Another prominent theory argues that there are 16 basic intrinsic desires that guide a person's daily life and determine who she or he is as a person.[13] These 16 basic desires are as follows:

1. Acceptance: the need for approval

2. Curiosity: the need to learn

3. Eating: the need for food

4. Family: the need to raise children

5. Honor: the need to be loyal to the traditional values of one's clan or ethnic group

6. Idealism: the need for social justice

7. Independence: the need for individuality

8. Order: the need for organized, stable, and predictable environments

9. Physical activity: the need for exercise

10. Power: the need for influence of will

11. Romance: the need for sex and for beauty

12. Saving: the need to collect

13. Social contact: the need for friends and relationships with others

14. Social status: the need for social standing and feelings of self-importance

15. Tranquility: the need to be safe

16. Vengeance: the need to strike back and to compete

This theory argues that although people share these basic desires, the relative importance and ranking of each desire depends on each individual and the circumstances. How people rank and combine these desires is what makes each individual unique.

Examine an example of two people in a work setting, Bob and Mary. Bob's top three desires are tranquility, social contact, and acceptance, and Mary's top three are social status, honor, and power. Bob might be likely to excel in an organization that emphasizes teamwork and camaraderie, whereas Mary might do better in a system that encourages competition and individual effort.

Leaders often fail to effectively motivate because of their failure to understand individual differences and their use of one-size-fits-all strategies to motivate. For instance, leaders who are highly motivated to achieve power and social status can have difficulty understanding why others might place these desires at the bottom of their priority list. Although they appreciate cognitively that others may have different desires and values, they have trouble accepting these differences emotionally. Leaders may even develop a disrespect for anyone who does not share their personal desires.

According to Reiss,[13] leaders need to motivate by appealing to each individual's values, not those of the leader. This approach can be difficult because individuals often believe their values are superior to those of everyone else. When this belief is combined with the confidence and competitive nature of many leaders, there is a natural desire to persuade someone toward one's own desires rather than listen to another person's perspective. Indeed, much of the leadership literature describes stories about a leader's personal journey and the way the leader was able to inspire others to follow his or her personal vision. In many of these stories, the leader is less interested in understanding what the followers care about and more interested in getting followers to do what the leader cares about.

The theory of the 16 basic desires makes a case that leaders need to truly seek to understand the relative importance of various desires of individuals and to use that understanding to tailor their behavior toward those individuals. If you want to motivate anyone—a classmate, coworker, subordinate, physician, or boss—be smart and consider what they care about.

■ ■ CONCLUSION

A large portion of every pharmacist's daily task is influencing others. A critical part of influencing is getting people to perform tasks that achieve the mission of the pharmacy. People do not always perform as expected for many reasons. Pharmacists must diagnose problems with performance and develop strategies to increase it.

This chapter reviews the most common theories of motivation and prepares readers for the next chapter, which continues with the topic of motivating change. Chapter 9 addresses how to use best evidence to motivate others and ourselves.

■ ■ KEY TERMS AND CONCEPTS

- Motivation
- Performance
- Job satisfaction
- Expectancy theory
- Reinforcement theory

- Carrot and stick approach

- Maslow's hierarchy of needs

- Herzberg's two-factor theory

- Extrinsic motivation

- Intrinsic motivation

- Equity theory

- Procedural equity

- Distributive equity

- Self-determination theory

- Engagement

- Theory of 16 basic desires

■■ DISCUSSION AND REVIEW QUESTIONS

1. Can dissatisfied pharmacists perform at a high level? Will they give their maximum effort? What are the primary sources of pharmacists' dissatisfaction in their jobs?

2. How can people-centered leaders put the mission first and still be people centered?

3. When is punishment a good way to motivate people? How about rewards?

4. How do you feel when you are threatened? What are you motivated to do when threatened?

5. What things do you do for intrinsic reasons?

6. Think about a time when you were unfairly treated. What was your response? How did you retaliate or act to reduce the inequity?

■■ REFERENCES

1. Corbin J. The Gallup 2017 Employee Engagement Report is out: and the results . . . nothing has changed. March 7, 2017. theEMPLOYEEapp. https://www.the employeeapp.com/gallup-2017-employee-engagement-report-results-nothing -changed/. Accessed May 31, 2018.

2. Oxford English Dictionary Online. http://www.oed.com/.

3. Heneman HG, Schwab DP. Evaluation of research on expectancy theory predictions of employee performance. *Psychol Bull*. 1972;78(1):1–9. doi:10.1037/h0033093.

4. Holdford D, Lovelace-Elmore B. Applying the principles of human motivation to pharmaceutical education. *J Pharm Teach*. 2001;8(4). https://www.tandfonline.com/doi/abs/10.3109/J060v08n04_01. doi:10.1300/J060v08n04_01.

5. Donnelly JH, Gibson JL, Ivancevich JM. *Fundamentals of Management*. 10th ed. Boston, MA: Irwin/McGraw Hill; 1998.

6. Kanfer R, Frese M, Johnson RE. Motivation related to work: a century of progress. *J Appl Psychol*. 2017;102(3):338–355. doi:10.1037/apl0000133.

7. Maslow AH. A theory of human motivation. *Psychol Rev*. 1943;50(4):370–396. doi:10.1037/h0054346.

8. Herzberg F. One more time: how do you motivate employees? *Harv Bus Rev*. 2003;81:87–96. doi:10.1108/eb055227.

9. Colquitt JA, Zipay KP. Justice, fairness, and employee reactions. *Annu Rev Organ Psychol Organ Behav*. 2015;2(1):75–99. doi:10.1146/annurev-orgpsych-032414-111457.

10. Ried LD, McGhan WF. An equity model of staff pharmacists' job satisfaction. *J Pharm Mark Manage*. 1987;1(3):3–24. doi:10.3109/J058v01n03_02.

11. Kim WC, Mauborgne R. Fair process: managing in the knowledge economy. *Harv Bus Rev*. 1997;75(4):65–75. doi:Article.

12. Ryan RM, Deci EL. Self-determination theory and the facilitation of intrinsic motivation, social development, and well-being. *Am Psychol*. 2000;55(1):68–78. doi:10.1037/0003-066X.55.1.68.

13. Reiss S. Multifaceted nature of intrinsic motivation: the theory of 16 basic desires. *Rev Gen Psychol*. 2004;8(3):179–193. doi:10.1037/1089-2680.8.3.179.

CHAPTER 9

Motivation Strategies
How to Motivate Yourself and Others

◼️◼️ OBJECTIVES

- ◼ Evaluate the benefits and difficulties associated with pay-for-performance motivational systems.

- ◼ Discuss the concept of job design.

- ◼ Describe the roles of key characteristics of job enrichment in increasing a person's engagement in his or her work.

- ◼ Identify strategies for motivating yourself.

Alone we can do so little; together we can do so much.

—Helen Keller

⬛⬛ INTRODUCTION

When you think about how to motivate people, your intuition tells you that you need to give something to get something. This transactional viewpoint is an incredibly simplistic way of viewing human performance. When considering what drives people, you may note that numerous variables are involved in motivating yourself and others.

Many motivational strategies have been proposed in the social science and management literature. The best-known strategies fall into three primary categories: linking pay to job performance, creating job design that increases intrinsic motivation, and facilitating self-motivation. Each strategy has relevance to pharmacists who want to maximize their own performance and the performance of the people with whom they work.

⬛⬛ LINKING PAY TO JOB PERFORMANCE

Linking pay to the performance of good work is commonly recognized and supported by individuals in work settings. The idea is built into the structure of most work settings and acts as a foundation of our capitalistic system. *Pay-for-performance* (P4P) plans make intuitive sense because the idea of rewarding individuals who achieve results seems fair in western cultures.

⬛ Support for Linking Pay to Performance

Linking pay to work output is supported by many well-known theories of motivation. Expectancy theory, reinforcement theory, Maslow's hierarchy of needs, and equity theory all suggest that behavior can be encouraged with the right rewards under the right circumstances. Herzberg's two-factor theory also supports rewards in limited circumstances to motivate. Newer motivation models, such as self-determination theory, claim that rewards can motivate when they are associated with an individual's personal needs, desires, and drives.

⬛ Difficulties Linking Pay to Performance

Implementing P4P plans well is difficult, and many P4P plans fail to achieve desired goals.[1-4] Failure can occur from flaws in P4P design and implementation, the plan's inability to affect nonmotivational reasons for performance, its potential to damage professional relationships, and the fact that P4P plans can encourage the wrong behaviors. Motivating with rewards requires programs to do the following:

- Accurately measure and assess change in performance.

- Convince payers and performers to agree on the measures and the rewards used.

- Assign a reward that is significant but not too significant for that performance.

- Assign rewards often enough to reinforce desired behavior.

- Communicate how the change in performance resulted in the reward being given or not being given.

Measuring Performance Is Difficult

Many aspects of the P4P process can go wrong. Accurately measuring performance is difficult for many jobs, especially for jobs that require technical skill, personalization, and complex problem solving—capabilities increasingly being expected of pharmacists.

Consider the job of filling prescriptions. The act of dispensing medication consists of both routine and cognitively complex tasks. The routine elements of the job are well-defined actions such as receiving the prescription, checking it for clarity, finding the drug, repackaging it, labeling it, and handing it to the patient. These are discrete tasks that can be accurately evaluated for speed and quality such as measuring the number of prescriptions filled per hour without dispensing errors.

However, simplistic metrics of work output may not accurately convey the complexity of a pharmacist's cognitive performance. They do not evaluate how well a pharmacist reviews the appropriateness of a prescription against the patient medication record or the quality of a patient interview about medication-related problems.

Therefore, P4P programs tend to reward behaviors that *can be measured* instead of performance that *should be measured*. Consequently, an employer may base pay raises on the number of prescriptions filled or the time spent per prescription filled instead of the number of medication-related problems prevented. Indeed, a pharmacist can often maximize P4P performance numbers by cutting corners on the difficult-to-assess cognitive tasks in favor of the easy-to-evaluate routine ones.

Disagreements About Assessments are Common

Performance evaluations are often viewed as unfair by the individuals being assessed.[4] Sometimes, perceptions of unfairness are due to a difference in opinion where individuals involved in performance evaluations reach conflicting conclusions. In other circumstances, the person being evaluated overestimates his or her own performance, a cognitive bias termed *illusory superiority*. Illusory superiority is also known as the Lake Wobegon effect, named after a place where all of the people are above average.

This difference in perception means that any P4P process that rates individuals at average or below will be perceived as wrong or unfair even when the assessments are valid. If a P4P plan is seen as unfair, individuals who are assessed will be more inclined to game the system, cheat, or reduce their effort—all unintentional negative side effects of P4P systems.

Reward Differentials Are Usually Too Small to Change Behavior

To motivate performance, P4P plans need to provide sufficient rewards to encourage heightened effort. However, the reward differentials between poor and outstanding pharmacists are too small with most incentive systems. The typical reward differences of 1 percent or 2 percent between poor and outstanding workers have little influence on long-term behavior. To change performance, differentials must be noticeable.

Rewards Are Given Too Infrequently to Have a Long-Lasting Effect

Most P4P programs give rewards once a year. This schedule is too infrequent to have any long-lasting effect on motivation. Individuals quickly become acclimated to rewards, and their effect on performance quickly wanes. To be more effective, P4P programs should give awards more often to continuously encourage effort.

P4P Programs Do Not Often Address the Real Reason for Poor Performance

Many P4P programs fail to improve performance because they do not address the nonmotivational reasons for poor performance. Rewards cannot address deficiencies in an individual's job-related knowledge, skills, or abilities. Monetary rewards might motivate an untrained or unknowledgeable individual to work harder, but the rewards will not result in better performance unless they are accompanied by job training and development. Incentive systems cannot substitute for useful feedback, support, clear goals, and leadership.

P4P Programs Often Get in the Way of Professional Relationships

P4P programs tend to reward individual behavior, which can damage relationships by increasing competition and conflict and by decreasing teamwork. Incentive systems can reduce cooperation by pitting individuals against each other to compete for rewards. Information sharing and help are less likely to occur if people know that doing so may affect their bonuses or raises. P4P programs can even encourage some workers to sabotage the efforts of their own team members.

These conflicts are accentuated when people perceive P4P systems to be unfair. In pharmacy settings, conflict can occur when new pharmacists start at salaries that are close to or even greater than those of experienced pharmacists with long tenure. In a similar manner, the large pay differences between pharmacists and technicians can foment conflict, especially when pharmacists are insensitive to the differences or they appear to put less effort into their work than the technicians. Incentive systems can also be seen as manipulative and stir resentment between employees and management.

P4P Programs Motivate People Only to Receive Rewards

The quest for rewards encourages people to work toward only getting the rewards, not necessarily toward performing well. People are able to cut corners, push off work onto others, and employ other selfish strategies and be highly rewarded for doing so. Reward systems tend to emphasize individual effort over teamwork. P4P programs also discourage people from taking any risks that might hurt their chance to receive a reward. For example, if you know that identifying a problem at work might make your boss angry and hurt your potential for a raise, you are more likely to avoid mentioning it.

Pharmacists who practice at high professional levels often do so in spite of the reward systems, not because of them. Instead, they perform their jobs well for personal, internally motivated reasons. Box 9.1 indicates the difficulty in managing reward systems.

▦ ▦ JOB DESIGN

Although compensation and rewards are important for motivating pharmacists, such incentives are not enough to sustain and engage them throughout their careers. They also want interesting and challenging work where they can

BOX 9.1 Leadership in Action: Distribution of Pay Raises

Thomas Wesley, PharmD, has been the Director of Pharmacy Service for the past 2 years at Buckeye Pharmacies, a small community pharmacy chain in Ohio. Thomas has managerial responsibility of 40 full-time and part-time pharmacists, technicians, and clerks employed at the chain.

On Monday, Thomas received a memo from the chain's owners that there would be a 2 percent increase in the pharmacy's current payroll budget. This increase was over and above the 3 percent cost-of-living raise that all employees received at the beginning of the fiscal year. The extra money was the result of tight budgetary control policies adopted by the chain. Thomas believed that much of the savings occurred because of the diligence and efforts of the pharmacy's employees. The memo directed Thomas to identify how the extra money would be dispersed across pharmacy personnel and to provide a clear justification for the decision.

The next day was the pharmacy's regularly scheduled monthly staff meeting. Thomas thought that this meeting would allow him an opportunity to announce the raises as well as his decision regarding how the money would be dispersed across all pharmacy personnel. He had several options to consider:

* Option 1. Give everyone the same percentage raise.
* Option 2. Give everyone the same dollar increase in salary. This approach would give technicians an average increase of 3.5 percent, and clerks and pharmacists would receive an average increase of 1 percent.
* Option 3. Give the raise to only the technicians and the clerks. The reason behind this option is that a recent salary survey found a significant disparity between the salaries of technicians and clerks at Buckeye Pharmacies and the salaries of employees at competing pharmacies. In contrast, the survey found pharmacists' salaries at Buckeye to be competitive with those at other pharmacies.
* Option 4. Distribute the raise according to each employee's annual evaluation: significantly above-standard employees will receive a 3 percent increase, above-standard employees will receive 2 percent, and standard employees will receive 1 percent.
* Option 5. Distribute the reward to only the most outstanding employees (i.e., significantly above standard). The reason behind this option is that a recent study found that top performers contribute much more to the success of firms than do average or slightly above-average employees. This option would give top employees at least a 7 percent raise.

Questions

1. What problem is Thomas facing?

2. Who are all of the parties involved? What are their interests?

3. Discuss the potential risks to Thomas's relationships with various employee groups depending on his decision. How might this decision positively or negatively affect the trust between Thomas and others?

4. Identify what Thomas's primary objective should be in the distribution of pay raises.

5. Discuss the positive and negative aspects of each option based on what you know.

6. Recommend a course of action for Thomas to follow that provides a clear justification to the chain's owners. Describe how the course of action will be communicated to the department's staff (e.g., e-mail). Identify the group most likely to be dissatisfied with your course of action and why.

make a difference in the lives of their patients and others. Their coworkers want the same thing.

Nevertheless, certain jobs and tasks in the pharmacy profession can be seen as boring and monotonous. They consist of repetitive, mindless routines that vary little throughout the day. Even the most interesting jobs include tasks that can be viewed as dreary. Job enrichment is a strategy used to address the dull routine of many work settings.

Managerial Strategy

Job design is a managerial strategy used to enrich employees' jobs. Job design tries to alter jobs to increase intrinsic motivation in workers and to provide greater personal achievement and growth. It has been associated with job satisfaction in pharmacy settings.

Job design counters those management strategies that attempt to dehumanize jobs through their treatment of workers as parts of a machine. In the early twentieth century, management theory revolved around the work of efficiency expert Frederick Taylor.[5] Taylor argued that performance in work settings can be maximized with a top-down approach in which managers design tasks. The only responsibility of employees is to complete the tasks exactly as designed. This management philosophy is used in the management of fast-food workers and unskilled employees on an assembly line.

Taylor envisioned workers acting as cogs in a smoothly running machine. In this machine, work is standardized, tasks are simplified as much as possible, and responsibilities are clearly defined. Workers are allowed little input into decisions about their jobs, and they never see the effect of their work on the end product. The problem with this approach is that it makes the work setting boring and dissatisfying. Completing repetitious, meaningless tasks can choke the meaning out of work, and it ignores the humanity of workers. Bored and unengaged workers tend to do shoddy work, quit their jobs more often, and require significant time and effort by management.

Job Enrichment

The most important element of job design is job enrichment. *Job enrichment* is the designing of work to make it more meaningful to people (Table 9.1). Job enrichment involves changing the variety of skills employed, the task identity, the task significance, autonomy, and feedback in work.[6] These five elements help workers find meaning in their work and help workers attain mastery of

TABLE 9.1 Elements of Job Enrichment

Element	Description
Task variety	Do different things each day to keep the job fresh and engaging.
Task identity	Follow a job from beginning to end to see the result of one's effort.
Task significance	Do jobs that are meaningful.
Autonomy	Do jobs without the need to be told.
Feedback	Have a feedback loop that allows learning and improvement to occur.

their job, while intensifying perceptions that the work itself is worthwhile and important. Each of the five elements of job enrichment are described below.

Task Variety

Tasks are more interesting when people use a variety of their skills to complete them. In a community pharmacy, variety can be increased by having individuals rotate responsibilities in the daily workflow. Rather than staying on the same task every day, workers are given tasks that change periodically to keep them fresh and engaged.

Increasing task variety requires balancing specialization (where individuals focus on becoming excellent in a defined area) with generalization (where individuals perform many tasks in a good but not necessarily exceptional way). On the one hand, specialization allows workers to employ a relatively limited skill set and knowledge base that they can do well (e.g., when an intravenous room technician in a hospital becomes really skillful at preparing sterile products for patients). On the other hand, job enrichment discourages too much specialization because it can lead to boredom and reduced engagement. Even the most interesting and challenging tasks can become tedious once they are mastered.

The downside of increasing task variety is that individuals may be assigned tasks and responsibilities at which they do not excel. This situation can slow down work and increase the stress on workers. Nevertheless, the loss of performance associated with task variety can be more than offset by the increase in engagement and attention to tasks.

Task Identity

Task identity describes the extent to which jobs allow individuals to follow their work from start to finish. When individuals can see the fruition of their labor, the job is perceived to be more meaningful. This view contrasts with that of assembly line workers. In assembly lines, workers tend to be restricted to tasks within a limited area of focus and never see the end result of their contributions. For example, an auto worker on an assembly line who is responsible for tasks associated with only the door panel or windshield will never see how his or her work contributed to the automobile rolling off the end of the assembly line.

Lack of task identity can occur in pharmacy practice when tasks in the medication-use process are separated into silos. For example, a physician sees a patient in her office and prescribes a drug. The pharmacist receives the prescription with little information about why the physician chose that drug for the patient. The pharmacist then fills the prescription but allows the technician to give the medication to the patient (after encouraging the patient to agree that counseling is not needed). The patient then goes home and is never seen again, because the patient's insurer convinces the patient to receive future medications through mail-order outlets. In this process, pharmacists may see themselves as little more than assembly line workers completing just a small piece of the entire medication-use process.

Many recent innovations, such as team-based patient care, can increase the task identity of a pharmacist's work. By working in teams, all professionals, including pharmacists, can participate in decisions throughout the patient-care process. By teaming up with other professionals, pharmacists can influence drug choice, monitor the effect of their efforts on patient outcomes, and have a more comprehensive understanding of their role in the health care profession. These changes in practice can help enrich the pharmacist's job as well as improve patient health outcomes.

Task Significance

Task significance describes an individual's perception that his or her work has a substantial and detectable effect on the world in which he or she lives. It is based on the powerful drive in humans to lead meaningful lives and to contribute to the world. Task significance is similar to task identity, which deals with the ability to associate individual tasks to the meaningful outcomes of a job, but task significance addresses the meaningful outcomes of the overall job.

Pharmacists put too much time, effort, and money into their education and training to land in jobs without meaning. Most pharmacists get into the profession, at least in part, to make a difference in the lives of patients and their community. In addition, work takes up a significant part of one's waking hours, and the belief that time spent at work should achieve some greater purpose makes sense.

Increasing task significance does not necessarily require changing the job itself. Often, it merely requires a reframing of one's perceptions. Pharmacists who see their jobs as simply a paycheck will find their work days to be monotonous and dispiriting. However, pharmacists who believe they are responsible for their patients' health needs are likely to find their work days to be energizing.

The importance of having a good attitude and a feeling of purpose is illustrated by the famous story about President John F. Kennedy and a janitor. On a visit to the National Aeronautics and Space Administration center in 1962, President Kennedy interrupted his tour to speak with a janitor carrying a broom. After introducing himself, President Kennedy asked what the janitor was doing. The janitor responded, "I'm helping put a man on the moon." Rather than seeing his job as mopping floors and taking out the trash, he linked his work to a higher purpose.

Task significance can be increased by helping pharmacy workers appreciate their contributions to the process. Pharmacy technicians can reframe their jobs from "filling prescriptions" to "saving lives." Instead of "running the pharmacy," pharmacists are "building the best pharmacy in town."

The antithesis of task significance is the belittling of the contributions of others. Pharmacy technicians, clerks, janitors, and others may not have the title and prestige of a pharmacist, but their contributions to the team are just as important as those of the pharmacist. A simple show of appreciation for their efforts can do much to improve others' perception of the significance of their jobs.

Autonomy

Job autonomy occurs when workers have more control over their jobs. It is associated with perceptions of self-control, lower job stress, and less burnout. Perceived autonomous characteristics include self-determination, free will, freedom of choice, and self-direction. Autonomous pharmacists exert control over their practice settings by setting their own goals, making decisions regarding the pharmacy and the patients being served, and advocating for the good of the patient. Autonomy is necessary to achieve Maslow's self-actualization.

Pharmacists who perceive themselves as owners of their practice setting are more likely to feel autonomy. This perception contrasts with that of pharmacists who practice with the employee mindset, "Hey. I just work here." Employees with an employee mindset tend to be more disengaged and unwilling to take responsibility for the success or failure of the pharmacy.

Pharmacists with an ownership mindset are more likely to feel in control because they are willing to do anything necessary to satisfy patients and help with patients' needs. This mindset might be one of the reasons that independent owner-operated pharmacies are consistently rated higher in consumer surveys than corporate-owned pharmacies, which have employee pharmacists. However, one cannot generally state that employee pharmacists cannot or will not take ownership of their practices. Rather, the proportion of pharmacists with an employee mindset are more likely to work in corporate settings.

Perceptions of job autonomy can be encouraged with the right employees and leaders. Hiring employees with the willingness to accept responsibility for the business is an essential first step. Once these employees are engaged, leaders need to coach and train the employees to accept greater responsibility for the pharmacy itself. Of course, this approach requires leaders who are willing to share responsibilities. Individual pharmacists should search for employers who encourage them to act with greater independence, and then they should make the best of that autonomy once they are hired.

Feedback

Workers who receive feedback on their job performance can better understand how they can achieve their goals. This feedback is part of a *feedback loop* that helps them assess their performance, learn what works best, and improve their skillset.

Ideally, feedback is most beneficial—more intrinsically motivating—when it is a derived from the work completed rather than from opinions of someone such as a manager. This is seen in the classroom where students who develop their own feedback loops for course work are more likely to master the learning material than those whose sole source of feedback is a grade.

Self-motivated, autonomous pharmacists set their own goals and deadlines in serving patients (e.g., "I will complete 10 medication profile reviews in the next hour"). If they are really competent at their job, they may need little input from their boss.

Management can facilitate feedback loops by aggregating performance data and sharing them with workers. Employers increasingly provide *performance dashboards*, which are data visualization tools that provide feedback at a glance of job progress. Dashboards help pharmacists compare their work with that of other pharmacists in the organization or other organizations. When provided formatively as a way of improving performance, dashboards can engage individuals to improve how they perform their jobs. This approach contrasts with feedback that is provided in a judgmental and punitive way (e.g., "You need to do better or you are out of here"). This response to employee efforts is often counterproductive, causing stress, conflict, and distraction.

Feedback and all of the other variables associated with job enrichment help pharmacists and workers be more engaged in their work. Every job has activities that are tedious, repetitive, and seemingly unimportant. Understanding the elements of enriched work settings can help leaders make these tasks more bearable—even enjoyable. However, individuals do not need leaders to enrich their work for them. They can enrich their jobs by applying basic principles of self-motivation. These principles are discussed in the following section.

⬤ ⬤ SELF-MOTIVATION

The idea of self-motivation is based on the principle that humans have a choice in this world. They can choose to motivate themselves or they can wait on others to motivate them. Figure 9.1 illustrates potential consequences of each path. The *motivate yourself path* typically results in either you reaching a mutually agreeable accommodation with your employer or you going elsewhere. The *let others motivate you path* results in either career dissatisfaction or satisfaction through good luck.

Either path can lead to good or bad results for pharmacists. The motivate yourself path requires pharmacists to take control of their own lives and choices. This proactive path requires more effort and planning and may still result in failure. The easier path in the short run might be to act reactively, waiting for someone else to motivate through rewards or an enriched work environment. In recent years, many pharmacists have been quite lucky and successful taking this path—receiving generous salaries and good working conditions. At the same time, many others have questioned whether they made the right choice in their career.

Self-help guru Wayne Dyer once said, "Be miserable. Or motivate yourself. Whatever has to be done, it's always your choice."[7]

Pharmacists who wait for others to solve issues are often destined for misery. No one cares about your interests as much as you, and self-motivation is the only motivational strategy that lies completely within the control of each individual pharmacist. Of course, self-motivation requires pharmacists to take ownership of their job and their responses to it. However, this perception of empowerment over their lives can help reduce stress and increase engagement in work environments. Rather than waiting and hoping for their employers to

FIGURE 9.1 Motivating Yourself or Letting Others Motivate You

satisfy their desires, pharmacists must develop ways of doing so for themselves. The steps are relatively simple in concept, but they take a lifetime to master.

Know What You Want

If you truly want something, you will do whatever is necessary to achieve it. If you know your purpose in life, this knowledge will inspire and sustain you over long and difficult periods. Without a purpose, you can quickly lose enthusiasm.

Knowing your purpose is difficult because most people have only a vague idea of what they want in life. They may know they want a well-paying job, time for friends and family, a house and a car, and so on, but the details are fuzzy.

This fuzziness can cause pharmacists to take actions that lead them away from the life they want. Pharmacists often pursue a higher-paying, less challenging job after graduation rather than one that pays less but helps them grow professionally. Blinded by the high salaries, they purchase expensive, high-status products and live paycheck to paycheck; this lifestyle prevents them from exploring other career options that might contribute more to their happiness. They tell themselves that they will be happy if they can just buy the newest electronics or car, get that new title, or attain another degree, but when they achieve those goals, happiness is still illusive. The reason for this unhappiness is that these individuals have not expended the time and effort to understand what is really important to them.

Self-reflection is essential for understanding what you really want out of your career and life. Numerous books, Web sites, self-administered tests, and professionals can help you work through this process. Most self-reflection processes start by helping you identify your passion(s) in life and work.

If you know your passion, you can make it a larger part of your daily work and life. Identifying your passion often comes from asking yourself the following series of questions:

- What would you do if you won the lottery today and never had to work again for a living? How would you spend the remaining days of your life? Removing the constraint of working for a living helps you understand what is intrinsically valuable to you.

- What do you like to do in your spare time? These are the activities that bring you pleasure and should be an integral part of your life.

- What did you like to do when you were a child? Did you like to explore? Draw pictures? Play with friends? The activities you loved at 10 years of age are probably those you still love.

- What is something in which you believe very strongly? Or, if you were given one wish that you could use to change one aspect about the world, what would it be? If you really care about this aspect, you will want to do something about it.

● Find Your Career Path

A career describes the professional journey through the work phase of one's life. It is more than a series of jobs held, titles earned, and tasks completed over time. Instead, it is a search for meaning and purpose in one's work and profession.

Like any journey, a career starts with a first step. In pharmacy, it starts with the first job after graduation or the steps (e.g., school, work experiences) leading to the first job after graduation. That first job will probably not be your last job. For one reason or another, it will eventually lead to your next job. Therefore, enjoy your first position after graduation, learn and accomplish as much as you can, and use your first position to prepare yourself for your next job. Likewise, enjoy your second position, make a difference, and use it to prepare yourself for the next job.

The mindset of always viewing your current job as preparation for your next job simply reflects the reality that few people stay in one job all of their lives. Also, if a current position does not continue to develop your capabilities and skills, your career will likely stagnate and your options for future positions will dry up. Pharmacists who fail to develop their career skills typically find themselves in unsatisfying, dead-end jobs that lack meaning or purpose.

First jobs are typically entry-level positions. As time passes, entry-level positions become routine and less challenging. Even the rare individual who finds his or her dream job directly out of pharmacy school often outgrows the job and needs new challenges. Therefore, people should gain as much as they can from their first job so that it can prepare them for their next, even better job.

A good job is engaging. Table 9.2 lists elements of engaging jobs. An engaging job is consistent with a worker's goals and values (i.e., mission). When mission and work align, a job becomes more meaningful. A good job also encourages personal growth, allowing people to build on their strengths and improve on their weaknesses. Finally, engagement occurs when jobs allow workers self-determination. Self-determination allows people to control stress and manage their work life.

TABLE 9.2 Elements of Engaging Jobs

Element	Why the element leads to self-motivation
Is consistent with your personal mission	Commitment to an employer and a career path is greater when they both align to your personal values and professional goals.
Builds on and uses your strengths	Work on tasks that use your strengths. You will do good work, and careers are built on jobs at which you excel.
Helps improve on your weaknesses	Weaknesses can damage careers if they are in fundamental parts of your work. Develop weaknesses to at least a minimum level of acceptability.
Allows self-determination	Work that encourages personal growth with conditions promoting autonomy, competence, and relatedness will be self-motivating. Careers that allow the aspects of self-determination will allow professionals to do their best.

■ ■ INTEGRATING AND APPLYING THEORIES TO LEAD OTHERS

No single motivation theory or strategy answers every question about motivating people. People and situations are more complex than any single theory can explain or predict. Still, there are basic rules to follow that might help in motivating oneself and others. Just remember that for every recommendation, there are exceptions when the advice may not work. With experience, pharmacists will learn when to use motivational rules of thumb and when not to use them.

■ *Stop Trying to Motivate People*

When people try to motivate others, they take responsibility from the people who really should be held accountable—the individuals charged with completing the tasks. When leaders and managers motivate, the individuals being motivated stop taking ownership of the work and become passive participants in the process. With the onus on the leader, motivation becomes something that is inflicted on followers, rather than something that they own. Consequently, workers can blame their poor performance on leaders by using the excuse that the leaders were not motivating them enough.

Manipulative motivational strategies demean people because they imply that people are too irresponsible to do good work without carefully crafted motivational interventions. Low expectations of professional responsibility are communicated to workers, and perceptions about the work are devalued, "It must be unpleasant if I have to be made to do it." Workers who take pride in their performance often feel disrespected by efforts to manipulate them. They respond by becoming more transactional in their approach to work, "I will do this if I get that."

Instead of motivating, leaders need to have an honest conversation with followers regarding their mutual expectations of performance. Responsibilities for performing need to be explicitly stated together with the consequences for good and bad work. Leaders should ensure the responsibility for performing rests with the individual worker. The leader's responsibility is to become an adviser and coach, help remove the barriers that impede performance, and provide the tools and feedback that followers need to succeed.

Motivation evolves from something that is imposed on others to the development of an environment and culture that encourages, engages, and builds desired behaviors. Motivation is less about judgment of others and more about mutual problem solving to increase performance. When approached this way, motivational conversations then revolve around questions such as, "What is getting in the way of doing your job better?" instead of "What are you doing wrong?"

Avoid Demotivating People

Leaders should "Do No Harm"; they should not say or do anything that demotivates people. Unfortunately, demotivating ideas and actions often occur in work settings. For instance, organizational politics are a significant demotivator because they use unwritten, subjective rules to guide behaviors. Organizational politics force people to play political games to compete for power and influence, which is demoralizing because the rules constantly change and people rarely know where they stand in an organization. Instead of focusing on a shared vision, people focus on giving attention to the most popular or powerful person in the organization.

Numerous demotivators exist in the workplace—scheduling too many meetings, micromanaging the tasks of others, chasing the newest managerial fads, and accepting poor performers on teams. Leaders should identify the demotivating practices in a work setting and change them.

Provide Adequate Compensation

Workers' perceptions about inadequate compensation can be real or imagined. Whether valid or not, a person's belief that he or she is undercompensated can hurt performance by causing dissatisfaction and feelings of being slighted. A preoccupation with compensation distracts everyone—employers and employees—from the issues that really matter.

This preoccupation can be avoided by identifying whether those perceptions are real or not by completing compensation comparisons for similar jobs. The human resource department of a business usually conducts salary surveys of local competitors to ensure that employee salaries are competitive. If compensation is truly lower than other comparable salaries, it should be raised to a more equitable level or a valid reason for the lower pay should be provided (e.g., other benefits of the job make up for the lower salary).

In many cases, however, pay is competitive but workers do not perceive it as such. In these situations, a conversation must occur to discuss misperceptions and disagreements. The discussion should be conducted with delicacy because of the emotional nature of compensation disagreements. When these discussions are handled well, both parties can come to a mutual understanding and agreement regarding compensation rules and their application.

◼ Try to Be Fair

Trying to be fair is the best that anyone can hope for because perceptions of fairness are so subjective and biased. Pleasing everyone with regard to fairness is rarely possible. Therefore, attempts should focus on practices associated with being fair.

One practice is to consistently communicate performance expectations to people through speech, writings (e.g., policies and procedures), and actions and then to follow these rules as consistently as possible. When people perceive unfairness, gain an understanding of the source of those perceptions and address them openly and honestly. Correct any real inequity when possible, and when it cannot be corrected quickly, explain why. Then try to resolve the issue over time, keeping relevant parties updated with any progress.

Most people are forgiving about acts of unfairness if they feel that the overall system governing behavior is fair. Therefore, to be fair, ensure that procedures are clear, impartial, and consistently applied.

◼ Never Make Threats

People in positions of formal authority have an advantage over the people they manage. This inequity increases the perceived danger of any interaction with authority because there is always an unspoken threat, "If I am dissatisfied with your behavior, I have the ability to do something you will not like." Therefore, leaders should avoid explicit or implicit threats, even in jest, when interacting with the people they manage. If people feel threatened, their energy will move from being productive to protecting themselves. Although a leader might joke about firing people, the joke is lost on the people who could be fired. Do not do it.

◼ Facilitate Positive Feedback Loops

When people do a good job, recognize their accomplishment in a genuine manner. This genuine recognition will encourage them to repeat their good performance. In addition, allow people to develop their own feedback loops by sharing performance data. When performance data are provided to individuals, they can use the data as a benchmark against the work of others, which can in turn increase motivation and performance.

◾ Communicate a Higher Purpose

Leaders should inspire people toward a noble, shared purpose. Humans have a basic desire to make a difference; leaders can help people understand the higher purpose of an organization, task, or initiative. Engaging in a higher purpose can make even mundane, everyday tasks bearable.

Simon Sinek uses a golden circle to describe the importance of explaining purpose.[8] He states that many leaders see their job as managing processes and outcomes. They spend most of their efforts regulating behavior and assessing performance. They emphasize WHAT people should do and HOW they should do it. However, Sinek says that few leaders or companies clearly articulate WHY people should do what they do.

Great leaders start by communicating the WHY—the purpose. WHY does your business exist? WHY do you get out of bed every morning? WHY should you care?

When leaders verbalize the WHY, they give people a clear sense of an organization's purpose and priorities. When people know an organization's mission and priorities, greater engagement, creativity, and customer service can occur.[9] By starting with the WHY, team members are entrusted with the responsibility to think and act independently in the best interests of the organization and its mission. This approach also allows team members to take ownership of their own contributions to the organization and to build their professional portfolio of accomplishments.

◼◼ CONCLUSION

Pharmacy employees have the capability to be high performers. For the pharmacy profession, the costs of reduced performance are missed opportunities to help patients. Humans are complex, and no single solution exists to solve issues with motivation. Nevertheless, understanding the best practices described in this chapter can help pharmacists better manage themselves and their coworkers.

◼◼ KEY TERMS AND CONCEPTS

- Pay-for-performance (P4P) plan

- Job design

- Job enrichment

- Task variety
- Task identity
- Task significance
- Autonomy
- Feedback loops
- Performance dashboards
- Self-motivation

DISCUSSION AND REVIEW QUESTIONS

1. Should employers share pay information with employees? What are the positive and negative aspects for doing so?

2. What performance metrics should determine the pay of a typical staff pharmacist working in a community pharmacy chain? What is the best way to reward pharmacists for their work?

3. Rank the five elements of job enrichment according to your personal preferences in a job. Which element is most important to you, and which element is least important to you? How much salary would you require to work in a job that lacked significance, variety, task identification, autonomy, and feedback?

4. What feedback loops do you use in your life to achieve personal and professional goals?

5. Can inspirational speeches or posters motivate people? Why or why not? What type of motivation does this involve?

REFERENCES

1. Eijkenaar F, Emmert M, Scheppach M, et al. Effects of pay for performance in health care: a systematic review of systematic reviews. *Health Policy*. 2013;110(2–3):115–130. doi:10.1016/j.healthpol.2013.01.008.

2. Magrath P, Nichter M. Paying for performance and the social relations of health care provision: an anthropological perspective. *Soc Sci Med*. 2012;75(10):1778–1785. doi:10.1016/j.socscimed.2012.07.025.

3. Aguinis H, Joo H, Gottfredson RK. What monetary rewards can and cannot do: how to show employees the money. *Bus Horiz*. 2013;56(2):241–249. doi:10.1016/j.bushor.2012.11.007.

4. Kohn A. Why incentive plans cannot work. *Harv Bus Rev*. 1993;71(5):54–63.

5. Locke EA. The ideas of Frederick W. Taylor: an evaluation. *Acad Manag Rev*. 1982;7(1):14–24. doi:10.5465/AMR.1982.4285427.

6. Herzberg F. One more time: how do you motivate employees? *Harv Bus Rev*. 2003;81:87–96. doi:10.1108/eb055227.

7. Wayne Dyer Quotes. BrainyQuote.com. 2018. https://www.brainyquote.com/quotes/wayne_dyer_165697.

8. Sinek S. *Start with Why: How Great Leaders Inspire Everyone to Take Action*. New York, NY: Penguin Group; 2009.

9. Gulati R. Structure that's not stifling. *Harv Bus Rev*. 2018;96(3):69–79.

SECTION III

MANAGING RELATIONSHIPS

CHAPTER 10

Professional Relationships
Developing and Maintaining Them

■ ■ OBJECTIVES

- Identify the causes and benefits of good professional relationships.
- Suggest actions that managers and pharmacists can take to develop and maintain strong professional relationships.
- Discuss how to foster strong professional relationships.

There's a difference between interest and commitment. When you're interested in doing something, you do it only when it's convenient. When you're committed to something, you accept no excuses—only results.

—Kenneth Blanchard, Leadership expert

●● INTRODUCTION

On any given day, pharmacists engage in multiple interpersonal contacts with other employees, customers, and physicians. A pharmacist's success depends in great part on his or her ability to manage these relationships.

A recent study[1] found that three of four new pharmacy practitioners said that managing staff relationships was a major part of their job. However, less than half of them felt competent at doing so.

Relationships are fundamental to pharmacy practice. Effective professional relationships are vital in leading others, teaching and coaching performance, negotiating win-win solutions, and resolving conflict in pharmacy organizations. Good professional relationships help improve communications, make work more enjoyable, and increase opportunities for success.

Fortunately, scholarly research conducted by psychologists, sociologists, and other social scientists is available to help identify predictable patterns that can help guide pharmacists in managing their professional relationships.[2-4] Most findings are consistent with the same basic advice offered by most parents to their children—choose your relationships carefully, be polite, keep your promises, work hard, do a good job, and treat people with respect.

Yet pharmacists and other health care managers continually fail to establish and maintain effective professional relationships. The following sections provide suggestions on how to address this recurring and avoidable problem.

●● TYPES OF PROFESSIONAL RELATIONSHIPS

Professional relationships often fail because partners want different things from each other. Relationships vary depending on the benefits desired, the levels of power between partners, and the amount of reciprocity expected of partners (Table 10.1).

Partners need to understand the type of relationships they have in order to manage expectations and satisfaction. Mismatched expectations, such as one partner wanting a friendship and the other wanting a fling, will ensure a rocky relationship full of conflict and emotions.

Many pharmacists have a sharp intuitive sense of how to develop and maintain good relationships with coworkers and other professionals. Other pharmacists need guidance on how to strengthen their relationships because they have no framework with which to assess relationships. Often, this is because people put

TABLE 10.1 Common Types of Professional Relationships

Type	Description
Transactional	This relationship is based completely on benefits received from the relationship. The bonds between partners are purely transactional and are broken as soon as one of the partners perceives a better offer is available from someone else. Partners have equal power, and emotional attachments are minimal.
Authoritarian and submissive	Like a transactional relationship, it is based completely on benefits received. However, one partner has power over the other, and the relationship lasts as long as the weak partner is willing to submit. An example is the command-and-control relationship that bosses have with subordinates.
Friendship	In this relationship, partners like each other and enjoy each other's company. The relationship is founded on shared values and interests. Partners have equal power, and emotional attachments are significant.
Collaborative partnership	Partners in this relationship work together to achieve a desired long-term outcome. The partnership is based on the partners' reliability and ability to contribute to a successful outcome. Partners typically have equal power, and emotional attachments may develop over time if the collaboration is a success.
Fling	In this type of partnership, the bonds between parties are fleeting. Sometimes flings are an experimentation with partners that does not last (e.g., a short-term gig with an employer). Other times, they are meant to be brief. Flings are types of transactional relationships that typically start with great enthusiasm and end when the excitement and passions of one or more of the partners diminishes.

little thought into developing relationships; they just let relationships emerge because of personal chemistry or closeness. As a result, people are careless in managing relationships, and they commit errors that hurt their connections with other professionals. Sometimes, the errors result in missed opportunities to network. Other times, a blunder can turn a potential ally into an adversary.

■ ■ IMPORTANCE OF COMMITMENT

Commitment between partners is essential for strong professional relationships.[2] Commitment is an enduring desire to maintain a valued relationship. It is very similar to engagement in that both concepts describe an enduring desire to maintain a relationship with a person or thing.

Commitment between individuals and groups must be a shared desire because relationships need reciprocity and mutual benefit to be strong. Research indicates that commitment to an employer is strongly affected by perceptions of the employer's commitment to the employee.[5]

■ Components of Commitment

Commitment has affective, normative, and continuance components.[6] *Affective commitment* to a relationship is manifested through emotional attachment to and identification with partners. It is a process based on feelings about partners and involvement with them. *Normative commitment* describes a perceived obligation to remain with partners. The more positive the feelings about and obligations to the relationship, the stronger the commitment. *Continuance* or *behavioral commitment* reflects the economic and noneconomic benefits of the relationship in comparison to alternative relationships. It is a cognitive process that weighs what is given versus what is received. The more people perceive a benefit from a relationship, the stronger their likelihood to remain in it.

Affective, normative, and behavioral commitment all contribute to lasting relationships. When loyalty is based solely on the benefits received, relationships last only until something better comes along. For example, a pharmacist with little emotional or normative attachment to an employer or coworkers can easily be persuaded to quit for a better opportunity. However, with strong affective and normative bonds, a relationship is more difficult to break.

Commitment varies in strength along a continuum consisting of several levels (Table 10.2). Commitment can vary from none at all (i.e., noncompliance) to complete commitment (i.e., ownership).

● Benefits of Commitment

Commitment is important because committed partners are less likely to leave a relationship—either physically or mentally.[2] They are less likely to terminate the

TABLE 10.2 Degrees of Relationship Commitment

Degree of commitment	Description
Ownership	Ownership is complete commitment to a relationship where individuals will exert whatever effort is necessary to make it work no matter what obstacles exist. It describes a commitment so strong that partners feel a sense of ownership toward the relationship.
Partial commitment	Partial commitment is a relationship where a person sees the benefits of the relationship and is willing to do what is expected and more to maintain it. However, limits exist to the amount of time and effort a person will expend with partial commitment.
Full compliance	Full compliance is a relationship where a person sees the benefits of the relationship and will do what is expected to maintain it, but no more. The individual will maintain the relationship only when doing so is convenient or beneficial. Bonds between individuals melt away if too much effort is needed to maintain them.
Grudging compliance	A person in this relationship does not see the benefits of the relationship, but still exerts the smallest effort necessary to maintain it. Apathy and disinterest typically accompany grudging compliance. Motivation to maintain bonds is often tied to habit, inertia, or fear of missing out. People in this relationship are the type to exert the least effort necessary to avoid trouble, and then goof off when no one is looking.
Noncompliance	A person in this relationship sees no value to the relationship and makes no effort to maintain it under any conditions. Indeed, noncompliant partners often consciously or subconsciously seek to damage the relationship.

relationship completely (e.g., "I'm leaving and never coming back") or partially (e.g., "We will still see each other, just not as often"). Committed partners are also more likely to be mentally and emotionally invested in a relationship.

Committed partners value the relationship and are motivated to work to maintain and strengthen it. This commitment means complying with what is asked of you by your partner and cooperating with each other to work together toward a common goal. The stronger the commitment, the greater the level of enthusiasm and participation in the relationship.

▥ ▥ HOW IS COMMITMENT DEVELOPED?

▥ *Commitment as a Characteristic and a Choice*

Commitment is both a personal characteristic and a choice. It is a characteristic because some people more freely commit themselves to people and causes, while others are reticent to get involved. This characteristic may be instinctual or it may be learned from past experience. Commitment is a choice; people make a conscious or unconscious decision to commit to a relationship. Partners choose to engage or not to engage in relationship-building activities on the basis of their commitment.

▥ *Situational Commitment*

Commitment is also situational because people are more committed to things they care about. For example, parents with school-aged children may become involved in the Parent and Teachers Association at their children's school; but they will often end their involvement once their children graduate. The same is true for any relationship with a person, group, or thing. Once the circumstances of the relationship change, the commitment often does too.

Situational characteristics of professional relationships fall into four main categories: perceived benefits, termination costs, shared goals and values, and level of trust.[2,7]

Perceived Benefits of the Relationship

People enter into relationships because they receive tangible and intangible benefits for doing so. Friendships are made to have someone with whom to talk, to do activities and to share things. People take jobs to earn money, help others, make friends, and find mental stimulation. The strengthening effect of benefits depends on the perceived value of the benefits in the eyes of the relationship partners and the way those benefits compare to available alternatives. People choose specific friends and jobs for the benefits that they provide.

Perceived Relationship Termination Costs

Many people stay in unfulfilling and dissatisfying relationships (e.g., jobs, marriages), not because of the benefits, but because of the fear of what may be lost if that relationship is terminated. For example, pharmacists may pass up desirable job opportunities because they do not want to give up benefits such as accumulated vacation, saved sick days, or the comfort of knowing what to expect in a job. Note that these termination costs (e.g., financial, emotional, temporal) may be real or imagined. However, real or imagined makes little difference. The greater the cost of ending a relationship, the more likely inertia or fear will keep a person in it.

Shared Goals and Values Between Partners

When partners share goals and value systems, they are likely to be committed to a relationship. Shared goals and values help partners better predict and understand each other's motives. When individuals have similar motivations and perceptions of the world, they are less likely to attribute negative causes to the actions of their partner. For instance, when a boss and an employee share a strong work ethic, the employee is less likely to attribute a negative motive to the boss's assignment of extra work.

Mutual Trust Between Partners

Trust, more than any other condition associated with strong relationships, is necessary for the highest levels of commitment between partners (i.e., ownership, partial commitment). *Trust* is defined as confidence in a relationship partner's reliability and integrity.[2, 8] It refers to questions such as, "Does my partner act in a consistent, reliable manner?" "Can my partner be relied on to keep promises?" "Will my partner let me down given a chance?" and "Does my partner care about me as a person?"

■ ■ IMPORTANCE OF TRUST IN RELATIONSHIPS

Commitment is difficult if a partner cannot be expected to act in a consistent, predictable manner and with integrity and honor. Employers who act arbitrarily in how they communicate with and treat employees will receive less commitment from employees. Similarly, employees who are unreliable or fail to meet ethical standards have difficulty earning and keeping the trust of their employers. The same holds true for relationships between pharmacists, coworkers, patients, and other people. Trust is necessary for strong and lasting relationships.

Trust is essential for engaging in productive conflicts.[9] *Productive conflicts* are disagreements that attempt to improve relationships through communication and cooperation. In any professional relationship, conflicts can occur, but conflicts do not need to escalate into bitter feelings or even warfare between partners.

Conflicts can be productive when they lead to open and amicable resolution of disputes. Disagreements create opportunities to clarify misunderstandings between partners and work through problems. For example, a pharmacist may be aggravated by a supervisor who assigns extra tasks. However, if the pharmacist trusts the supervisor, he or she may initiate a discussion that leads to a greater understanding between these two partners and an improvement in the relationship.

Trust improves communications between partners.[10] Partners who trust each other spend less time trying to decide if one of them is being truthful and or has a hidden agenda. Trust also allows for easier clarification of facts that might be obvious to one partner but not to the other partner. A person who says, "There is no such thing as a stupid question," will not be believed without trust.

Leaders in positions of formal power face unique barriers in their ability to develop and maintain trust. The power they wield over subordinates makes the encouragement of openness and honesty especially difficult, as illustrated in Box 10.1.

■ ■ HOW TO EARN AND KEEP STRONG PROFESSIONAL RELATIONSHIPS

The ability to foster relationships is a dimension of being emotionally intelligent. This ability includes the broad set of social skills that are needed to manage relationships and to influence people into a desired direction. These social skills include the following abilities:

- Build bonds

- Persuade and advocate

- Communicate

- Manage conflict

- Collaborate

- Influence

These social skills are what differentiate effective pharmacist leaders from ineffective ones. Effective pharmacists use this mix of social skills to foster professional relationships, to keep a pharmacy running smoothly, and to interact with pharmacy stakeholders. These practices are relevant for fostering all relationships.

Identify and Understand What Partners Seek in a Professional Relationship

Partners need to know and understand what each other seeks from the professional relationship. A pharmacist who expects high levels of maturity and commitment to patient care is likely to be dissatisfied with coworkers who lack the same work ethic. Knowing if partners seek a collaborative relationship, a friendship, or a fling is helpful.

Increase Human Contact with Partners

Relationships benefit from human contact. Relationships are stronger when partners are both physically present and mentally present. Face-to-face interactions

---

BOX 10.1 Leadership in Action: Trusting a Boss Is Difficult

Jill is a good manager who works very hard to be supportive of her pharmacy staff. No matter how much she tries, however, she has difficulty convincing them to confide in her about problems at work. Jill is worried that her subordinates are afraid to share bad news with her.

One coworker, whom she considers a friend, confided to her that, "No one should ever trust their boss, even you. The boss can always do bad things to people they have power over. Anyone who trusts the boss not to react badly to bad news is just being naïve. It is the boss's job to punish people for mistakes and bad work."

This conversation really worried Jill because she knows the importance of convincing workers to share unpleasant news. The sooner a problem is recognized, the sooner it can be fixed. Indeed, silence is likely to mean that serious problems will never be addressed. In a pharmacy, this can lead to potentially fatal mistakes for patients.

Questions
1. Should subordinates ever really trust their boss? Isn't wariness about one's direct supervisor perfectly natural?

2. What can Jill do to increase trust in her subordinates?

3. What is the responsibility of subordinates in this relationship?

provide the opportunity for people to give their full emotional and intellectual attention to the relationship. When partners schedule time to chat with each other, and cell phones and other distractions are put away, they can give each other their full attention.

Give as Much or More than You Receive in Every Interaction

Pharmacists can strengthen the value of relationships by going out of their way to ensure that partners benefit from the relationship. For example, collaborative practice agreements between physicians and pharmacists are strengthened when both parties see how their relationship benefits their businesses and patient care. Pharmacists who provide clear value to physician practices will receive more referrals and gain more willing partners.

Avoid Even the Hint of Untrustworthy Behavior

Perceptions are important, so be attentive to how circumstances appear from your partner's viewpoint. No matter how noble your motivations for doing something, relationships will be determined by how your partner perceives your actions. Managing perceptions to ensure that misunderstandings do not impede valued relationships is important.

Be Consistent in Your Words and Actions

Trusted relationships require consistency. The well-known phrases, "Walk the talk," "Do what you say, and say what you do," and "Actions speak louder than words," all emphasize the importance of matching your words with your actions. Conflicting words and actions define hypocrisy, and hypocritical behavior is an enemy of trust.

Engage in Productive Conflict, But Do So Judiciously

Sometimes, conflicts are the best way to air grievances and solve problems, but other times, they are not productive. The key is to understand when to engage and when not to engage. Pharmacists must be willing to speak up when needed but be judicious in selecting the best time and the best way to do so.

Always Keep Your Promises

Promises are personal pledges to do something. When they are broken, reputations suffer. Broken promises, even small ones, suggest to a partner that the other partner lacks integrity and reliability. The breaker of the promise may disagree, making excuses for his or her actions or arguing that a broken promise is not significant. Yet, broken promises convey the message that partners are not important and that the relationship is not important enough to honor one's word.

◼ *Repair Damaged Professional Relationships*

A worthwhile professional relationship can take years to develop and only a moment to destroy. Rebuilding lost confidence in partners is difficult but not impossible, as described in Box 10.2.

BOX 10.2 How to Repair Damaged Professional Relationships

All pharmacists have workplace conflicts. Misunderstandings and unprofessional behavior can get out of control and damage professional relationships. The good news is that damaged professional relationships can be repaired. The bad news is that repairing those relationships is an uphill battle.

Broken relationships are difficult to repair because perceived behavior resulting in negative feelings has an overwhelming effect on relationships when compared to positive actions. A single negative moment in a professional relationship can destroy all of the goodwill built by years of positive moments. Therefore, the key is to avoid damaging professional relationships in the first place. If a relationship is damaged, however, the following are some best practices for repairing them.

- *Acknowledge it.* Avoiding damaged relationships ensures that they will never be fixed. A key step to fixing the problem is to sit down with your partner and say, "We seem to be having a problem, and I hope that we can resolve it."
- *Come to an agreement on the problem.* If partners agree that a problem exists and are willing to take steps to improve it, then basic conflict negotiation processes can begin. Questions to discuss include preventable causes of the problem, acceptance of mutual roles in its causes, and a focus on future behaviors to repair the situation. For example, partners might discuss how the future will look if the relationship is not fixed. Discussion might examine the conflict's effect on patient care or general working conditions for coworkers.
- *Ask whether the relationship can be saved.* Relationships are difficult to repair when partners hold grudges or are just too hurt to trust again. Some people do not believe in giving second chances. For them, a second chance is just giving someone another opportunity to hurt them again. If the relationship is important, however, there is a chance that differences can be resolved after both sides have an opportunity to have their voice heard.
- *Ask whether it is worth saving.* Some relationships are damaged because they were never meant to exist. Partners may not really offer anything of value to each other, or their values may be incompatible. As Bob Marley reportedly said, "Truth is everybody is going to hurt you: you just gotta find the ones worth suffering for."
- *Ask for a reset.* Agree to acknowledge the past but emphasize the future in the relationship. Partners cannot fix the past. They can change only the future. Agree to what a future relationship should look like, and then focus on achieving it.
- *Make time your ally.* The saying that "time heals all wounds" may not be quite as applicable to the wounds of a broken professional relationship, where the wounds are scars that are often not forgotten. However, with time, relationships can improve if the parties want that to happen.

■■ CONCLUSION

Developing and maintaining professional relationships is a critical responsibility of managers and pharmacists. It is also important for career and job success. This chapter discusses the components of strong professional relationships and the way to foster these relationships.

■■ KEY TERMS AND CONCEPTS

- Commitment
- Affective commitment
- Normative commitment
- Continuance commitment
- Compliance
- Trust
- Productive conflicts

■■ DISCUSSION AND REVIEW QUESTIONS

1. Can you be committed to a long-term relationship with someone you do not trust? Why?

2. What is the average level of commitment you see in people at your school or job? What would be needed to increase this commitment?

3. What is more likely to keep people in a relationship, the benefits received or the perceived termination costs? Why?

4. Why do people with shared goals have a greater commitment to relationships?

5. What differentiates productive conflicts from unproductive conflicts?

■■ REFERENCES

1. Mospan CM, Casper KA, Coleman A, et al. Managerial skills of new practitioner pharmacists within community practice. *J Am Pharm Assoc.* 2017;57(3):S265–S269. doi:10.1016/j.japh.2017.03.003.

2. Morgan RM, Hunt SD. The commitment-trust theory of relationship marketing. *J Mark*. 1994;58(3):20–38. doi:10.2307/1252308.

3. Graen GB, Uhl-Bien M. Relationship-based approach to leadership: development of leader-member exchange (LMX) theory of leadership over 25 years: applying a multi-level multi-domain perspective. *Leadersh Q*. 1995;6(2):219–247. doi:10.1016/1048-9843(95)90036-5.

4. Turner Parish J, Cadwallader S, Busch P. Want to, need to, ought to: employee commitment to organizational change. *J Organ Chang Manag*. 2008;21(1):32–52. doi:10.1108/09534810810847020.

5. Rama Devi V. Employee engagement is a two-way street. *Hum Resour Manag Int Dig*. 2009;17(2):3–4. doi:10.1108/09670730910940186.

6. Allen NJ, Meyer JP. The measurement and antecedents of affective, continuance and normative commitment to the organization. *J Occup Organ Psychol*. 1990;63(1):1–18. doi:10.1111/j.2044-8325.1990.tb00506.x.

7. Holdford D, White S. Testing commitment-trust theory in relationships between pharmacy schools and students. *Am J Pharm Educ*. 1997;61:249–256. doi:aj6103249.

8. Ozawa S, Sripad P. How do you measure trust in the health system? A systematic review of the literature. *Soc Sci Med*. 2013;91:10–14. doi:10.1016/j.socscimed.2013.05.005.

9. Overton AR, Lowry AC. Conflict management: difficult conversations with difficult people. *Clin Colon Rectal Surg*. 2013;26(4):259–264. doi:10.1055/s-0033-1356728.

10. Thomas GF, Zolin R, Hartman JL. The central role of communication in developing trust and its effect on employee involvement. *Int J Bus Commun*. 2009;46(3):287–310. doi:10.1177/0021943609333522.

CHAPTER 11

Trust in Professional Relationships
Strategies for Developing and Maintaining Trust

▪▪ OBJECTIVES

▪ Discuss the role of trust in professional relationships.

▪ Identify determinants of trust in relationships using the CREDOS framework.

▪ Suggest strategies to develop and maintain trust in professional relationships.

Trust is like blood pressure. It's silent, vital to good health, and if abused, it can be deadly.

—Frank Sonnenberg

■ ● INTRODUCTION

According to the Gallup Poll,[1] pharmacists have been one of the most trusted professional groups in the United States for decades. They have been deemed to be one of the most honest and ethical groups of professionals.

Although highly trusted, pharmacists are undervalued and underutilized in the health care profession by patients and the health care system. In general, people do not understand the job of pharmacists, and they are hesitant to use pharmacists for services beyond basic dispensing. Even the federal government has shown a lack of faith in pharmacists by failing to give them provider status.

A possible reason for the discrepancy between polls and public perceptions is that the concept of trust is more complex and more difficult to measure than the perceptions of honesty and ethical behavior measured by Gallup. Trust includes dimensions such as transparency, communication, competence, consistency, and predictability.

Trust is important in professional relationships because it affects cooperation, conflict management, commitment, and uncertainty in decision making.[2] Pharmacists must work every day to gain trust and to hold that trust in their various relationships with professionals, patients, employers, and others. Trust between individuals is a crucial component of strong professional relationships.

■ ● TRUST DEFINED

Trust in relationships refers to beliefs about a person's reliability, truth, and ability to perform a role in a relationship.[2,3] It describes perceptions of a person's character and capability in terms of moral traits, tendencies, and behaviors in relationships. Trusting others involves risk; it entails depending on others and believing that they will look out for your best interests. Trust also requires consistent and predictable behavior; partners need to be able to depend on each other. Trust accumulates over time, and it needs to be cultivated and nurtured to last.

Trust has both cognitive and affective dimensions.[4] *Cognitive-based trust* is a thoughtful judgement about the reliability and the competence-based aspects of the relationship (e.g., "I trust her to get the job done"). In contrast, *affective-based trust* describes how people feel about partners, such as perceptions of mutual respect and caring for each other (e.g., "I trust her to back me up when things get tough").

ELEMENTS OF TRUST

The literature on trust in relationships is extensive, but it can be distilled into a framework of behaviors or perceived characteristics.[2,3,5,6] These characteristics can be spelled out by the mnemonic memory aide CREDOS—competence, respect, equity, dependability, openness, and support.

The word "credo" defines a set of fundamental beliefs or principles guiding general behavior. In a related way, the CREDOS framework offers a set of guiding principles for gaining and keeping trust in professional relationships. If pharmacists continually demonstrate *competence, respect, equity, dependability, openness,* and *support* to others, they will be able to build deep and long-lasting professional relationships (Table 11.1).

Elements of the CREDOS framework for managing trust are interdependent. Like most frameworks of human behavior, the six elements are distinct but also overlap. For example, role competence might be associated with other elements such as equity and dependability, and openness might be related to respect and support. Therefore, a deficiency in one element of the CREDOS model can diminish perceptions of the remaining elements. For instance, a perceived lack of openness can hurt a leader's image regarding his or her competency, show of respect, or other element.

TABLE 11.1 Elements of Trusting Professional Relationships

Element	Definition
Competence	Ability of partners to effectively fulfill expected roles in the relationship
Respect	A feeling about and treatment of partners in a way that makes them feel valued and admired
Equity	Perceptions that partners are treating each other in a way that is evenhanded and free from bias
Dependability	Degree to which partners are seen as demonstrating dependable and predictable behavior
Openness	Views that partners share relevant information and engage in frank communications as needed
Support	Behavior of empathy, advocacy, compassion, and encouragement that indicates approval for partners and helps them be successful

▦▦ CREDOS MODEL

▦ *Competence*

Individuals have expectations of partners' responsibilities and obligations in professional relationships.[7] Competence is a partner's ability to effectively fulfill these expected roles. For example, employees expect a manager to be able to solve problems and coordinate work, and they perceive any failure to do so by the manager as incompetence. In some relationships, employers define employee responsibilities and obligations in contracts or other formal documents, and they provide position descriptions and performance criteria for roles expected of employees. Employees who fail to meet the terms of these expectations are judged to be less than competent in their role in the employment relationship.

In other relationships, however, mutual responsibilities and obligations of partners are not clear. Indeed, the lack of clarity about expected behavior is common enough to have a formal name, *role ambiguity*.

Role ambiguity typically refers to employee roles in work settings, but it can describe uncertainty in any professional relationship. It results when a partner is unclear about his or her role responsibilities or expectations in a relationship. Role ambiguity results in difficulty judging competence fairly and can cause conflict that damages professional relationships.

Role conflict often results because partners have not taken the time to discuss their mutual roles. For instance, employees often label managers as "paper pushers" because much of what the manager does is invisible to employees. They may only see a manager going to meetings or filling out paperwork without understanding the role of these tasks in helping an organization run smoothly. In fact, a competent manager who prevents major conflicts, manages resources, organizes workflow, and plans for the future may receive little credit from employees for doing so. Instead, employees tend to notice when problems arise, attributing much of the blame to their managers.

People rarely see themselves as the source of a problem in a relationship. An outsider is often needed to raise this point, similar to the situation described in Box 11.1

Misunderstandings about competence in professional relationships can be improved by understanding partners' roles and responsibilities. Partners can be more forgiving and trusting by recognizing their other partners' roles and the difficulties those partners face in balancing the expectations of multiple roles. Realizing that conflicting obligations may require tough choices (e.g., a

BOX 11.1 Leadership in Action: Your Coworkers Do Not Trust You

Patty invited Gary into her office for a serious talk about his relationships with other employees in the pharmacy. As Gary's supervisor, Patty believed she had a responsibility to let him know that he had lost the confidence of his coworkers.

Patty began, "How do you think things are going with your other coworkers in the pharmacy?"

Gary said, "I am starting to think that everyone here is a jerk. I've noticed that they have been avoiding me. They never ask me to work with them on special projects. They also make snide comments to me about my work— that I am working too slow, or I make too many mistakes, or I am not nice enough to the customers. I'm even getting a little irritated with you about your management style. You always seem to be monitoring my work and offering unwanted advice to me. You don't seem to be doing this to other employees. I am starting to think that you do not trust me."

Patty replied, "Have you thought about why people might be acting this way to you?"

Gary said, "Nope. No idea."

Patty responded, "Some of the other employees in the pharmacy told me that they do not feel comfortable asking for your help and that they can't trust you to get your assigned work done on time and without errors. I have come to a similar conclusion. That is why I have been monitoring your work more and stepping in to offer help."

Patty continued, "You are going to need to earn back my confidence and the confidence of your coworkers. Let's talk about some specific circumstances to illustrate what I am talking about and come up with a game plan to improve your work."

Questions

1. How self-aware is Gary?

2. What is the main reason that people do not trust Gary? Do you think that if he addressed this reason that his problem will be resolved? Why?

3. Will Gary ever be able to earn back the complete trust of his coworkers and Patty? Why?

---

manager might need to put the customer first over an employee even when the employee is right) is important. Partners need to forgive each other for making difficult choices.

Perceptions of competence also require partners to build a history of success in roles. A track record of competency can help partners be more forgiving when inevitable letdowns occur in long-term relationships.

Respect

Respect is a crucial element of relationships that means different things to different people. It is defined in the dictionary as both a feeling and a way of treating someone.[8] It is a feeling of admiration for someone's personal qualities, achievements, or status, and it is a way of treating someone by being polite and showing them kindness. Thus, pharmacists can respect their technicians and can demonstrate this respect by exhibiting certain behaviors, such as those shown in Figure 11.1.[9,10]

The meaning of respect differs between individuals because perceptions vary depending on the situation and individuals involved. Indeed, behavior that is seen as respectful in social situations may be highly disrespectful in work circumstances, and behavior acceptable between friends may be unacceptable between coworkers.

Respect can be seen as a clear recognition of an individual's humanity.[11] Every time you interact with people, you face a choice. You can treat that individual as a human being with hopes, problems, fears, capabilities, and weaknesses, or you can treat that person as an object who is in the way of what you want to do or accomplish.

FIGURE 11.1 Behaviors Associated with Showing Respect to Others

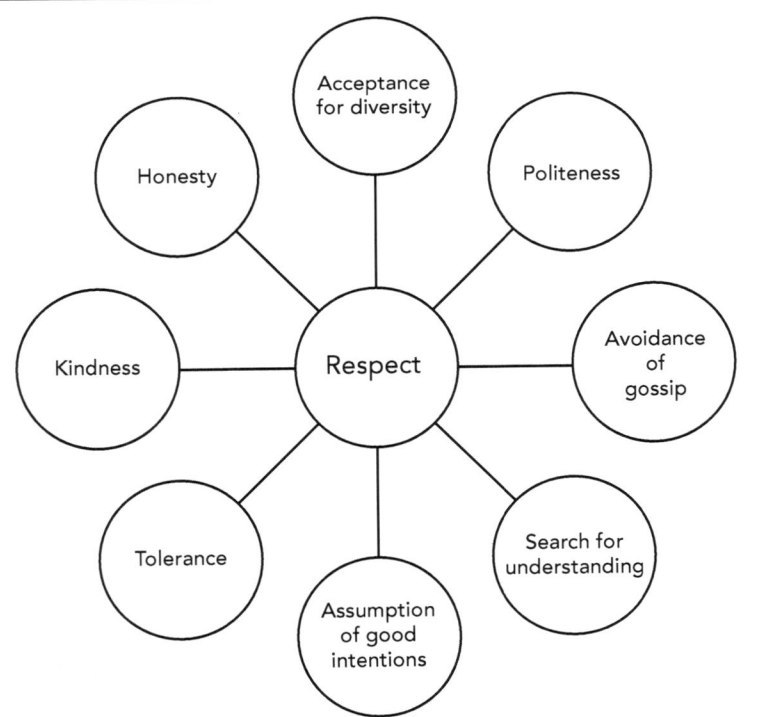

In automobiles, people might rage at other drivers on the road during the morning commute. Angry drivers usually see other drivers not as humans but as barriers keeping them from getting to work. Objectifying the other drivers often leads to horn honking, rude gestures, and rude language. In contrast, making eye contact with the other drivers and seeing them as humans frequently helps rage subside, resulting in a return to normal polite behavior.

Treating people as humans is the idea behind adopting the *10/5 way* in businesses and organizations. The 10/5 way recommends that if you are within 10 feet of someone, you should acknowledge them with a nod or smile. When you are within 5 feet, you say "hello." Of course, the rule might be impractical in large crowds or inappropriate because of cultural norms, but it can promote behaviors that give a face to individuals in organizations.

Finally, respect is shown through basic courtesy.[9] Courtesy consists of the following basic rules of etiquette:

- Acknowledge a person's presence.
- Give people your full attention (especially putting down your cell phone).
- Say "please" and "thank you."
- Speak clearly.
- Do what you say, and say what you do.
- Do not waste people's time.
- Value diversity.
- Listen to and acknowledge words, feelings, and differences.
- Assume the best intentions.
- Treat others as you would like to be treated.

■ Equity

Equity (also known as fairness) is the quality of making judgments that are evenhanded and free from bias. It refers to the equality of outcomes received (i.e., distributive equity) and the fairness of procedures used to decide an outcome (i.e., procedural equity).[12]

Perceptions of *distributive equity* between partners occur when each partner is satisfied with the allocation of rewards and costs in a relationship. These perceptions differ from those of *procedural equity*, which emphasize the rules and norms that delineate how allocations of rewards and costs are distributed over time.

Perceptions of equity are influenced by cultural and societal norms. For some cultures, the norm is distributive equity—everyone gets the same no matter what. For other cultures, fairness occurs when those who have more share with those who are less fortunate. Conflicts occur when individuals disagree about the norms guiding behaviors in relationships.

Disagreements revolve around the rules of conduct and whether they are fairly applied. With that in mind, the following list suggests ways to improve perceived equity in professional relationships:

- Understand the written and unwritten rules of any professional relationship. Rules are formal standards of conduct (e.g., respect the chain of command) found in an organization's policies and procedures. Unwritten rules are cultural norms (e.g., acknowledging colleagues in elevators) that also guide behavior. Both types of rules are important in guiding the perception of fair treatment.

- Agree upon fair procedures as early as possible in the relationship; try not to wait until a conflict arises. As disagreements occur, respectfully negotiate a new agreement regarding fair procedures.

- Clarify with partners what would be perceived as fair outcomes. Identify what each partner wants to achieve from the relationship. Then discuss how these outcomes can be achieved through the agreed-on fair procedures.

- Address conflicts as soon as possible. Perceptions of mistrust can grow over time if left unresolved.

● Dependability

People gain the trust of others when they demonstrate dependable and predictable behavior day after day. Dependable partners in relationships maintain composure and do not exhibit emotional outbursts or moody behavior, even if they are having a "bad day" because of personal stress, fatigue, or other stressor.

Dependability requires promises to be kept, no matter how small. Breaking promises is one of the easiest ways to damage professional relationships. Credibility is lost because breaking a promise suggests that you cannot be relied on to do what you say you will do. Broken promises convey to the other partners that your professional relationship is not important enough to you to keep your word.

What happens when a person feels the need to break a promise? Are there any circumstances when going back on one's word to another is acceptable? Box 11.2 explores these questions.

Excuses are inadequate to prevent broken trust (Table 11.2). Everyone gives occasional excuses to explain themselves, but each excuse has the potential to chip away at the trust between partners. Excuses can indicate incompetence, disrespect, inequity, undependability, lack of openness, and unsupportive behaviors, depending on the type and frequency. The more excuses a person makes, the less likely he or she will be trusted.

■ Openness

Openness is a way of communicating in which partners are transparent and do not keep secrets from each other. It denotes the extent to which partners are perceived to share information and engage in frank communications about important issues.

Openness does not mean that anything goes when sharing information. Rather, it requires judgment about what information to share and what to keep confidential. Openness also concerns who should or should not have information and when. A major problem with perceptions of openness is that people may reasonably disagree on what information should be shared, with whom it should be shared, and how it should be shared.

Lack of openness really refers to instances when partners do not share information for reasons that are difficult to justify. Some people hoard information because it makes them feel more important or powerful (e.g., "I have a secret but can't share it"). Others may hide information out of self-protection (e.g., not reporting a medication error). Often, information is not shared because of laziness (e.g., it may require extra explanation) or insensitivity (e.g., "I didn't know that this information was important to you"). Distrust occurs when partners are perceived to disrespect the information needs of others.

A good rule of thumb for being open in professional relationships is for partners to share important matters that relate to their professional and personal roles. Openness in a boss-and-employee relationship means having accurate and timely conversations about topics that are necessary for both sides to do their jobs.

BOX 11.2 Leadership in Action: Help! Should I Keep My Promise or Break It for a Better Opportunity?

When is breaking a promise acceptable? Bob, a graduating pharmacist who has accepted a job offer with one employer, wants to break his promise to this employer for a better opportunity. What options should Bob consider in making the decision?

The simple answer is "No. It is never okay to break a promise." Going back on a promise is unprofessional, and a pharmacist's word is a pledge that should never be broken.

However, not keeping one's word may be justifiable in some circumstances. The real and more complex answer to the question "Should I keep my promise?" is, "It depends."

It depends on a variety of issues. Chief among them is, "What is best for Bob?" How much better is the new opportunity for him? Will it offer significantly more chances to learn, help patients, work with a great team, and make a difference? If breaking the promise allows Bob a greater chance of achieving his professional mission, it might be personally justifiable.

Another concern for Bob should be, "How does breaking the promise hurt others?" For the employer, Bob's decision could cost the organization tens of thousands of dollars in wasted time and money spent on interviews, communications, and lost productivity. The decision might put the employer in a difficult spot by forcing it to postpone or cancel plans. Less evident to Bob, however, might be the effect of his decision on the reputation of his pharmacy school and the individuals who wrote him letters of recommendation. His decision sends a bad message about the school and the people who vouched for his character.

The final concern for Bob is, "How morally defensible is it to break a promise?" The answer to this lies in identifying under what conditions the choice can be justified. This includes considering questions such as the following:

* Can the employer easily fill the position with someone else?
* Has the employer kept all of its promises to Bob and treated him with respect?
* Have circumstances changed with the employer that might affect the agreement? For instance, the employer may have merged with another company or announced the closing of parts of its business.
* What would his potential new employer, alma mater, or advisers think if they heard that Bob broke his promise?

Before Bob breaks his promise, he needs to make certain that he has a full understanding of all the facts relating to his choice.

Questions

1. What information does Bob need?

2. Is breaking a promise ever acceptable? Why?

3. What is the worst-case scenario for Bob if he breaks his promise?

TABLE 11.2 Excuses That Damage Trust

Excuse	What it means to partners
You never told me to do that.	This excuse attempts to shift blame back to a partner for not doing something instead of taking responsibility and learning what needed to be done. In many cases, the partner was told but there is no documentation of that fact. Thus, this excuse forces people to document everything in order to hold partners accountable.
I did not understand what you wanted.	This defense attempts to shift blame back to a partner for not being clear. It demonstrates insufficient commitment to the relationship to seek clarification.
I forgot.	This excuse suggests to a partner that there is insufficient concern about the relationship to remember.
I don't know how.	This response essentially tells a partner to "Do it yourself," "Get someone else to do it," or "Drop whatever you are doing at the moment and take time out to teach me." All three options disrupt the partner's schedule and throw the problem back on the partner. A better response is, "I have never done it before but would love to give it a try. Can I ask questions if I hit a roadblock?"
That's not my job.	This response suggests to a partner that commitment to the relationship is limited to the responsibilities laid out in a job description. When told to a boss, it often results in a discussion about a person's future with an employer.

When information cannot be shared, partners should explain why. For example, if job cuts are impending, the boss might say, "I do not know when or if any of us will be affected. I will let you know as soon as I learn for certain."

Yet, maintaining openness in many professional relationships is difficult because human interactions offer so many opportunities for miscommunication. Perceptual and organizational barriers tend to cloud the delivery and receipt of ideas. Emotions, distractions, and one's own unique personal characteristics and idiosyncrasies inhibit the transmission of accurate messages.

Communications are further complicated when one partner has authority over another.[13] People in positions of authority have difficulty establishing trust in their subordinates because the role of a boss is to judge subordinates. If that judgment is negative, the boss may withhold rewards or inflict punishment. Therefore, employees are less candid with their boss out of a sense of self-protection.

The formal power of a manager or supervisor over subordinates can complicate the interpretation of seemingly innocent comments, written notes, and e-mails and can send unintended messages. When a boss responds to a question with, "Let's see," the subordinate could interpret the response as "No," "Maybe," "I have no idea," "Go away," or "I don't want to deal with this now." In addition, there is a tendency to interpret communications negatively if individuals lack a good relationship.

People in positions of authority must choose their words and the communication medium carefully. Messaging through e-mails and texting can be more easily misinterpreted than face-to-face conversations. A simple e-mail comment, without the facial expressions and tone of voice associated with verbal discussion, can be interpreted to be a command, criticism, or sarcastic comment. Sometimes, communicating by phone or in person is much more effective and efficient.

People in positions of authority must recognize the difficulty of gaining subordinates' trust. They must work especially hard to build and keep that trust. Failure to do so in pharmacy settings can put patients at risk.

● Support

Support in professional relationships occurs when people show approval for their partners and help them be successful (e.g., "My boss supports my career"). Support also means being compassionate with a partner when he or she is experiencing difficulties (e.g., "My boss supported me during my child's illness"). Supportive partners encourage each other to reach their highest potential by helping each other get ahead. They are also considerate during adverse times.

Support is similar to respect in that both are based on feelings of admiration that are reinforced by behaviors. However, the goals of respect and supportive behaviors differ. The goal of respect is to make clear that a partner is respected. It recognizes the humanity and value of people through words and actions. In contrast, providing support is to act in ways that enhance a partner's ability to be successful. It means advocating for them, protecting them, backing them, and encouraging them to succeed.

Like respect, support shows concern for partners as people. Support means being invested in the success of partners—mentoring them, encouraging their ideas, defending their positions, and helping out whenever needed. Support encourages gratitude and reciprocity, which further cement the professional relationship.

Support can be shown in a variety of ways. Partners who mentor others show their support by freely sharing expertise and offering guidance. Mentors facilitate networking by introducing mentees to others, and they offer a friendly ear for mentees to share frustrations and achievements. Support also occurs by taking an active interest in the success of partners. This can include knowing the names of a partner's spouse and children, personal background and interests, and career aspirations. Knowing a little about each other on a personal level helps partners better communicate, gain more understanding of differences, and resolve misunderstandings more easily.

CONCLUSION

Developing and maintaining their professional relationships is a critical responsibility of pharmacists and pharmacy managers. It is important for career and job success, and it is important in their care for patients. Pharmacists who follow the guidance of the CREDOS framework can diagnose the strengths and weaknesses of any professional relationship and develop strategies to shore up any gaps.

KEY TERMS AND CONCEPTS

- Trust in relationships
- Cognitive-based trust
- Affective-based trust
- CREDOS framework
- Competence
- Respect
- Equity
- Dependability
- Openness
- Support
- Role ambiguity

DISCUSSION AND REVIEW QUESTIONS

1. Can you trust a person who is a competent, reliable coworker but likes to gossip about other people and spread false rumors? Why or why not?

2. How do you define competence in your role as an employee? Would your employer define competence the same way? How would your coworkers

define competence in your relationship with them? How would you define competence in the relationship between patients and pharmacists?

3. What behaviors were acceptable before entering the pharmacy profession but are now considered disrespectful by peers?

4. How do workplace rules, regulations, and laws help ensure equity in work settings?

5. Where do you get your support at work? At home? What does support look like at work and at home?

6. What do you think is meant by the anonymous quote, "Trusting you was my decision, and proving me right is your choice"?

■ ■ REFERENCES

1. Gallup. Nurses keep healthy lead as most honest, ethical profession. December 26, 2017. https://news.gallup.com/poll/224639/nurses-keep-healthy-lead-honest-ethical-profession.aspx.

2. Dirks KT, Ferrin DL. Trust in leadership: meta-analytic findings and implications for research and practice. *J Appl Psychol.* 2002;87(4):611–628. doi:10.1037//0021-9010.87.4.611.

3. Lewicki RJ, Tomlinson EC, Gillespie N. Models of interpersonal trust development: theoretical approaches, empirical evidence, and future directions. *J Manage.* 2006;32(6):991–1022. doi:10.1177/0149206306294405.

4. Johnson D, Grayson K. Cognitive and affective trust in service relationships. *J Bus Res.* 2005;58(4):500–507. doi:10.1016/S0148-2963(03)00140-1.

5. Morgan RM, Hunt SD. The commitment-trust theory of relationship marketing. *J Mark.* 1994;58(3):20–38. doi:10.2307/1252308.

6. Erdogan B, Bauer TN. Leader–member exchange theory. In: *International Encyclopedia of the Social & Behavioral Sciences.* Smelser N, Baltes PB, eds. 2nd ed. Amsterdam, The Netherlands: Elsevier; 2015:641–647. doi:10.1016/B978-0-08-097086-8.22010-2.

7. Twyman M, Harvey N, Harries C. Trust in motives, trust in competence: separate factors determining the effectiveness of risk communication. *Judgm Decis Mak.* 2008;3(1):111–120.

8. Oxford English Dictionary Online. http://www.oed.com/.

9. Clarke N. An integrated conceptual model of respect in leadership. *Leadersh Q.* 2011;22(2):316–327. doi:10.1016/j.leaqua.2011.02.007.

10. Spagnoletti CL, Arnold RM. R-E-S-P-E-C-T: even more difficult to teach than to define. *J Gen Intern Med.* 2007;22(5):707–709. doi:10.1007/s11606-007-0164-x.

11. Arbinger Institute. *Leadership and Self-Deception: Getting Out of the Box.* 2nd rev. ed. Oakland, CA: Berrett-Koehler Publishers; 2010.

12. Thibaut J, Walker L. *Procedural Justice: A Psychological Analysis.* Hillsdale, NJ: Lawrence Erlbaum Associates; 1975.

13. Bartolomé F. Nobody trusts the boss completely—now what? *Harv Bus Rev.* 1989;67(2):135–142.

CHAPTER 12

Conflicts and Negotiations
Formulating Win-Win Solutions

■ ■ OBJECTIVES

- ■ Describe the characteristics of conflicts.

- ■ Compare negotiation with other forms of conflict resolution.

- ■ Contrast win-lose negotiations with win-win negotiations.

- ■ Identify key elements in any negotiation.

- ■ Identify common strategies used in negotiations.

So much of life is a negotiation—so even if you're not in business, you have opportunities to practice all around you.

—Kevin O'Leary

◼◼ INTRODUCTION

Whenever people work together on an important issue, there will be disagreements and conflict. Sometimes conflicts stem from simple miscommunications, but often they originate from differing opinions on the processes and desired outcomes of the work. Understanding conflicts and how to resolve them is a key responsibility of professionals and leaders. When handled well, conflicts can improve relationships, solve difficult problems, and influence change in organizations.

Conflict management is crucial for managing professional relationships. Conflicts between partners have the following characteristics:[1]

◼ Interdependence between the parties: "I need you, and you need me."

◼ Perceived incompatible goals: "We want different things."

◼ Scarce resources: "There is not enough available for us both to get what we want."

◼ Interference: "You are in the way of getting what I want."

◼ Social interaction: "Our relationship is subject to the peculiarities of human behavior."

Pharmacists experience conflicts daily because they often interact with people to induce action. For example, they may be encouraging a patient to take a medication as directed, convincing a physician to change a prescription, or persuading a manager to alter the schedule of technicians. Interactions that result in conflicts are sometimes uncomfortable and stressful. Any pharmacist who is not encountering conflict is probably not doing his or her job.

Many pharmacists have problems managing conflicts. Some of them find conflicts unpleasant and avoid them. They just want everyone to get along with each other, so they shun disputes when possible or gloss over any differences. Other pharmacists are comfortable with conflicts but are ineffective in resolving them.

The better pharmacists negotiate conflicts, the more successful they will be in furthering their personal interests and those of patients. This chapter introduces the practice of conflict management, emphasizing the use of negotiation to resolve conflicts faced by pharmacists.

■■ COMMON RESPONSES TO CONFLICT

There are many ways of responding to conflict, and each way is situation specific. Most responses differ by the degree to which the parties involved focus on their own concerns (i.e., are selfish) and the concerns of the other parties (i.e., are selfless). Conflicts also differ by the degree to which parties cooperate in meeting each other's concerns. The degree to which parties assert their personal interests and cooperate describes four standard responses to conflict: *opportunism*, *avoidance, accommodation*, and *collaboration* (Figure 12.1).[2]

Opportunism is the practice of taking selfish, unfair advantage of others, possibly in a devious, unscrupulous manner. Opportunistic behavior is driven by self-interest. Opportunists do not shy away from conflicts because conflicts offer opportunities for personal gain and exploitation of others. In its extreme form, opportunism damages relationships, increases distrust, and often leads to bad outcomes over the long term. Opportunistic behavior can be expected in win-lose negotiations in which parties try to take advantage of the others for maximum gain.

Avoidance occurs when individuals steer clear of altercations because of fear, shyness, apathy, or another reason. When avoidance is a consistent pattern of behavior in pharmacists, it can be a significant problem. Chronic avoiders dodge confrontations whenever possible—even at the cost of their own interests and

FIGURE 12.1 Approaches to Managing Conflicts

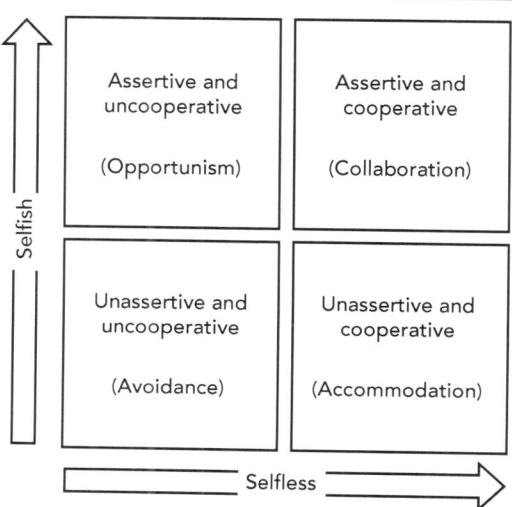

those of their patients—because their primary concern is to stay out of conflicts. Avoidance is an uncooperative response to conflicts because cooperation requires engagement. Without engagement, collaborative problem solving cannot occur. However, avoidance may be the correct reaction in some situations, such as when people try to drag others into a petty argument or when the engagement has little chance of having a positive influence.

Accommodation is an approach to conflict in which individuals placate others by yielding on issues. Accommodation is selfless, because it seeks to address the concerns of others without consideration of one's own interests. It is also unassertive because one's own needs and desires are deferred. Accommodation in conflicts is efficient because the conflict is over when one side concedes. In addition, it can build goodwill and preserve fragile relationships, unless the other party sees accommodation as a form of weakness to exploit in the future. The problem with accommodation is that it can build resentment in the accommodating party. By not asserting one's own interests, the accommodating party is shortchanged and becomes bitter about the unfair partnership.

Collaboration occurs when parties cooperate to resolve conflicts in creative ways that satisfy all of the parties involved. Collaboration is a common feature of win-win negotiating. Collaborators seek to understand the concerns and interests of the other side while asserting their own interests as well.

■■ NEGOTIATING TO RESOLVE CONFLICTS

Typically, pharmacists think of negotiations as something that is done by business people, lawyers, or diplomats in formal settings. However, everyone negotiates. You negotiate whenever you interact with others. Sometimes, you may not realize it.

■ Aspects of Negotiation

Negotiation is the process of resolving conflicts between individuals or groups through dialogue and problem solving.[3,4] Thus, people negotiate whenever they engage with others who have conflicting goals. Pharmacists negotiate with patients, physicians, insurance companies, coworkers, supervisors, and many others.

Negotiations can occur at any time and any place—not just at formal occasions with everyone sitting at a conference table or desk. In reality, many important negotiations are conducted informally, during normal day-to-day interactions.

Negotiations also occur between groups of people, including associations, regulatory agencies, businesses, and other institutions. The dynamics and tactics of group negotiations are beyond the scope of this chapter, so the remainder of this discussion will focus on negotiations between individuals.

■ Misconceptions about Negotiation

There are many misconceptions about negotiation—typically based on widespread stereotypes.[3,4] One common misconception is that negotiation is about winning and losing. In this stereotype, opportunistic individuals seek to triumph over others, often through the use of deceit and trickery. Another misconception is that the very process of negotiating damages relationships because someone loses and may respond negatively. Even if the negotiation results in a compromise whereby both sides yield, there is an incorrect assumption that hardball tactics are needed to reach a compromise and that these tactics can harm a previously cordial relationship. In stereotypical negotiations, individuals believe they need to argue, act rudely, and be pushy to "win" a negotiation (as seen in Box 12.1).

Negotiation does not have to function according to stereotypes. Negotiation can involve finding ways where both sides win. It can be conducted in a respectful, cooperative, and professional manner. In fact, it can actually enhance relationships by resolving conflicts in ways that encourage trust and commitment.

■■ TYPES OF NEGOTIATIONS

Of the four standard responses to conflict, only two are associated with negotiating—opportunism and collaboration. The other two responses, avoidance and accommodation, are responses that seek to avoid conflict by dodging it or conceding.

■ Win-Lose Negotiations

Opportunism is commonly seen in *win-lose negotiations*. Win-lose negotiations occur when one or more parties have something to gain from the deal and that party's gain is another party's loss. Also called *zero-sum game* or *fixed-pie negotiations*, a win-lose negotiation is similar to divvying up a pizza—it is a contest to get as much of the pie as possible.

Negotiations for the purchase of a new car are commonly win-lose negotiations. When purchasing a car, the buyer and seller face off with the goal of

BOX 12.1 Leadership in Action: Conflict with the Store Manager

Ron, the store manager of a pharmacy, and Natalie, the pharmacist in charge, do not get along with each other. They have had several disputes, primarily because Ron makes unilateral decisions about pharmacy operations without consulting Natalie. Their most significant disagreement concerns how Ron alters the staffing of pharmacy interns without talking to Natalie. This frustrates Natalie because it often leaves her without sufficient staffing to run the pharmacy. On one hectic day, Mrs. Berber, a long-time but somewhat cranky customer, dropped off a new prescription to be filled. Mrs. Berber was told by the technician, Angie, that the medication could be picked up in 30 minutes. Hearing Angie's promise, Natalie worried to herself, "I hope we can meet that promise. I only have Angie helping me, and work is starting to back up."

Normally, two interns were helping Natalie, but Ron felt that only one would be needed that day. Ron was wrong, because in the next 30 minutes, several new prescriptions were dropped off, and six individuals came in to receive flu shots.

Exactly 30 minutes after dropping off her prescription, Mrs. Berber approached the pharmacy counter to pay for it. When told that her medication was not ready, Mrs. Berber became very angry and told Angie, "You didn't keep your promise. You're a liar." When Angie explained that the pharmacist had to administer six flu shots to patients in the past half hour, Mrs. Berber turned her anger on Natalie, responding, "You made a promise and did not keep it! Why do flu shots take priority over filling my prescription? I was here first! I want to register a complaint against you!"

Upon hearing the commotion, Ron came over to help. Sizing up the situation, he told Mrs. Berber, "You are absolutely right, Mrs. Berber. Thirty minutes is more than enough time to fill a prescription! I will write up a complaint against Natalie and counsel her about her mistake. Also, she will personally deliver your prescription to your house at the end of her shift, if you like. There's no reason to wait around if it was Natalie's fault."

Natalie gaped at Ron in disbelief.

Questions

1. Is this a situation that can be negotiated to achieve a win-win solution?

2. What are Natalie's other options in managing the situation?

3. What should be Natalie's goal in resolving the conflict?

---

getting as much as possible from the transaction in exchange for giving as little as possible. The seller wants to negotiate the highest possible price for the car, and the buyer wants to pay the lowest possible price. The two haggle until they agree on a price. Win-lose negotiations are associated with several tactics:

■ **Withholding information.** Individuals' interests can be used against them in win-lose negotiations. If a car salesperson knows the maximum amount a customer is willing to spend on a specific car on his or her lot, the salesperson will structure an approach to have the customer pay the maximum price. In contrast, if the salesperson does not know what the customer is willing to pay, the customer can more easily negotiate a lower price.

- **Hiding emotions.** Expressing eagerness or desire to opponents indicates a weakness that can be exploited. For example, when purchasing the car of his dreams, a customer lets it slip to the salesperson that he really wants to make a deal on his dream car that day. This information gives the salesperson an enormous advantage because a motivated buyer is easier to influence. However, if the customer is able to convince the salesperson that he is "just looking" and likely to leave without making a deal, the customer has the upper hand.

- **Being stingy with concessions.** If a party concedes something to the other side, it should be done only after receiving something of equal or greater value. The typical process consists of "I will give you this, if you will give me that." The one who concedes the least, while gaining the most, wins.

Some situations inevitably result in win-lose negotiations. One circumstance where this is likely to occur is when individuals are unlikely to interact with each other again. In this situation, there is no relationship to build or maintain. Another example is when the stakes of the transaction are extremely high and the benefits of winning outweigh the goodwill that might be lost in beating a partner, such as the purchase of a business or a house. Finally, win-lose negotiations may be the only option if one partner in a conflict insists on taking an adversarial, opportunistic stance. Unless both partners are willing to collaborate toward a mutually agreeable solution, win-lose negotiations are likely the only option to resolve the conflict.

Pharmacists should always try to mitigate any potential fallout from a win-lose negotiation. They should always be cognizant that their actions have a direct effect on the image of their profession. Pharmacists should be cordial and respectful of adversaries during negotiations, no matter the outcome.

● *Win-Win Negotiations*

Win-win negotiations are discussions in which both parties seek mutually satisfactory outcomes. In win-win negotiations, parties are not seen as adversaries but as partners, and each interaction with that partner is an opportunity to build a relationship. Win-win negotiators are always thinking long term regarding relationships and often use the partnerships formed in one negotiation to lay the groundwork for future negotiations. For example, the process and outcomes of one salary negotiation will likely influence future salary negotiations.

Consider a conflict between a supervisor and a pharmacist over work schedules. In this conflict, the parties have competing goals—the supervisor needs the pharmacist to work overtime, while the pharmacist wants to go home to be with his family. In a win-lose contest, one party must lose. However, in a win-win negotiation, the pharmacist and supervisor may reach a mutually beneficial solution, such as the pharmacist working overtime in exchange for not working on a holiday.

Win-win negotiators reject the assumption that there is a fixed-pie. Instead, they believe that if both parties in a negotiation are flexible and creative in formulating solutions, the pie can be expanded in ways that satisfy everyone.

This belief can be illustrated with the Parable of the Orange. In the parable, two cooks are haggling over a desired orange. Both cooks want and need the orange to bake a dessert. They resolve the stalemate with a compromise by agreeing to split the orange into halves. However, neither cook is satisfied with the compromise because each cook can make only half of the desired dessert with half of an orange. Furthermore, they missed an opportunity for both to be satisfied. One cook wanted only the orange's juice, and the other cook wanted only the rind. If they had worked together, each could have acquired the part of the orange needed to make a full dessert.

The Parable of the Orange illustrates how a compromise is less desirable than a win-win solution. A *compromise* results when conflicting parties make concessions to resolve a conflict. Neither party gets exactly what it wants, but the parties are willing to settle for what they can get. In the Parable of the Orange, the compromise is one-half of an orange.

Compromise typically occurs when two or more strongly positioned parties are pressured to resolve an issue but are unwilling to yield unless concessions are made by the other party. However, the focus on concessions can blind negotiators to potential, mutually beneficial solutions. Compromising often results in rushed decisions and negative outcomes that a more collaborative process might have avoided. To achieve win-win solutions, the following are required:

- **Cooperation.** Cooperation is necessary because parties need to work together to find mutually beneficial solutions to conflicts. Cooperation does not mean that negotiators need to be best friends—they just need to show a willingness to work together.

- **Trust.** Trust is necessary for partners to share information without feeling that it will be used against them opportunistically. Trust is also needed for partners to make concessions. Partners have to trust that a concession by one partner will be reciprocated. Without trust, neither partner will make the first move necessary to break an impasse.

■ **Imagination**. Imagination is essential because many negotiations revolve around a multitude of issues of varying importance to the parties. Imagination and creativity can help parties look beyond the one or two easily recognizable paths to a solution.

■ ■ COMMON ELEMENTS OF EVERY NEGOTIATION

Most pharmacists have a basic understanding of how to negotiate. They just need to hone their skills. The first step is to realize that all negotiations revolve around three important elements: power, time, and information.[4]

■ *Power*

Power describes the relative influence of each party in a negotiation. The party with the most influence can set the terms and outcomes of a negotiation. Inexperienced negotiators often misjudge their power in conflicts—either adopting a level of powerlessness or overestimating their power. Thus, they may give away their interests or overplay their hand, leading to poor outcomes or a stalemate. An assessment of the relative power of parties in a negotiation is important, and it typically comes from three sources (Table 12.1).

TABLE 12.1 Sources of Negotiating Power

Source of power	Description
BATNA	BATNA, the **b**est **a**lternative **t**o a **n**egotiated **a**greement,[a] refers to the course of action a party will take if a negotiation fails and no agreement is reached. In negotiating employment, one's BATNA might be the next best job available. BATNA is an important source of power because an individual has greater power when others perceive him or her to have equal or better options to the deal being offered. Thus, the most powerful party in c negotiation is the one who can most easily walk away from an offer.
Authority	Authority describes formal or official power bestowed on individuals. Greater authority gives one greater flexibility in negotiating. One rule of negotiating is that individuals should partner with those that have the authority to make a deal. Avoid working with subordinates who might say, "My hands are tied."
Attitude	People with positive and confident attitudes are perceived to be powerful negotiators. Effective negotiators exude an aura of confidence. Projecting confidence, even when one does not feel confident, changes a partner's response. Partners who face a confident negotiator are less likely to be opportunistic than if they were to face an unconfident one. Projecting confidence also helps other people feel confident. Confident people worry less about making a mistake, are more likely to take chances, and are less likely to become emotional.[b] Of course, confidence must be matched with skill and preparation for the best outcomes. Indeed, an overconfident individual without the requisite negotiating skills can be exploited by good negotiators. Nevertheless, confidence can increase one's power in a negotiation.

a. See reference 4.
b. See reference 4.

BOX 12.2 Good Cop, Bad Cop

Lack of authority is often used as a negotiation tactic to delay negotiations or to make an argument that a higher authority needs to be satisfied before a deal can be made. That way, the negotiator can play the *good cop* while the higher authority can play the *bad cop* in the negotiation. The good cop (who lacks authority) appears supportive, understanding, and sympathetic to the negotiating partner, when in reality, the good and bad cops are conspiring together to obtain a better deal.

A common tactic of car salespersons is to claim that negotiated agreements need to be approved by a manager. After returning from seeing the manager, the salesperson might say, "I really fought for this deal, but the manager won't accept it. Can you come up two hundred dollars on the price of the car?" If the customer agrees, the salesperson may repeat the same process in seeking concessions on financing, trade-in, or other points.

Experienced negotiators have two responses to the claims of authority. First, the experienced negotiator will refuse to accept it by asking, "I know that your policy does not permit this, but is there anything you can do to help me here?" If asked pleasantly, the partner will often bend or ignore the rules to make an agreement. In circumstances where the other side is unwilling to assume authority to seal an agreement, the experienced negotiator will ask, "If you don't have the authority to make this decision, can I speak to someone who does?" Depending on the conflict being negotiated, one might need to go up the chain of command to gain satisfaction.

Box 12.2 describes a well-known tactic in which the negotiator pretends to have little power to make decisions but promises to work in a partner's best interests. The tactic is called *good cop, bad cop.*

◼ Time

Time refers to the period during which a negotiation takes place. The end of this time period, the deadline, is where most negotiating occurs. Everyone knows the importance of deadlines in getting things accomplished—the closer the deadline, the more motivated the parties will be to act. Either party can set a deadline, and either party can benefit from it.

There are several issues associated with deadlines in negotiations. One issue is the importance of knowing a partner's deadline, which will help in judging the partner's desire to make a deal. There are three types of deadlines: explicit, secret, and implicit.

- *Explicit deadlines* are clearly stated by the parties, "This deal goes away if not accepted by the time I leave this office" or "We would like to have your answer by the end of the week."

- *Secret deadlines* are undisclosed by parties because parties can use them as a form of leverage to gain concessions. For instance, if a buyer learns that a car dealer will lose a manufacturer's rebate on a car if it is not sold by the end of the month, the buyer can use that deadline to persuade the car dealer to share part of the rebate or offer better financing terms. Therefore, the car dealer's incentive is to keep that deadline secret.

■ *Implicit deadlines* are neither secret nor explicit. Rather, they are implied by the circumstances. Many implicit deadlines are self-imposed because of an individual's impatience. For example, when a negotiation drags, people can become impatient. This impatience can pressure individuals to make concessions or rash decisions.

The best recommendation for dealing with deadlines is to exercise patience. Impatience is an enemy in negotiations. Allowing the process to unfold on its own time is better. If neither side is ready to make a decision, forcing a premature conclusion may not result in the best outcome.

In negotiations, knowing the range of options for responding to deadlines is important. The first option is to give in and accept the offer. The second option is to walk away from the deal. A third, frequently overlooked, option is to negotiate a new deadline.

Deadlines are not inflexible. They can be changed or eliminated altogether. If more time is needed and there is a mutual desire to come to an agreement, partners may renegotiate. Asking never hurts.

● Information

The third and final element of any negotiation is information. When entering into negotiations, you should have facts and knowledge about your objectives, about yourself, about the individuals with whom you negotiate, and about the object of the negotiation.

Information About Yourself

Capable negotiators have a clear understanding of (1) the goal of a negotiation and (2) self-awareness about their personal style of negotiation. Knowing this information helps them in setting objectives and developing strategies to achieve those objectives.

Before any conflict, negotiators need to ask themselves, "What do I want to achieve with this negotiation?" Although this is a common-sense question, many individuals enter into negotiations with only a vague idea of their objective. A new graduate might apply for a pharmacist position with a plan to "get a job that pays good money." However, this hazy objective leads to difficulty in communicating one's desires to negotiating partners or in knowing what to concede in a negotiation.

Losing your bearings in a negotiation is easy without a clear understanding of what you desire. Without goals and boundaries, you may have difficulty keeping track of the various issues being negotiated or you may become emotional over trivial issues.

You also need to know about your personal negotiating style. Capable negotiators have a realistic understanding of their emotional temperament, habits, assertiveness, and negotiating capabilities. This understanding is used to develop strategies to overcome any characteristics that may hinder the negotiation. For instance, a pharmacist who is aware that he has trouble acting assertively during confrontations might role-play an important negotiation with a mentor to identify areas that need improvement.

People are often their own worst enemy when negotiating conflicts because they allow their emotions to take control. They can easily become upset when other individuals act as barriers to their goals, and controlling these negative feelings can be challenging. Anger, anxiety, or other emotions can get in the way of negotiating a satisfactory outcome.

Information About Your Partners

Successful negotiators learn as much about the other parties as possible. At a minimum, they try to find out what the other parties want and how much the parties want it. Having this information will help them determine their possible negotiating positions and any advantages. Negotiators should try to learn the answers to the following questions regarding the individuals with whom they negotiate:

- What are their underlying interests and concerns?
- What are their time constraints and deadlines?
- Who will make the final decision, and how will the decision be made?
- What is their negotiating style and experience?
- What are the limits of their negotiating authority?
- What incentives do they have to make this deal?
- What is their track record for honesty and integrity?

BOX 12.3 Leadership in Action: Knowing Additional Information

The following are two descriptions of a real-life scenario. One has minimal information and the other provides more information.

Minimal Information Scenario

A staff pharmacist who has been working at the same store for a number of years is rude to the customers and staff members. Pharmacy policy requires that all pharmacists participate in immunizations and medication therapy management counseling, but this staff pharmacist refuses to participate. You, the manager, must address this refusal. What do you do? Your first impulse might be to reprimand him and threaten to fire him. How might your response change when faced with the scenario with more information?

More Information Scenario

John, the pharmacist who refuses to participate, has been an excellent pharmacist and is well-liked among staff members, but he is currently going through a divorce. He is not managing it very well. His rudeness to customers and staff members has been only recent. Indeed, it is completely uncharacteristic of his past behavior.

Several years ago, he accepted his position at the pharmacy. At that time, employee turnover was a constant problem and the store was chronically unprofitable. Since then, John was instrumental in turning it around financially, and employee turnover is no longer an issue. You, the manager, must address John's refusal to participate. What do you do?

Questions

1. How might you approach the two scenarios differently?

2. Does the second scenario add empathy that might soften your response?

Discovering information about a negotiation and the individuals involved can make a significant difference in a negotiation. Box 12.3 reveals how knowing additional information about a partner can change everything.

Information About the Object of Negotiation

Negotiations can focus on issues, positions, or interests (Table 12.2). Win-win negotiators know the difference between these three elements. *Issues* are the

TABLE 12.2 Differentiating Issues, Positions, and Interests in a Job Negotiation

Issues	Positions	Interests
Annual salary	At least $100,000	Financial independence
Retirement plan	401(k) plan with an employer match of 3%	Financial security
Health insurance	A plan that contains dental coverage	Financial and physical security
Work schedule	40 hours per week with one weekend per month	Work-life balance

variables being negotiated. *Positions* are a party's stand on an issue, with each party having competing positions on issues. *Interests* are the parties' motivations for taking positions.

A key principle of win-win negotiating is to avoid bargaining over positions.[3] When negotiators bargain over positions, they tend to lock themselves into a specific stance and argue that viewpoint. Positional bargaining quickly becomes a contest of wills instead of an attempt to meet the underlying concerns of the other party. The more people focus on a particular position, the less attention they devote to the interests of others.

Focusing on interests in negotiations allows more flexibility in crafting agreements. Win-win negotiators are empathetic listeners, and they try to learn the intent behind the other party's position. Listening not only to the words but also to the meanings behind the words can help parties identify creative ways to solve an impasse that will satisfy both parties.

CONCLUSION

Negotiation is one of several methods available for pharmacists to manage conflicts. The manner in which negotiations are conducted depends on the situation and the desired outcome. There are four primary outcomes for partners in negotiations:

1. I win. You lose.

2. I lose. You win.

3. We compromise. Neither of us gets what we want, but we are willing to accept what we get.

4. I win. You win.

Win-lose negotiations may be the only option available when one party takes an adversarial approach to the negotiation. A compromise might be the only option when parties are unable or unwilling to come to an agreement. However, the ideal outcome for any negotiation is one where both sides win. This outcome benefits both parties and can strengthen relationships.

Win-win negotiations occur when both sides stand up for their needs while considering the needs of others. These negotiations require parties to balance self-interest with the interest of others. Successfully managing the balance between cooperation and competition requires practice and experience. At the conclusion of win-win negotiations, pharmacists will know if they are successful if they can answer "yes" to the following questions:

- Are we both satisfied with the result?

- Did we conduct our negotiations in a cooperative and respectful manner that will maintain or strengthen our professional relationships?

■ ● KEY TERMS AND CONCEPTS

- Conflicts

- Opportunism

- Avoidance

- Accommodation

- Collaboration

- Negotiation

- Win-lose negotiation

- Win-win negotiation

- Zero-sum game

- Fixed-pie negotiation

- Parable of the Orange

- Compromise

- Power

- BATNA

- Good cop, bad cop

- Deadlines

- Issues

- Positions

- Interests

■ ■ DISCUSSION AND REVIEW QUESTIONS

1. How do you typically respond to conflicts? Do you pay attention to your interests more than your partner's interests? How does this approach generally work for you?

2. What is the difference between collaborating and compromising? What is the downside of compromising?

3. How do fixed-pie negotiations limit your ability to come up with a win-win solution?

4. When are win-lose negotiations needed in workplace settings? When is winning over a partner acceptable?

5. What information do you need when negotiating a salary for a new job? What is your BATNA for a new job? Why is focusing on a party's interests in a job negotiation important?

6. There is a cardinal rule of negotiation, "Never negotiate against yourself." What does this mean? Give an example.

■ ■ REFERENCES

1. Hocker JL, Wilmot WW. *Interpersonal Conflict*. 9th ed. New York, NY: McGraw-Hill; 2014.
2. Thomas KL, Kilmann RH. *The Thomas-Kilmann Conflict Mode Instrument*. Mountain View, CA: CPP, Inc.; 1974.
3. Fisher R, Ury WL, Patton B. *Getting to Yes: Negotiating Agreement without Giving in*. New York, NY: Penguin; 2011.
4. Cohen H. *You Can Negotiate Anything*. New York, NY: Bantam Books; 1982.

Index

Note: Page numbers followed by *b, f,* or *t* indicate material in boxes, figures, or tables, respectively.

Made in the USA
Lexington, KY
14 December 2019